THE Customer Experience EDGE

THE Customer Experience EDGE

Technology and Techniques for Delivering
an Enduring, Profitable, and Positive Experience
to Your Customers

Reza Soudagar, Vinay Iyer, and Dr. Volker G. Hildebrand

NEW YORK   CHICAGO   SAN FRANCISCO
LISBON   LONDON   MADRID   MEXICO CITY   MILAN
NEW DELHI   SAN JUAN   SEOUL   SINGAPORE
SYDNEY   TORONTO

The *McGraw-Hill* Companies

1 2 3 4 5 6 7 8 9 0   DOC/DOC   1 6 5 4 3 2 1

ISBN   978-0-07-178697-3
MHID   0-07-178697-X

e-ISBN 978-0-07-178696-6
e-MHID   0-07-178696-1

Design by Lee Fukui and Mauna Eichner

McGraw-Hill books are available at special quantity discounts to use as premiums and sales promotions, or for use in corporate training programs. To contact a representative please e-mail us at bulksales@mcgraw-hill.com.

This book is printed on acid-free paper.

To my biggest fan and best critic,
my wife, Karen, for her encouragement and support.
—Reza Soudagar

To my patient wife, Rupa, who did the harder work of taking care
of our kids, Rudradaman and Mandakini, so that I could write.
—Vinay Iyer

To my kids, Romy, Ryan, and Kay, for consistently creating the
most important and most delightful experiences in my life.
—Volker Hildebrand

Contents

Foreword

THE WORLD IN WHICH WE HAVE TO DO business today is certainly different. Dramatic shifts in technology, social networking, the democratization of information, globalization, and the recent economic climate have all altered the old ways of doing business and engaging with customers. In the 1990s, companies focused on reengineering their internal processes and operations to achieve greater supply chain and manufacturing efficiencies. In the early 2000s, the focus shifted to taking full advantage of the efficiencies that were possible by using the Internet to sell goods and provide services.

However, in the second decade of the twenty-first century, the focus is shifting from the inside out to the outside in. Our company, CEMEX, is a leading global supplier of building materials such as cement, ready-mix concrete, and aggregates. At CEMEX USA, we have realized that running the business from the customer's point of view is our competitive advantage.

As I read the case studies and other insights in this book, I realized that we are not alone in this journey. The experience that companies create for their clients and prospects is driven not by industry, company size, or geographic location, but by a much broader customer perspective. CEMEX is in the building materials business, but when we are talking about the customer experience, our competitors are not only companies within our industry, but also FedEx, Apple, Amazon, Marriott, Disney, and other customer experience–focused companies discussed in this book.

The people who deal with us day-in and day-out are also consumers of other products and services. The customer experiences that they realize in their personal lives have influence in their professional lives. When a consumer can easily buy a book or a video or reserve a hotel room through his smartphone, he questions why he cannot get the same level of effortless shopping when he is buying products from us.

The Customer Experience Edge is not just a high-level view of how organizations should improve the experience they offer their clients. I am a process guy—I want to know what is behind the curtain. This book describes how the corporate culture, strategy, execution, and technologies need to be harnessed to provide a positive and profitable customer experience. While it is easy for a customer to ask for a better experience, we have learned, and this book shows, that it is difficult for a company to become customer-centric—especially if it has to deliver that experience consistently and profitably to thousands of customers.

First, there must be top-down support from management and then a bottom-up commitment from the organization. As my colleague Ven Bontha explains in the book, in 2003 we used a customer survey to determine what our customers liked and did not like about our service. Those data provided both top management and the rest of the organization with a road map on how best to implement an effective customer experience program.

Second, the only way we can provide a great experience to our thousands of customers is to make sure that information is readily available and accessible. We receive 250,000 calls a year from our customers, placing orders, asking about the status of a delivery or of their account, or other inquiries. Without the right technology in place, providing great customer experiences on that scale is challenging, if not impossible.

The technology that we utilize must match the desired customer engagement needs. We have a saying at CEMEX that we used to have a 180-degree interface in our call center. That is, the customer service representative would have a number of desktop computers, each connected to one of the disparate systems that held customer information. The rep would swivel in her chair from one screen to the next to obtain different pieces of information to answer a customer's question. As a result of the obstacles to finding the required information, not only did we waste the rep's and the customer's time, but we incurred unnecessary back-office costs. We realized that empowering our employees by having all the relevant information easily accessible in one place is critical to our success in dealing with our customers. We invested in the right technology platform to enable this, and we are realizing the benefits. This book makes this point very clearly through several case studies.

In addition, the book and our own experience show that improving customer experience is a journey. The screws are never tight, and they always need adjusting as our customers increasingly expect more. At CEMEX, we continue to look for ways to position ourselves as the provider of choice, and *The Customer Experience Edge* is an excellent how-to book that will help you understand how to deliver a positive, profitable, and sustainable experience for your customers. I hope you find the case studies in this book helpful as you begin or redesign your own customer experience program.

—JUAN CARLOS HERRERA
EXECUTIVE VICE PRESIDENT, CEMEX USA

Acknowledgments

MOST PEOPLE DON'T REALIZE that it takes a village to create a business book. The image of an author locked in a room alone, churning out insights by the ream, may be true for a novelist, but not for a business writer. *The Customer Experience Edge* is the result of scores of individuals sharing their views, their experiences, and their time.

While the three of us developed the ideas concerning what it takes to create the customer experience edge, we want to thank the practitioners, the consultants, our SAP colleagues, and our publishing partners for their collaboration and support.

First, of course, is the debt that we owe to the implementers of a positive and profitable customer experience. For almost a year we searched for and contacted those people from around the world who we thought were the leading practitioners of the customer experience edge vision. Dozens of individuals from a wide variety of companies were willing to share their experiences and provide feedback on our views. We are especially grateful for the contributions by the following individuals and organizations:

Mike Bidwell, president of the Arizona Cardinals Football Club

Ellen Brasse, head of marketing and sales at coop@home

Ven Bontha, customer experience management director for CEMEX USA

Deborah Dexter, director of customer service for business operating systems at Cardinal Health

Frank Eliason, senior vice president of social media

Ed French, senior vice president of Marriott Rewards at Marriott International, Inc.

Rick Germano, senior vice president of national customer operations at Comcast Corp.

Conny Kalcher, vice president of consumer experiences at The LEGO Group

Gil Katz, CIO at Colmobil

Mike Keppler, senior vice president, sales, marketing, and revenue management systems at Marriott International, Inc.

Greg Langston, vice president of sales for the Harris Products Group, a subsidiary of Lincoln Electric Company

Aaron Magness, senior director of brand marketing and business development at Zappos

Vito Mazzarino, vice president of field support operations at Synopsys

Manish Mehta, vice president of social media and community for Dell

Ajay Waghray, the CIO of Verizon Wireless

Customer experience management has become an active subindustry, and several consultants, industry analysts, trusted advisors, and others have developed a national or international reputation in this area. The following individuals shared their research and their views, and we appreciate their collaboration:

Lior Arussy, president of Strativity Group

Ginger Conlon, editor of *1to1 Magazine*

Paul D'Alessandro, partner at Diamond Advisory Services at PricewaterhouseCoopers

Leigh Durst, principal of Live Path

David Gardner, author, consultant, and mass customization expert

John Goodman, founder of the customer experience agency TARP Worldwide

Doug Hurley, managing director at PricewaterhouseCoopers

Andy Main, principal, customer transformation, for Deloitte Consulting

Denis Pombriant, founder of the consulting company Beagle Research Group, LLC

Don Peppers, founding partner of the CRM consultancy Peppers & Rogers Group

Phil Reed, an analyst at the automotive information website Edmunds.com

Martha Rogers, founding partner of the CRM consultancy Peppers & Rogers Group

Patricia Seybold, president and CEO of the Patricia Seybold Group

Gary Smith, chief analyst at Gary Smith EDA

Shaun Smith of the CE consultancy Smith i co

Bruce Temkin, principal with the customer experience consultancy Temkin Group

Fred Van Bennekom, principal at Great Brook Consulting

Ray Wang, principal analyst and CEO of Constellation Research

More than a dozen individuals at our employer provided ideas, support, and encouragement. In particular, the following members of the SAP management team enabled this book to happen:

Jonathan Becher

Heather Deason

Anthony Leaper

Jujhar Singh

Jeff Stiles

In addition, Saswato Das of SAP was generous in offering valuable strategic advice and continuous and ongoing support. We also are indebted to the assistance provided by Karen Herrerias and Guy Bardsley in identifying companies for us to approach.

These days, the life of a publisher couldn't be more complex. In addition to all the traditional challenges—finding the writers, shaping their ideas and their words, and getting the books printed, distributed, and sold—the rise of the Internet and the digitization of the printed word have presented a new series of obstacles. The publishing team at McGraw-Hill—Mary Glenn, Niki Papadopoulos, Ron Martirano, Mark Trosino, Julia Baxter, Pamela Peterson, Ruth Mannino, and others—not only were invaluable in helping to shape and package our ideas into a publishable manuscript, but also provided outstanding ideas about how to get the word out. And thanks to Karen Schopp for her ideas as well.

And finally, a big thank you to the research and editing team at Triangle Publishing Services. Lauren Gibbons Paul, Mary Brandel, Esther Shein, Alice Shimmin, Christina Williams, Davis Barber, and Chris Lewis provided invaluable support for this project. And in particular, we are grateful for the guidance from Triangle's Larry Marion.

While the vision and ideas in the book are our own, it did take a village to realize them in the form of this book. We are truly grateful to all those who contributed.

Introduction

THINK OF THE LAST FIVE INTERACTIONS you had with a business, either as an employee or as a consumer. They can be any type of encounter: a phone call to address a billing problem; using your smartphone to research product information while standing in a store aisle; seeking recommendations through your social media connections; an in-store visit to make a return; receiving a discount or marketing message via short messaging service (SMS); navigating a vendor's website to purchase an item or troubleshoot an issue; or spending time on Web forums to research the future purchase of construction equipment, a load of cement, or a thousand microprocessors to embed in robots that your company builds.

Considering all of those interactions, what is the average rating you would give your overall experience as a customer of these businesses? Use a scale of 1 to 5, with 1 being "poor" and 5 being "excellent." Remember that number.

Now, consider the following facts:

- In a recent survey by Bloomberg Businessweek Research Services (BBRS), more than 80 percent of companies named "customer experience (CE)" as being among their top five strategic priorities in the coming year.

- When asked to rate themselves on the customer experience that they provide, the same companies scored themselves a mediocre 3.62 on a scale of 1 to 5. Although the ratings may vary by industry, company size, and role of the person giving the rating, a sizable gap remains between many companies' intent and their reality.

So, which of these perspectives does your customer experience rating align with? Is it evident that the businesses that you patronize are working hard to delight you? The fact is, it is hard to find a company today that is not investing in its "customer experience." Across industries, and in business-to-consumer (B2C) and business-to-business (B2B) companies alike, investments are being made to map customer journeys, identify "moments of truth," empower employees, create innovative ways to close the gaps between performance and expectations, or otherwise "wow" and "delight" customers.

Companies can no longer compete on product and price alone; they are now working to sell an experience that is highly valued by customers and difficult if not impossible for competitors to replicate. To do this, they are trying to better manage the cumulative impact, both emotional and practical, of all of the encounters and interactions, both direct and indirect, that their customers have with them. Creating such an experience is the new business battleground. If it's done right, it's what will define your competitive edge. If it's not done at all, the very future of your business will be in question.

But, in many cases, the work that is being done is not reflected in the profits and other positive results that executives—and customers—want to see. Examples of poor customer experiences have only become more visible (and entertaining), thanks to social media videos, blog rants, and Twitter dispatches that go viral. A small sampling of the more famous of these "interactions" includes film director Kevin Smith's "too fat to fly" Twitter rant, musician Dave Carroll's "United Breaks Guitars" hit video, journalist Jeff Jarvis's "Dell Hell" blog posts, and writer/ad critic Bob Garfield's now-defunct ComcastMustDie.com.

And businesses have horror stories of their own. After the Mayo Clinic, the University of Texas, law firms, and thousands of other companies received desktop computers with defective components, users who complained were told that the problems were not caused by hardware issues, but by improper use. Unsealed documents from a lawsuit, reviewed by the *New York Times*, soon proliferated throughout the Internet and humiliated the company.[1]

And then there is the other side of the spectrum—businesses that throw so many resources at providing such a fantastic customer experience that they cannot sustain their level of customer centricity for very long. These are the grocers that order specialty items that one customer requests while ignoring the negative impact of the unsold inventory. These are the businesses that extend extremely customer-friendly policies that cause trouble for their bottom line. Costco, for instance, had to end its lenient return policy on consumer electronics in 2007 after finding out that setting no time limit for fully refunding returns was not financially feasible. It was all too easy for people to take advantage of the Costco policy by returning older items and upgrading to new ones while benefiting from the price drops.[2]

The bottom line is, it is as dangerous to throw too many resources at the customer experience without giving enough thought to sustaining the experience and profiting from your investment as it is to put too little into the customer experience. Equally common are the numerous technology investments, made with the best of intentions, that are intended to improve the customer experience but simply fail to deliver on the promise. Think of the self-service and automated voice response systems that backfired as companies tried to do the right thing by their customers but ended up frustrating them.

That is why we wrote this book: to help executives and managers smartly and sensibly leverage the right technologies at the right time to create a customer experience that differentiates them from their competitors, is difficult for others to replicate, and uses both foundational and disruptive technologies to accomplish this in a cost-effective, agile, scalable, and sustainable manner that leads to profitability. Much has been said and written about the business value of delivering a great customer experience, but very few books explain how smart technology investments play a strategic role in helping companies consistently offer a customer experience that leads to top- and bottom-line-focused goals.

We call this sensible, smart, sustainable approach "the customer experience edge." This edge is the new competitive weapon that all businesses need in order to create a differentiated offering that customers value, transforming them into not just loyal but passionate advocates who promote your offerings to others and co-create and co-innovate with you, boosting your revenues and profits. Technology is the secret ingredient in achieving the customer experience edge, as it enables companies to create a strong customer experience on a large scale and at lower cost. After all, it's not just about delivering a great customer experience—it's about doing so in a sustainable and ultimately profitable way.

We have learned the right and wrong ways of providing the customer experience edge during our collective 60 years as business school professors, consultants, and software industry executives. We have consulted with large international companies, worked at the biggest names in the consulting and software industries—including Accenture, Siebel, Oracle, and SAP—and played pioneering roles in creating the original customer-related software concepts and applications. As leaders of the SAP team that develops software designed to deliver positive and profitable customer experiences, we want to share our perspective and expertise with you. Already, SAP has helped many companies, large and small—from a global cement manufacturer, to a billion-dollar semiconductor design automation company, to a family-owned automobile importer, to the biggest retailer in Switzerland—excel at honing the customer experience edge.

Using the customer experience for competitive advantage means not only a well-thought-out strategy, leadership support, the breaking down of organizational silos, and skilled management, but also an often-overlooked element: the smart use of both foundational and disruptive technologies. You need the right type of IT infrastructure, layered with the clever use of traditional technologies (such as analytics) and newer technologies (such as social media), some of which are still emerging. The fact is, you can provide a great customer experience without great information technology. But you cannot scale that customer experience, deliver it consistently, sustain it indefinitely, or provide it profitably unless you have the right technological infrastructure and strategy.

Scaling and sustaining the customer experience are key to profitability, because the funny thing about the customer experience is that it does not stand still. Especially with the rising use of new technologies, the more you work at improving the customer experience, the higher the bar goes. With ever-expanding ways for customers to interact with companies, the job of providing a consistent, synchronized experience across all of those channels only becomes more difficult.

The snowball effect is enormous. Interactions can occur on the Web (through research, the company's site, social media, and online forums); on smartphones, tablets, and other mobile devices (through mobile point-of-sale capabilities, Twitter, and location-based services); on the phone (through customer service and sales); and in the real world (through face-to-face encounters and physical locations), just to name a few. It does not help that one bad experience can quickly become a PR nightmare once it hits the electronic grapevine that we call social media.

But there is no turning the other way and letting this phenomenon pass. In today's world, there are fewer ways to grow, and widespread commoditization makes differentiation increasingly unobtainable. Digitally engaged customers, who are seldom found without their mobile device of choice, trust the information, anecdotes, and reviews that they hear from one another or that they find online—not what they hear directly from companies. If they want to find a better deal, all it takes is one click, and they are gone.

In today's environment, the economics of securing customer loyalty are both compelling and necessary. Companies today are reaching not just for high levels of customer satisfaction, but for "customer loyalty" and "customer advocacy." Various studies have demonstrated that passionate, emotionally bonded customers are also highly profitable. In fact, a new science is being applied to measure the cost impact of a customer's bad experience and all of the resulting negative outcomes. Costs include the lost revenue opportunities from that customer (and probably from others who were affected by that customer), in addition to the resource costs of attending to the customer complaint and fixing the problem. This science makes it clear that the cost of not investing in the customer experience is great enough to outweigh any doubt that the customer experience should be done—and done in a focused manner that aligns with business goals. It is no longer affordable for companies to just let the customer experience "happen."

According to research reports, it is predicted that more than 75 percent of products and services will be undifferentiated in 10 years' time, exhibiting similar capabilities and features. To avoid the downward spiral of a commodity market price war, the main competitive differentiation that companies can build is through their customer experience delivery, that is, creating and delivering on their customer experience edge.

Creating the customer experience edge means going far beyond a company's traditional comfort zone. Companies are now competing on unfamiliar terrain, moving beyond the use of traditional incentives, such as guaranteed lower prices or loyalty programs, to keep customers from turning to competitors. They are increasingly relying on the murkier world of emotional and psychological incentives that are based more on behavioral science than on economic realities.

Achieving the customer experience edge also requires a new focus on employee empowerment. In most cases, employees are motivated to satisfy customers' needs and desires, but they often do not have the technology tools, data access, incentives, or organizational standing to do so. There are two sides to this coin: customers get frustrated when service reps and other customer-facing employees cannot help them, and the feeling is mutual among employees who do not have the right tools. With younger employees—sometimes called millennials—entering the workforce, this frustration will only grow, as these professionals increasingly expect to make use of the technology tools that are a constant presence in their personal lives.

Throughout this book, we will share anecdotes, examples, and best practices from a wide range of businesses. Among them are those that are at the top of their game (such as Marriott, CEMEX USA, and The LEGO Group) and those that are climbing the learning curve (such as Comcast). In Part I, we set the stage for the rest of the book. Throughout this section, we describe the state of the customer experience as it stands in today's "new normal"; describe what "the four essentials of the customer experience" are and what they look like in action; define what the customer experience looks like, from the perspective of both customers and businesses; and describe how the customer experience is just as applicable for B2B as it is for B2C.

Part II is our "Making It Happen" section, in which we explore how customer experience initiatives mean throwing out the old playbook for companies, employees, customers, and the technologies that companies choose. We also delve into the "recipe" for the customer experience—the practices, processes, and organizational structures that need to be in place in order to achieve the customer experience edge. In addition, we touch on the financial results that companies can expect to achieve.

In Part III, we detail the core role that technology plays in achieving the customer experience edge by delivering customer experience on a large scale and at lower cost. We discuss this from two angles: how to create the right technology foundation, and the disruptive technologies that enable you to advance the game. Customer experience initiatives also pose opportunities and challenges for IT leaders to secure a spot at the table when business leaders are setting CE strategy. The CIO is in a prime position to be a key player in making the CE initiative successful.

Finally, in our last section, Part IV, we explore how to continue the momentum of your customer experience initiative. This section includes a look at creating "quick wins" along the customer experience journey; how to measure the value of your customer experience program; the role of technology in exporting the customer experience to emerging economies; what the future of the customer experience will look like; and our summary of actions that companies should take when developing their customer experience edge.

Our objective in writing this book is to illustrate how companies can deliver a differentiating, sustainable, and profitable customer experience by making strategic technology investments. Our goal for you, after you read this book, is that you feel empowered to champion a profitable customer experience initiative at your own company.

Armed with the customer experience edge, your company will be prepared to compete not only in today's business world, but in whatever new market and economic forces tomorrow brings. When you deliver highly valuable experiences to your customers in a scalable, sustainable way, the reward is loyal, engaged advocates who help you propel your business forward in exciting and profitable ways.

PART I

Customer Experience: The New Competitive Battleground

CHAPTER 1

Customer Experience in the "New Normal"

*80 percent of companies say getting closer to customers
and providing them with a differentiated experience
is a top strategic objective. Their average rating of the
customer experience they provide, however, is just 3.6
on a scale of 1 to 5.*

— BLOOMBERG BUSINESSWEEK
RESEARCH SERVICES SURVEY, 2010

EVERYONE HAS A CUSTOMER EXPERIENCE horror story. The cable
company technician who never shows up. The parts supplier that
you have to call repeatedly for an update on a spare part order. The
support person who cannot help you with your billing question, even
after you have waited on hold for an hour. The building materials
supplier whose late delivery costs you thousands of dollars in lost labor and causes you project delays.

WHAT IS: *Customer Experience?*

> Customer experience is the cumulative impact—both emotional and
> practical—of all of the encounters and interactions that a customer
> has with a company.

It's ironic but true: in an age in which a large majority of companies profess to rate a positive customer experience among their top strategic objectives—about 80 percent in two recent surveys by Bloomberg Businessweek Research Services (BBRS)[1]—examples of bad customer experiences abound. Executives, it seems, are doing a lot of talking about the importance of customer experience, but they are failing to back that up with technologies, processes, and policies that can consistently and cost-effectively foster customer happiness. These same executives will even admit to this failing, with most of them rating the customer experience offered by their own firms only slightly higher than mediocre, according to BBRS data (see Figure 1.1). Walking the talk they are not.

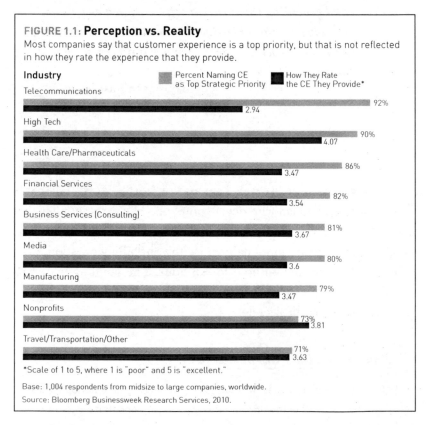

FIGURE 1.1: Perception vs. Reality
Most companies say that customer experience is a top priority, but that is not reflected in how they rate the experience that they provide.

Industry — Percent Naming CE as Top Strategic Priority / How They Rate the CE They Provide*

Telecommunications — 92% / 2.94

High Tech — 90% / 4.07

Health Care/Pharmaceuticals — 86% / 3.47

Financial Services — 82% / 3.54

Business Services (Consulting) — 81% / 3.67

Media — 80% / 3.6

Manufacturing — 79% / 3.47

Nonprofits — 73% / 3.81

Travel/Transportation/Other — 71% / 3.63

*Scale of 1 to 5, where 1 is "poor" and 5 is "excellent."

Base: 1,004 respondents from midsize to large companies, worldwide.

Source: Bloomberg Businessweek Research Services, 2010.

The fact is, there are two sides to a successful and profitable customer experience: the employees are on one side, and the customers are on the other. In most cases, employees are motivated to satisfy customer needs and desires—but they are not empowered to do so.

Imagine, for example, a customer phoning the call center of a large bank. Say this customer has just discovered something disturbing in her online bank account: a check for $10,000 that she deposited a few days ago is marked "hold," and the funds are not available. After toying with the idea of trying online chat support, she decides instead to call the support center. Once she is in the interactive voice response system, she punches in her account number and listens to a list of options until she can finally press zero to speak to a customer service representative (CSR). The CSR asks for her account number—*Why? She just entered it.*—and then for the "verbal password" on her account.

WHAT IS: *The Customer Experience Edge?*

The customer experience edge

- Differentiates a company from its competitors.
- Is difficult for competitors to replicate.
- Uses well-designed foundational and disruptive technologies.
- Accomplishes its goals in a cost-effective, scalable, flexible, and sustainable manner that leads to profitability.

This edge is the new business weapon that all businesses need if they are to create a differentiated offering that customers value, transforming them into not just loyal but passionate advocates who engage with you in co-creation and co-innovation and promote your offerings to others, boosting your revenues and profits.

Increasingly anxious, the customer replies that she does not recall ever choosing a verbal password, whatever that might be, so she could not possibly know what it is. The CSR then asks her a series of questions, from her social security number to her address to her phone number to her mother's maiden name to the amount of a recent deposit. Once she has supplied all of that (three minutes into the exchange), the customer can finally ask why the check was being held, only to be told that the bank does not have any specific information on that check. Her options at that point: get in the car, drive to her local branch, and wait in line for a supervisor, who might be able to make an exception; or wait until the date when the hold is lifted and accept whatever consequences that might have for her bills in the meantime. It is no wonder the customer's stomach is in knots when she hangs up the phone.

Meanwhile, the CSR is in no better shape. During the call, he has been well aware of the customer's anxiety, and he has had to see-saw between two computer screens, switch between two keyboards, and use several applications to track down all the pieces of information he needed in order to access the customer's various accounts and try to resolve her questions. He ends the call feeling frustrated that, once again, the best he has been able to do for yet another customer is simply apologize.

As everyone knows, banks have stringent processes and security practices in place—as they should. These measures are there to safeguard our money. But if the CSR in this example had had easier access to the right information, and if the bank had had business applications that enabled a 360-degree view of the customer, our customer would not have had to repeat her information. Also, the CSR could have quickly discovered the reason for the hold—this was an out-of-state check for a large amount. In addition, he could have looked up historical information on the customer's account and discovered that she is a high-value individual with a variety of different types of accounts at the bank. With this information at his fingertips, the CSR could have either lifted the hold himself or quickly gotten a supervisor on the phone with the necessary authority to do it. How far this action would have gone toward making the customer happy! How much lighter of heart—and stomach—this customer would have been, and how much more likely she would have been to become a customer for life.

Not to mention, think of how much more satisfied the customer service representative would have been with this increased level of empowerment. People who go into the field of customer service have a strong motivation to help other people and solve their problems. And just as customers get frustrated when CSRs cannot help them, the CSRs themselves also get frustrated when they do not have the right information to help customers.

Loyalty vs. Lock-In

The sad reality is that many customers of large banks stay only because the costs of switching to a new institution are too high. New fees, combined with the time investment of notifying the numerous entities that deposit into or withdraw from the existing account, are a daunting deterrent to switching banks.[2] Being locked in, however, does not create loyalty. Once a better option presents itself, any customer who has endured a stressful or frustrating experience anything close to what we have just described will go for it—not to mention all of those customers who have simply had just "OK" service.

Like everyone else, large companies do not intentionally offer a poor customer experience; rather, it happens simply because a good customer experience is hard to provide. Traditional business processes, organizational structures, and cultural practices all tend to place the needs of the company above the needs of the customer, creating many obstacles to creating the customer experience edge.

And then there is the matter of cost. Superior customer experience tends to be viewed as being expensive customer experience, although that is certainly not always the case. Often, doing the right thing for the customer will result in lower costs (for example, higher product quality or better service delivery leads to fewer support calls). But executives are leery of funding initiatives that promote customer centricity because they are unsure of what the real impact of a particular investment will be. More than half of the executives responding to the North American BBRS survey cited inadequate funding as an obstacle to improving the customer experience.

The trick is not to throw money at an undefined customer experience initiative. Rather, companies should raise the overall customer experience bar and then concentrate their resources where the superior experience repays the investment—for example, with customers who have a high lifetime value.

Profitability is a necessary component of the customer experience equation, although early leaders have not always seen it that way. Zappos, for example, prides itself on free shipping and no-hassle returns for all customers for up to a year after purchase. The self-described customer-obsessed online shoe seller also maintains a blog that recounts stories of "wow" experiences that its employees have extended to individual customers.

Customers Really Are in Charge

From the dawn of commerce, companies have developed products and offered them on the market. Consumers either bought them or didn't. Except in extreme cases, communication flowed from the company outward. Internal experts did their best to gauge the drift of future demand and prepare products accordingly.

Today, globalization, mass customization technology, digitally engaged customers, the mobile Web, and the widespread use of social media, among other factors, have created a landscape in which the consumer or business buyer has more information and, therefore, more control than ever before. Customers increasingly feel empowered to tell companies exactly how they want to be treated, down to their preferred product delivery mechanism, while demanding ever more personalized solutions and real-time response times to suit their individual tastes and needs. Consumers talk to one another and hold their peers' product reviews in higher esteem than any information they can glean from a corporate website.

WHAT IS: *A Digitally Engaged Customer?*

A digitally engaged customer is one for whom it is second nature to use social media, mobile devices, the mobile Web, and other technologies to engage with a business, conduct research, and complete transactions.

This shift is true not only in the world of business-to-consumer marketing (B2C), but also for business-to-business companies (B2B). Increasingly, there is little differentiation between the two business environments—employees expect the same level of customer experience from their business partners that they expect as customers in their private lives. Business employees also are apt to spend their free time on social media sites on work-related topics. Hence, B2B companies are developing Web portals where partners can order goods, remember preferences, obtain information on popular products, view other products or services they might want to consider, and see real-time order status. In addition, these companies are building online communities and monitoring social forums to ensure that they are aware of what is being said, and they even engage in conversations.

We would go so far as to say that the distinction between B2C and B2B is increasingly a meaningless one; both belong to a single category: P2P, or people to people. After all, that is the new framework dawning on businesses of all types. We are all people serving people, and we all spend time on both ends of the transaction. (We will talk more about the customer experience for B2B companies in Chapter 3.)

The upshot of all of this is that it is no longer good enough to "treat customers well." Now, companies must offer a superior "experience"—and a differentiated one, at that. And different experiences need to be created for different types of customers to ensure that the value they are seeking is provided.

WHAT IS: CRM?

Traditionally, customer relationship management (CRM) systems focused tightly on sales, marketing, and customer service and support. Today, the boundaries of CRM are being stretched to include all customer-facing interactions, including billing, fulfillment, and other back-office processes with high customer impact. CRM strategies should seek to synchronize all these functions so that they operate as one and not as distinct elements.

Differentiation is also the path to a *profitable* customer experience. It makes sense to concentrate resources on those customers who promise to repay the investment—now or via an expanded lifetime value. The good news: foundational technologies [such as integrated CRM and enterprise resource planning (ERP) software] and disruptive technologies (such as the mobile Web and social media) can greatly reduce the cost of providing a successful customer experience, thereby enabling companies to provide all customers with a level of experience that would otherwise be cost-prohibitive.

WHAT IS: Integrated CRM and ERP Software?

Let's start with what integrated CRM and ERP software is not, which is easily seen with a visit to any call center. In many situations, call center reps sit in front of not one but two (or even more) screens just to access all of the data they need to answer customer questions on billing, delivery, troubleshooting, and so on. The problem is, the data are stored in multiple systems. With integrated CRM and ERP software, all employees would have a full view of customer information, including finance, manufacturing, sales, and service.

It is a mistake, however, to view investments in customer experience as a direct path to increased revenue. "Most executives think, 'How can we use this technology to sell more stuff?'" says Don

Peppers, founding partner of CRM consultancy Peppers & Rogers Group. "This attitude is doomed to failure. A better question is: how can we use this technology to deliver more value to our customers— better, faster, and cheaper?"

At a high level, improving the customer experience requires reorienting the whole organization—people, processes, and technology—to focus on the customer. This flips the dynamic that has been in place forever. Now, customers will tell you what they want, rather than passively receiving whatever you choose to offer. Such a major change is hard for any organization to assimilate. The bigger and older the company, the more entrenched its organization centricity is likely to be. It is difficult to align everyone around the same goal— giving customers what *they* want, on *their* terms. In this era, when all businesses are trying to balance the need to cut costs with seeking growth avenues and maintaining innovation, interacting with customers on an individual level and answering their needs provides a competitive advantage.

The Cost of Ignoring the Customer Experience

Realigning the company around the customer is indeed a major effort that affects every part of the organization. But sooner or later, the consequences of ignoring the customer experience can be dire. Even in a special case, where your company has a near-monopoly (think Microsoft a few years ago), you make yourself vulnerable to competition from new quarters (think Microsoft post-Google). As with all negatives, the cost of not improving the customer experience is hard to measure but cannot be underestimated. The stakes are as high as extinction.

Take Dell. In 2005, the company saw its customer satisfaction score slip by five points, according to the American Customer Satisfaction Score Index, which is conducted by the University of Michigan.[3] The dip was largely attributed to the viral response to the blog postings of journalist Jeff Jarvis, along with Dell's slow response to the online events.[4] Dell later hired a large team of people, led by a vice president of communities and conversations, to monitor and manage social media activities.

In 2011, that team monitors more than 22,000 online conversations a day, according to Adam Brown, Dell's executive director, social media, global marketing. He runs a Social Media Listening Command Center, launched in December 2010 at Dell's headquarters in Round Rock, Texas (a second center will be launched in China later in 2011), to coordinate and manage the company's response, around the clock, to those 22,000 conversations—70 percent of which are not in English. Dell can currently respond to conversations in nine languages, and it plans to add more.

The team includes assignment editors. These editors route critical conversations to one of the 7,000 social media–trained Dell employees, who have applicable, appropriate technical expertise and language skills, Brown explained at the Microsoft Global High Tech Summit in early 2011.

In the future, a radio icon on selected desktops around the company will let individuals "tune in" to online conversations that are relevant to them. For example, an engineer who is designing laptop hinges can see conversations about hinge-related issues, while a shop floor manager might monitor conversations about the build quality of the products produced in his shop. Other individuals will have the equivalent of a social telephone on their desktop, so that they can engage in and respond to conversations as needed, Brown explained.

Dell does not view the investments required to support its Social Media Listening Command Centers as an unrewarded cost, but, ultimately, as providing a return on the investment, Brown noted. Dell realized—and you should, too—that the costs of an unhappy customer are myriad. You also need to consider the costs of unhappy customers themselves—the cost of a complaint, a bad experience, and customer churn—and how much money you are leaving on the table by not providing a customer experience tailored to business objectives, says Lior Arussy, president of Strativity Group, a customer experience research, strategy design, and implementation firm, in our interview for this book. An example is a $300 million cost-reduction effort that could lead to a $1 billion loss of revenue because you have become irrelevant to customers, Arussy says.

Failing to invest in the customer experience also means risking not being differentiated and therefore having to compete substantially on price, according to David Gardner, author, consultant, and mass customization expert. In our conversation on the topic, Gardner points to the early days of the MP3 player as an example of how this lack of differentiation can play out. Sony, Nokia, and other companies each had its own version of a digital music player. Though initially—and widely—considered one of the weaker market entries, the Apple iPod succeeded in differentiating itself via a superior retail experience, product design, emotional appeal, and an easy-to-use solution to the vexing issue of downloading music. The other products were left to compete anemically on price.

In today's digitally engaged world, ignoring the customer experience also may have dire consequences for a company's reputation and, ultimately, its bottom line. On average, twice as many people will hear about someone's bad experience as will hear about his good experience, says John Goodman, founder of the customer experience agency TARP Worldwide. This outcome is even more dramatic on the Web, where four times as many people hear about a negative experience than hear about a positive one, he says.

Companies that have locked in customers—however temporarily—now understand that they need to join with their customers via love, not bondage. "In the past, companies invested hundreds of millions of dollars in [loyalty] programs that handcuff customers financially to their solution," says Paul D'Alessandro, partner at Diamond Advisory Services at professional services firm Pricewaterhouse-Coopers. "Today, they need to build up a bank of appreciation by addressing customer needs exactly how they want them addressed, and that's much more powerful than a loyalty program."

This "bank of appreciation" is built through the cumulative effect of three factors, according to D'Alessandro. The first is the stories people hear through word of mouth and the media, the second is direct interaction, and the third is the transcendent "moments of truth," which are profoundly positive or negative experiences that lead to long-lasting impressions, for better or for worse.

Clearly, for today's businesses, the focal point of doing business needs to shift to the customer and staying one step ahead of the curve in managing a consistently strong customer experience. The benefits of doing so are many. Delivering the customer experience edge can help you nurture engaged advocates who not only will stand by you into the future, but will help you grow your business through word of mouth and their own loyalty.

CHAPTER 2

The Four Essentials of a Profitable Customer Experience

According to 90 percent of companies, the most important elements of a positive experience are: reliable products and services, relevance of interactions, responsiveness of the company, and ease of doing business.

—BLOOMBERG BUSINESSWEEK RESEARCH SERVICES SURVEY, 2010

IF MONEY WERE NO OBJECT, just about any company could provide an amazing customer experience. Given unlimited resources, there is no end to the perks and extras you could provide your customers. And in industries such as luxury retail, where getting noticed is the name of the game, some companies have taken that approach. When you step through the doors of Neiman Marcus, for example, you know that you are in for a deluxe shopping experience. This is something that high-end retailers can afford to do, because customers are prepared for the price of the merchandise to reflect the chichi experience.

SPOTLIGHT ON: *Commerce Bank*

Commerce Bank in St. Louis sees itself as a retailer (as opposed to a financial institution), which has helped the bank create an experience that aligns with the customer experience essential of convenience. It uses its motto of "Ask. Listen. Solve." to rid itself of anything that unnecessarily robs customers of an enjoyable experience. For instance, it offers

- Convenience
- Seven-day branch banking
- Extended hours
- Free penny arcade coin-counting machines
- Hassle-free products
- Treats for children and dogs

No wonder the bank has had the highest customer satisfaction rating in retail banking in the Midwest region for three years in a row, according to J.D. Power & Associates.

But throwing all your money into dazzling the customer is not sustainable for most businesses, especially not in today's world, where customer expectations are constantly increasing. Companies can no longer compete on price and product alone; they need to spend intelligently to develop and offer services and experiences that truly matter to customers *and* that are difficult for competitors to replicate. "Treat the customer the way you would like to be treated if you were the customer," advises Peppers & Rogers Group's Don Peppers. "Use the Golden Rule. Imagine your best customer is sitting next to you when you're making decisions."

After all, the customer experience must—in the end—differentiate you from your competitors. And you need to achieve this differentiation in a way that is consistent and, ultimately, profitable. The "bank of appreciation" that we discussed in Chapter 1 needs to be valuable enough that customers become loyal advocates who trust you and want to engage with you. The value you offer needs to be delivered in a cost-effective way that leads to competitive differentiation and growth. Otherwise, simply put, there is no reason to do it.

"If there's no financial driver, we don't recommend companies do this," says Lior Arussy, president of Strativity Group and author of many books on the customer experience, including his most recent, *Customer Experience Strategy*. "It has to be something you can point to and say, 'We have moved the needle on either revenues or expenses.'"

Financial goals need to be front and center in the customer experience initiative as part of the business case. Companies can realistically aim for several financial drivers, in addition to new ways to measure business outcomes. (We will discuss these topics in more detail in Chapters 6 and 10.) Briefly, realistic business drivers can include higher revenues, the ability to institute premium pricing, improved customer retention rates, more word-of-mouth marketing, and reduced costs as a result of streamlined and innovative processes.

The Building Blocks of Trust

So how do you get there? How do you build that bank of appreciation without breaking the bank? How do you do it in a way that leads to profits and growth? We believe it is all about trust—a seemingly amorphous concept, but one that we strongly believe is the cement of a business relationship. Only when you have established trust between the business and the customer can you begin to form an emotional bond—"stickiness," if you will—that cannot be replicated by anyone else and will keep customers loyal to you.

We also have found that, on closer inspection, trust is not a blurry concept at all. In our customer experience work, we have determined that there are four building blocks of trust. We call these the *essentials* of the customer experience edge. These four customer experience essentials are reliability, convenience, responsiveness, and relevance (see Table 2.1 and Figure 2.1).

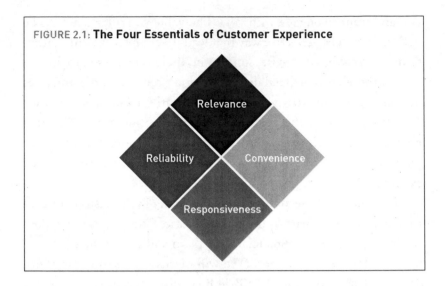

FIGURE 2.1: **The Four Essentials of Customer Experience**

TABLE 2.1: **Four Customer Experience Essentials**

Customer Experience Essential	What It Looks Like
Reliability	Living up to your promises. Example: Consistent on-time delivery, each and every time.
Convenience	Offering choice, consistency, and timeliness. Example: Using multiple channels to engage with customers.
Responsiveness	Listening and responding quickly. Example: Changing a process or policy when feedback reveals that it causes problems for customers.
Relevance	Ensuring that offerings are personalized and meaningful. Example: Gaining insight into, and delivering, what really matters to individual customers at a particular point in time.

Of these four essentials, reliability is the most fundamental and is really a prerequisite to the other three. After all, if you cannot consistently deliver on your promises, no one will care about your convenience, responsiveness, or relevance. Once you can deliver on reliability, you can look to the other essentials to develop your differentiation. Furthermore, you can use any one of these four customer experience essentials as a litmus test for assessing the ultimate worth of any action you take in the name of achieving a strong and profitable customer experience.

The importance of these customer experience essentials was validated in the North American survey by Bloomberg Businessweek Research Services (BBRS), in which respondents named the most important elements of a positive experience: reliable products and services, relevance of interactions, responsiveness of the company, and ease (or convenience) of doing business with the company (see Figure 2.2). Throughout this book, we will continue to show, through real company examples, how these four customer experience essentials—these building blocks of trust—form the basis of the customer experience edge.

Business strategy, executive ownership, and organizational alignment are the starting points in driving cross-functional processes to achieve a true 360-degree customer experience. The execution of customer engagement processes must be complete from start to finish, or else the nascent tendrils of trust can be trampled in an instant. To see why, let's look at the example of a pet owner who is shop-

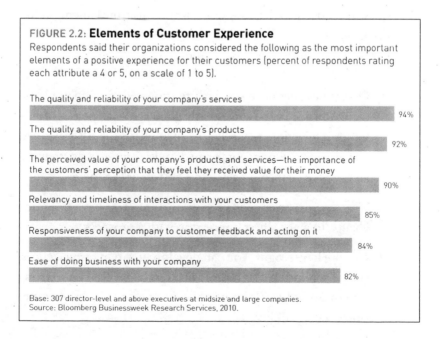

FIGURE 2.2: **Elements of Customer Experience**
Respondents said their organizations considered the following as the most important elements of a positive experience for their customers (percent of respondents rating each attribute a 4 or 5, on a scale of 1 to 5).

The quality and reliability of your company's services
94%

The quality and reliability of your company's products
92%

The perceived value of your company's products and services—the importance of the customers' perception that they feel they received value for their money
90%

Relevancy and timeliness of interactions with your customers
85%

Responsiveness of your company to customer feedback and acting on it
84%

Ease of doing business with your company
82%

Base: 307 director-level and above executives at midsize and large companies.
Source: Bloomberg Businessweek Research Services, 2010.

ping for medication for her yellow Lab at a Web-based pet supply company. Wondering about the difference between two competing brands, she clicks on the "chat" button and quickly gets a response to her question. Impressed, she places the order, specifying standard shipping, and over dinner that night with her family, she recounts the positive experience.

A week and a half passes, and the order has not arrived within the time frame promised. Having had good luck with chat, she tries this approach again. This time, however, the service rep is unable to help her, as he has no visibility into the order-tracking system. To make matters worse, he tells her that she needs to e-mail or call customer service. She sends an e-mail and then has to wait a full 24 hours before getting a response informing her that, indeed, her order had been shipped three days previously and that it "should" be arriving in the next few days. Eventually it does arrive. However, the customer is likely to examine other options and competitor sites before putting an order through this site again. The opportunity to retain this formerly satisfied customer—let alone turn her into an engaged, loyal advocate—has eroded (not to mention the increased likelihood that she will send a negative tweet or post her disgruntlement on her Facebook page).

This example illustrates several things:

- One-time experiences—no matter how terrific—do not build trust. You need to be consistently good across all phases of customer interaction, regardless of channel. In the BBRS survey, 82 percent of respondents named multichannel consistency as an essential element of a positive customer experience.

- The first experience is very important. You have only one chance to make a first impression with a prospect.

- Get the basics right. You can develop gratifying experiences, such as online chat, but these need to be layered on a strong foundation of working business processes and cross-functional data visibility.

- Once established, trust leads to stronger bonds between customers and the business. Without this bond, customers may be satisfied, but they will never become passionate, loyal advocates of the brand.

Without trust, you cannot hope for loyalty, advocacy, engagement, or participation—all of which are the cornerstones of the customer experience edge. It is only when trust develops that customers will be inclined to, say, provide feedback on how they would like to see a product evolve. Even then, you need to be able to act on that feedback (a customer experience element named by 84 percent of BBRS survey respondents). If your customers give you good ideas and you execute them well, differentiation is within reach.

"Too many companies are treating [the customer experience initiative] as *the* deliverable and whiffing on the practical delivery of service," says Denis Pombriant, founder of the consulting company Beagle Research Group.

The Cost of Broken Processes

In addition to building trust, getting the customer experience right the first time is also less costly than doing it wrong and having to backtrack. Imagine, for instance, the experience provided by the company everyone loves to hate: the cable services provider. The scenario is all too familiar. You are having problems with your TV, so you book an appointment and are given a three-hour time slot within which your technician is expected to show up. That window is irritating enough to begin with, and it's even more irritating when the technician does not arrive within it. Much as you hate to, you pick up the phone to find out what happened. The call center person usually does not have much information in this situation, but she promises to send an alert out to the field.

By the time the technician finally appears, your plans for the day are shot, and with them, your mood. The technician pokes around, rummages in his toolkit, and eventually pronounces the problem fixed. But when your kids try to watch the SpongeBob movie on demand that evening, it is apparent that the problem is very much alive and well. Another hour spent on the phone that evening brings another service "window" and a new promise to have the situation remedied. The result: an unhappy customer (you) and a lot of costly support for the company.

Any improvement in this scenario would produce both a better customer experience *and* lower costs to the company. What if the cable company had its quality control and business processes operating at a high level? What if the customer support, customer relationship management (CRM), scheduling, and dispatch processes and

---

SPOTLIGHT ON: *Comcast*

In the recent past, Comcast took a lot of heat for offering a poor customer experience. But the company has since taken many steps that are aligned with the essentials of the customer experience to respond to these complaints. For instance:

- **Reliability.** Comcast's seven-point Customer Service Guarantee promises that, among other things, it will issue a $20 credit if the technician fails to arrive for a scheduled visit during the appointment window—a testament to its desire for increased reliability.

- **Convenience.** The company is experimenting with whittling its two- to three-hour windows down to just one hour, to enhance customer convenience.

- **Responsiveness.** Comcast claims to have reduced its service calls by four million in the first four months of 2010 vs. 2009, because it monitors and responds to customer problems via social media. "That's a good thing, because that's four million fewer outstanding customer issues," says Rick Germano, senior vice president of national customer operations at Comcast.

systems all functioned together in a way that enabled automatic alerts to be sent—to your smartphone, e-mail, or landline, whichever you chose. That would eliminate the dreaded "window" and give you real visibility as to when the technician would arrive. Customers do not expect a product or service to be perfect, but they do expect the companies they patronize not to be riddled with broken processes. And if we are kept informed while problems are being fixed, we will see that as positive. And, chances are, we will tell our friends how well we were treated.

"There are numerous situations where investing in getting the experience right from the start is a good thing to do from a business standpoint," says Bruce Temkin, a principal with the customer experience consultancy Temkin Group. "And it has the benefit of being good for the customer, as well."

So, what are *you* doing as a company that would inspire people to spend their valuable money, time, and energy with you? For many businesses, the very first answer to that question is ensuring that the fundamental processes are in place and operating at an optimal level. If you promise a 24-hour turnaround on responding to a customer problem, you need to have the processes and people in place to do that. If you promise a discount on a particular product, your pricing across channels should consistently reflect that. If you say that something will arrive in three days, it had better arrive in that time frame. And you had better be able to do this in every channel in which you operate, whether the customer approaches you through an online or a brick-and-mortar channel.

The Customer-Centric Enterprise

The four essentials of a profitable customer experience need to be built into the culture of the company. The desire—and the ability—to offer convenience, responsiveness, relevance, and reliability has to be pervasive across every department in the company, not just something that only marketing and sales cares about. Product developers, engineering, finance, legal, the shipping department, and even store associates have to care about creating trust, too. We have determined that a cultural change is required to change the attitudes of everyone within the organization when it comes to how the customer is viewed.

Changing the culture and the attitude comes from the very top of an organization. Senior executives must reconfigure the enterprise, placing the customer—rather than the company's products and services—at the center. This means reengineering processes starting with the customer, from the outside looking in, rather than the converse. (We will discuss this topic in more detail in Chapter 4.) With that critical recasting of the corporate mindset, other decisions—including the choice of technology architecture to support the strategy—flow naturally.

It is one thing to work on the customer experience on the edges or at the margins. It is another to approach it as a transformative, profit-driven initiative that encompasses the entire company. A true customer experience is holistic, placing the customer at the center of the corporate universe. It demands integration of business processes, in which customer service, the call center, marketing, branding, product or service development, technology, manufacturing, and the other functions all work together to serve customers. The customer experience must be orchestrated across channels and touch points throughout the customer life cycle. Such a dramatic change can never be made without the dedicated commitment and vocal support of the company's top leaders. Indeed, the CEO is in the best position to articulate, on a regular basis, why the enterprise needs to focus on its customers, and what that means.

From inside the company, this means that the company is no longer focused on itself—its sales, product offerings, and future plans—but, instead, is focused on its customers and their desires. Such a holistic approach means that customers will never again suffer the problem of having to explain their problem over and over to different employees, with different outcomes. It means that customers who spend heavily through the website, for example, are recognized for their worth across all channels.

It is all too common for the customer experience to be a marginal rather than a whole-company undertaking. Consider an office goods superstore—one whose motto promises an easy shopping experience. A customer spends an hour in the store, analyzing the laptops on display. He decides on a particular unit, one that bears the sign, "Available in-store only." No big deal; he will buy it right now. So he flags down a service representative, who disappears into the back of the

---

SPOTLIGHT ON: *Coop*

When the Swiss grocer Coop began offering customers an iPhone grocery-shopping app, it ensured that the offering was not just a whimsical "come-on" that made it look hip to the 13 percent of Swiss citizens who carry iPhones. By connecting the app with its own integrated enterprise systems, the offering builds a whole new level of customer trust by aligning with the four customer experience essentials:

- **Convenience.** In Switzerland, stores close in the early evenings and are closed all day on Sundays. With a mobile app, customers can shop while they are commuting to or from work.

- **Responsiveness.** Coop continues to upgrade the mobile app, with improved navigation and search functionality.

- **Relevance.** Switzerland has one of the highest adoption rates of the iPhone in the world, making this a well-targeted platform for a mobile shopping app.

- **Reliability.** Customers can reserve one-hour windows to have groceries delivered before they place their order, so that they do not get locked out of available time frames. Real-time product availability means that customers receive exactly what they order.

(For more on Coop's customer experience edge, see the case study on page 26.)

---

store to retrieve the model. The rep returns with bad news: that laptop is out of stock. Ever helpful, the service rep checks the inventory in several nearby locations and tracks one down in a store about 20 miles away. Great, the customer says, asking when that store will be able to transfer it to this location so that he can pick it up. "I'm so sorry; we don't do that anymore," the rep admits. "It messes up our inventory."

Frustrated at having wasted his time—and mystified as to why the office supply store would not make this model available online—the customer leaves, with no intention of investing additional time (and gas money) traveling 20 miles out of his way. Two days later, he finds an even better deal on a similar model on eBay.

How close the office supply store had come, and how many things it had done right—a marketing message geared toward what customers want (easy shopping); a knowledgeable, helpful service rep; even the right product mix. But something important was missing: a multilocation, cross-channel, integrated inventory system, and order management system that was flexible enough to meet many customer desires. It is not enough for marketing to be customer-focused; the entire organization needs to be, and its applications need to enable that focus.

This type of customer-centric corporate alignment across every department and function is something that companies are just now realizing that they need to achieve. If the customer experience imperative resides in just one or two departments, it is not transformative; it is just marginal. And that will not be enough to build trust, without which a profitable customer experience is impossible.

CASE STUDY: COOP

Grocer Moves Shopping to the Palm of Customers' Hands

Leveraging both customers' attachment to their iPhones and their long commutes and time-compressed schedules, Switzerland-based Coop is boosting both loyalty and sales with an iPhone shopping app.

With about 13 percent of the population owning an iPhone, Switzerland has one of the highest adoption rates in the world for Apple's flagship mobile device. On any given day in any large city, Swiss citizens are compulsively surfing the Web on their iPhones, especially as they commute to and from work on public transportation. These two demographic tidbits—high iPhone penetration and long hours on the train—created fertile ground for Switzerland's largest retailer, Coop, to plant not just its new handheld grocery-shopping application but also its customer-driven strategy for boosting revenues and growth.

CE ESSENTIALS

- **Reliability.** Customers can reserve one-hour windows to have their groceries delivered before they place their order, so that they do not get locked out of available time frames. Real-time product availability means that customers receive exactly what they order.

- **Convenience.** In Switzerland, customers have limited grocery-shopping time, as grocers close in the early evenings on week-days and are closed all day on Sundays. With a mobile app, customers can shop while they are commuting to or from work.

- **Relevance.** Switzerland has one of the highest adoption rates of the iPhone in the world, making this a well-targeted platform for a mobile shopping app.

Like all retailers, $27 billion Coop fights fiercely for its share of the grocery marketplace. Basel-based Coop's 1,800 stores offer a wide variety of organic foods and wine, with a focus on sustainability. And like many companies around the world, in nearly all industries, the battle lines for Coop are now focused on engaging customers so intimately with its brand that they simply have no reason to turn to the competition.

The grocery business is, after all, highly traditional. As a result, profit margins are razor-thin, and spending on everything from technology to advertising to marketing campaigns is limited. However, a loyal customer's lifetime value can be great. The trick is to provide a low-cost but comprehensive experience that seals the deal.

To warm the weary hearts of time-pressed Swiss citizens, in May 2009 Coop created an iPhone grocery-shopping application as an adjunct to its already existing online store, coop@home. Coop was making a bold play to endear itself to customers by pioneering a valued capability before its competitors did, thus making it less desirable to use the other grocery brands and more likely that customers would stay with Coop.

CE PILLARS

- **Operational excellence.** Coop's iPhone application interacts with the retailer's integrated enterprise resource planning (ERP) and CRM systems, enabling real-time product availability, the ability to reserve one-hour delivery windows, and price synchronization across channels.

- **Interaction excellence.** Coop is continually refining its mobile interaction capabilities. It recently improved its navigation and search functionality with a practical filtering function. Customers can also add any item that is currently on their shelf at home to their order by scanning it in via the iPhone camera.

- **Decision-making excellence.** Coop had already created online shopping with home grocery delivery via post or truck. But by researching actual customer behavior, the team realized that putting grocery shopping literally in customers' hands for maximum convenience and relevance would be more compelling.

For a full discussion of the CE Pillars, see Chapter 7.

Already, customers are voting with their keypads. Coop@home sales now account for 80 million Swiss francs (CHF) per year. Orders through the iPhone account for 4 million CHF of that total, with higher growth expected. For a modest investment and two months of time, Coop's iPhone initiative has paid off handsomely for company and customers alike.

Such innovations are key to consumer satisfaction with retailers, which must continuously find ways to reinvent value for their customers, according to Dunnhumby, a U.K.-based customer behavior analytics firm. And, it seems, supermarket retailers are catching on. According to a recent Dunnhumby report, which surveyed 1,300 consumers on 59 major companies in eight sectors, U.K.-based supermarket retailers received the highest ratings and were regarded as nearly twice as customer-centric as airlines, which placed second. According to the firm, there is a direct correlation between the commitment that grocers make to their customers and the length of the relationship. This correlation is particularly true when the company delivers highly relevant customer propositions, the Dunnhumby report says.

Making Customers Feel @home

Lacking brimming coffers to draw from, coop@home focused on deconstructing its customer experience, zeroing in on areas that could be improved without requiring exorbitant investment. "We asked, what will it take to entice someone to shop with us—and then come back again?" says Ellen Brasse, head of marketing and sales at coop@home in Spreitenbach, Switzerland. "We needed to define services that would make customers depend on us more."

When commuters travel on the train, it might take them an hour going and an hour coming home. "Commuters tend to surf the Web, and we knew they had iPhones," Brasse says. Online grocery shopping had always been a natural for this demographic, as commuters have limited time to shop, and no one wants to lug grocery bags on the train.

You often hear that the customer experience is about creating "wow" experiences every day. For Brasse, though, the customer experience is first about meeting their needs in an elegant, efficient way. "As with any grocery retailer, our top priority is to meet our customers' requirements, then give them a beautiful experience along the way," she says. Coop gives its customers convenience, reliability, and relevant value—all essentials of customer experience.

Coop had already created online shopping with home grocery delivery via post or truck. But by researching actual customer behavior, the team realized that putting grocery shopping literally in customers' hands for maximum convenience and relevance would be more compelling. The Swiss love their iPhones—would iPhone grocery shopping make them love their grocery store?

Leveraging a Fully Integrated IT Environment

Coop began talking about the i-shopping application with its development partner, Movento Schweiz AG, in 2008. Designing the architecture was straightforward: like the e-shop, the iPhone application would interact with Coop's core SAP ERP and CRM systems.

The integrated CRM and ERP systems are an important linchpin for several key capabilities, including real-time product availability, says Christian Heim, managing director at St. Gallen, Switzerland–based Movento. "The integrated backbone is very valuable for Coop," he says. "We were able to use the latest technology for the Web and the iPhone, and we just extended the [backend] environment." Because of the integrated back end, there was already synchronization between products and prices, Heim says. "When they change a price in the back end, it automatically gets pushed through to the CRM system," he says. That integration also cut development time. In all, it took about two months to develop coop@home.

"Because Coop had this integrated system in place, we just had to build around the existing infrastructure," Heim explains. The moving parts were already connected, so creating an interface to the handheld was not overly difficult.

COOP AT A GLANCE

- Business description: Largest retailer in Switzerland, focusing on groceries

- Annual revenues: $27 billion

- Number of employees: 75,000

- Number of Coop member households: 2 million

- Number of subscribers to the coop@home weekly e-mail: 130,000

- Number of monthly unique visitors to the coop@home site: Approximately 300,000

- Revenues from iPhone application: 4 million CHF of the 80 million CHF per year from coop@home sales

Lastly, customers can select one-hour windows in which to have their groceries delivered. "You have to have an integrated system; otherwise, it would be impossible to offer that," Heim says. Customers have the option of reserving their delivery time before they place an order. Anyone who is not within Coop's delivery zone (60 percent of Swiss residents are covered) can get their grocery orders overnight via the postal service.

The customer experience will always have some constraints. Neither Coop nor the post office offers delivery on Sunday. But Coop sees a lot of activity on coop@home on that day, with customers placing their orders while they are out and about—another point of convenience for their busy lives.

Sustainable Value

Coop's major competitor now offers an iPhone shopping application. However, it lacks a key feature of Coop's offering: customers cannot see immediately whether their products are available. Brasse and her colleagues were adamant that their iPhone app show real-time prices and product availability, features that are also made possible by integration. This information is especially important when it comes to the purchase of wine, Brasse adds. Coop offers more than 1,000 different wines from around the world, arguably giving it an advantage over its competitor, which does not focus on alcohol. Wine enthusiasts are not big on product substitution. As prices are higher here, it is especially important for shoppers to get the exact bottle they want.

In a recent survey, customers report that they also appreciate features like the ability to add any item that is currently on their shelf at home to their order by scanning it in via the iPhone camera—taking interactivity in shopping to a new level.

Coop is continually refining its iPhone shopping experience. It recently released version 3.0 of the coop@home app, which uses state-of-the-art design elements in addition to improved navigation and search functionality with a practical filtering function. Brasse believes that coop@home increases the grocer's customer satisfaction levels and overall "stickiness," citing jumps in the app's usage on holidays and many Sundays, when stores are closed and customers are vacationing in the mountains. At 5 percent of all coop@home orders, iPhone sales are still only a small percentage of overall revenue, but that number is steadily increasing. "Mobile e-commerce is important to our customers," she says. Because of customer demand (and Web analysis statistics), a coop@home iPad app will be brought to market, as well.

CHAPTER 3

B2B Customer Experience: Same Animal, Different Spots

Mobility will increasingly be a hallmark of B2B customer experience, according to almost three-quarters of businesses who say they plan to offer sales and order status information to employees via handheld device by 2012.

—BLOOMBERG BUSINESSWEEK
RESEARCH SERVICES SURVEY, 2010

MOST DISCUSSIONS OF THE CUSTOMER experience revolve around the now-familiar examples of Starbucks, Disney, Apple, and other famed business-to-consumer (B2C) companies. However, we believe that the tenets and goals of building the customer experience edge are also important to the business-to-business (B2B) world and, indeed, are just as relevant to B2B companies as to their B2C brethren.

Like B2C companies, B2B firms can no longer compete on the basis of new product offerings and lower prices. Instead, these companies need to focus on value-adds that are relevant to their customers and that they can deliver consistently and cost-effectively. Indeed, according to the Corporate Executive Board's Integrated Sales Executive Council, only 9 percent of customers give price as a main differentiator when it comes to remaining loyal to their vendors, and 38 percent give brand and product/service quality as the main differentiator. The majority (53 percent) say that sales agents have a greater impact on customer loyalty than price, brand, and product/service quality combined.

We believe that the four essentials of a profitable customer experience (discussed in Chapter 2)—convenience, responsiveness, relevance, and reliability—are crucial for the B2B world. In fact, the impact of an inconsistent customer experience is potentially more damaging for B2B in terms of downstream implications. Consider the detrimental effects of mistimed deliveries, shipment delays, and incorrect quantities. Anytime a supplier is unable to honor its contract commitments, a manufacturer can be faced with thousands of dollars in budget overruns as a result of labor, waste, or other avoidable costs.

As we said in Chapter 1, we would go so far as to say that when it comes to creating and maintaining a positive and profitable customer experience, there is increasingly less and less distinction between B2C and B2B. In fact, we should simply think in terms of P2P—people to people.

TIP

There are ways to apply the human touch in the B2B world, says TARP Worldwide's John Goodman. For instance, he has advised terminal operators at a chemical company to simply start a conversation with the truck drivers who arrive at least twice a week and wait a period of time to load their tanks. This bond would encourage the drivers to speak positively about the company to anyone to whom they are delivering chemicals, Goodman says. It goes to show that it is possible to create an emotional connection even when the product you are selling does not evoke passion.

Nevertheless, executives in B2B companies can fall into the trap of believing that focusing on the customer experience is solely the province of companies that serve consumers. Consumer products are the ones that generate passion (think iPhone, Lamborghini, and Venti Caramel Macchiato). Did anyone ever wax poetic about a shipment of lumber or a load of cement?

Maybe not. But while the B2B customer experience is necessarily quite different from the B2C, the experiences that people have as consumers inform their expectations in the B2B arena. B2B clients are increasingly becoming habituated, as consumers, to businesses that provide a rich and personalized online experience, fulfill their unspoken needs, and provide opportunities for engagement. They are now turning to their business partners and vendors and asking, "Why don't we have that kind of relationship?" "Why aren't *you* supporting a robust and helpful community (online or physical) where I can engage with my peers?" "Where are *your* proactive alerts on order status?" "Why didn't *you* respond to that criticism I saw on the online forum I was on last night?"

In effect, nearly everyone who uses a B2B product or service is also an informed person who is connected to the digital world. Historically, opportunities for B2B clients to gather with their peers were limited to specialist communities that met in local chapters or at industry conferences held once or twice a year. Today, anyone can be plugged into a global network of ideas and information and be personally involved through Facebook, Twitter, and other social media. The line between social network interactions for personal and business reasons also is blurring. People who open their laptops after hours are likely to divide their time between an online forum for business and one with their friends. At SAP, for example, we now have more than two million business professionals in our online community network, a very large number for our industry. In fact, there is little reason anymore for any limitation on how people function in their jobs in a B2B context relative to how they interact in social communities in their personal lives.

Similarly, insights and information about B2B products, performance, and even pricing that previously could only be obtained through a salesperson or an exclusive group are now obtainable through multiple websites. The power of information control is no longer in the vendor's hands; in effect, access to information has been democratized. The ease of 24/7 information access has changed the dynamics of B2B companies and their customers.

That is why, even in industries like industrial manufacturing, we are slowly beginning to see companies offering B2C-like experiences through rich Internet application technologies and easier access to data for making buying decisions and online postpurchase support.[1]

SPOTLIGHT ON: *Colmobil*

For some companies, there is little distinction between the B2B customer experience and the B2C customer experience. Colmobil, an Israeli automobile importer, sells trucks to business clients, in addition to selling several brands of cars to consumers. In some cases, a business client might be a consumer client, too. This dual role served as one incentive for Colmobil to integrate its enterprise systems to obtain a 360-degree view of all of its customers and fulfill the reliability, convenience, and relevance essentials of the customer experience.

- **Reliability.** Sales and service employees record all customer transactions and interactions in a centralized system and follow standardized policies and processes.

- **Convenience.** Colmobil fitted its new cars with radio-frequency ID (RFID) tags and placed tag scanners at its entrance gates. When a customer arrives, reception agents can offer a personal greeting rather than an identification inquiry. When the customer leaves, the exit gate opens automatically, without further inquiry.

- **Relevance.** If a B2B client walks into a Colmobil sales outlet to purchase a Hyundai for a family member, the sales staff will know that he is a valued customer from a B2B context and can offer him a corresponding personalized experience, perhaps along with a special discount.

According to global IT, consulting, and business process outsourcing firm Cognizant Technology Solutions, B2B e-commerce is moving from primarily transactional to increasingly collaborative, influenced by key practices of B2C e-commerce such as better navigation and cart capabilities, improved pricing and availability, multiple search and display options, product comparison capabilities, and marketing tools that help cross-sell and upsell products through recommendations and promotions. B2B websites are starting to become embedded with social media tools, such as blogs and forums, to help with buying decisions or postpurchase support. Benefits, according to Cognizant, include larger average order sizes, lower dropout rates, fewer returns, and increased customer loyalty.

Central Role of Information Visibility

At the same time, while the customer experience is equally important in the B2B world, there are very different considerations compared to B2C. The customer experience can be more complicated to deliver in the B2B world, and it can be mission-critical for the customer. For instance, B2B transactions may involve large-volume orders, stringent security requirements, complex trade regulations, multiparty supply chains, contract offshore manufacturing, and intricate fulfillment issues. All of these factors drive the need for timely, accurate information. This is different from the B2C world, where one e-mail acknowledgment sent when the order is received and one e-mail sent when it is shipped are pretty much what a customer needs.

In many ways, access to information—deeper, richer information than just the order shipment data—is at the heart of the B2B customer experience. Customers and employees must be able to access relevant information at key points of interaction and product/service consumption, both within and outside the four walls of the organization. For B2B, this is one of the hallmarks of a customer-centric enterprise.

Senior executives are well aware of the need to serve up information to employees to enable them to better serve customers. In the global Bloomberg Businessweek Research Services (BBRS) survey, almost three-quarters of respondents said that they had plans to offer sales and order status information to employees via handheld device by 2012 (see Figure 3.1). Today, only a minority of the organizations surveyed empower their employees with information, such as customer order status and inventory levels, accessible via handheld. Being able to answer customers' questions and provide speedy access to relevant information is a clear priority across industries, according to the BBRS survey. Additionally, once companies provide employees with data via their mobile devices, they are one step closer to doing the same for customers.

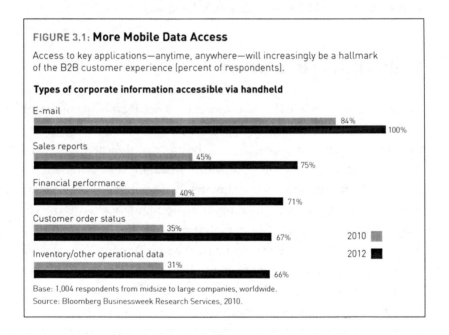

FIGURE 3.1: **More Mobile Data Access**

Access to key applications—anytime, anywhere—will increasingly be a hallmark of the B2B customer experience (percent of respondents).

Types of corporate information accessible via handheld

E-mail
84%
100%

Sales reports
45%
75%

Financial performance
40%
71%

Customer order status
35%
67%   2010

Inventory/other operational data
31%   2012
66%

Base: 1,004 respondents from midsize to large companies, worldwide.
Source: Bloomberg Businessweek Research Services, 2010.

In the B2B world, data visibility—into order status, inventory levels, and supplier status—is particularly welcome, as it enables companies to keep their own customers happy and their own operations humming along. CEMEX USA, a business unit of $15 billion global cement manufacturer CEMEX S.A.B. de C.V. of Monterrey, Mexico, installed sensors at customer sites to monitor and automatically replenish cement-inventory levels for customers who want a seamless and continuous supply of cement. In addition, customers can view their current stock levels and orders received via a self-service online portal.

Even CEMEX customers who are not part of this vendor-managed inventory program are kept apprised of the status of their cement deliveries. Delivery time is critical for CEMEX's customers, because of the nature of mixed cement. If it arrives too early, the batch can quickly become unusable, resulting in waste and project delays. If it arrives too late, work crews will need to be paid until it is delivered, resulting in escalating labor costs. For this reason, CEMEX has increased the visibility into its delivery operations and streamlined its bill of lading process by implementing an ERP and CRM system that reveals key information on process flows and sets system alerts when delays are likely. Not only has this increased on-time delivery, but CEMEX also notifies customers proactively of delays and how it intends to resolve them. CEMEX's overarching goal is to consistently and cost-effectively enable its

TIP

B2B companies are working to put the customer at the center of their processes. Doug Hurley, a managing director at PricewaterhouseCoopers, provides an example of an electronics manufacturer that revamped its processes and added new technologies at its inbound call center after analyzing how it could better serve its distributor base. For product repairs, the firm now follows up on the original phone call with an e-mail confirmation, which includes a bar-code label to be attached to the return so that it can be tracked throughout the repair process. It also continuously alerts the distributor to the status of the repair. "They're looking for ways to extend their customer service, where there is perceived value, with the intent that distributors will be more satisfied customers," Hurley says. In our view, the change also fulfills all four of our essentials of the customer experience.

customers to achieve their project and budget goals, and information is key to that. (For a full report on CEMEX USA's customer experience efforts, see the case study "Cementing Customer Bonds" in Chapter 8, page 157.)

Industrial robot manufacturer Yaskawa America makes it as easy as possible for its customers to quickly, easily, and consistently access product information and support, whether online or via its call center. Yaskawa support personnel have the full range of customer information available within one customer relationship management (CRM) system so that they can help customers speedily without having to put them on long holds, a more satisfying experience than the usual waiting game. At the same time, employees can gather information from customers during each interaction to help the company refine its product development and other strategies for the future, thereby helping to ensure that Yaskawa stays on track. This information is maintained in a knowledge base to inspire and inform anyone in the company.[2]

When Synopsys, Inc., a world-leading maker of electronic design automation software for semiconductors, decided to differentiate itself based on the customer experience, it created an online self-service portal that enables customers to initiate and check on service requests, in addition to other functions. It is currently used by more than 30,000 customers. In addition, Synopsys established a single "system of record" to store all customer interactions and support issues so that all employees can access the information they need to help customers. (For a full report on Synopsys's customer experience efforts, see the case study on page 42.)

Another key difference for B2B, as Strativity Group's Lior Arussy points out in an article, is what he calls "wallet share," where B2B customers give the vendor 100 percent of the available budget for a specific product or service, rather than distributing it among several vendors. As a result, the inherent loyalty in B2B is greater than that in the notoriously fickle consumer segment. And because one B2B relationship can be worth millions, there is all the more reason to nurture that relationship at all costs. This is difficult, because one B2B customer often requires dealing with a host of individuals in different departments with different needs. "B2B organizations face different challenges that require different business paradigms and customer experiences," Arussy writes.[3]

B2B companies have a genuine opportunity—one that is not quite achievable in the B2C realm—to get to know their top customers on a personal level. The bond is formed around the interpersonal relationship, as opposed to the product. "The smart B2B can—and should—tailor its product or service specifically to deliver the experiences wanted by that person they know directly," writes Richard Tait, blogger and principal at Product Development Consulting, which helps companies create product portfolios using customer-centric innovation management.[4] By contrast, many B2C companies are often unaware of who their best customers even are. Or, they know the demographics of their best customers—the types and personas—but they do not know these most valuable customers as individuals on a one-to-one level at all.

B2B companies can open a direct line of communication to their best, most influential customers, discovering what makes them tick, simply by asking. They usually have more data about their customers, their business challenges, and their competitive landscape. This is something that is virtually nonexistent in the B2C world, so theoretically, B2B companies are better positioned to know their customers and provide a better experience. At the same time, their customers also set the bar higher for them.

Differences aside, the important point for B2B companies to keep in mind is the human element, and that is what is being emphasized with customer experience initiatives today. The line between B2B and B2C is becoming increasingly blurred, especially as digitally engaged people from younger generations continue to enter the workforce. As you read through the rest of this book, you will see that we draw from examples in both worlds to create a complete picture of the customer experience edge.

CASE STUDY: **SYNOPSYS**

Focus on Customer Success Yields Substantial Cost Savings for Synopsys

Differentiated service at every stage of the chip design life cycle helps this electronic design automation leader's top and bottom lines.

Thanks to global demand for high-tech consumer devices like smartphones and tablets, the electronics industry is pulling out of the depths of the recession. With shorter consumer and business product life cycles, coupled with widely divergent demands in developing vs. developed economies, system makers and their semiconductor suppliers are always pushing for the next new thing. To deliver, chipmakers depend on electronic design automation (EDA) systems to infuse their intricate wares with ever more capacity and sophisticated features in a timely manner.

CE ESSENTIALS

- **Reliability.** Synopsys standardized on a single CRM system, which would enable its engineering support staff to follow a consistent process for supporting customers, no matter where in the company they resided.

- **Convenience.** Customers can use a self-service portal to initiate and check on service requests or upload a test case to a support engineer via Synopsys's web portal.

- **Relevance.** Synopsys's five-pronged strategy addresses the needs of a diverse customer base, from small start-ups to global companies.

- **Responsiveness.** Field consultants set up notifications and subscriptions in the CRM system, enabling the sales rep who is in charge of each account to see and respond to all issues, even if they come in via different channels.

Despite this reliance, chip manufacturers' success during boom periods does not, for the most part, spill over to EDA vendors. This counterintuitive fact keeps the three leading players—Synopsys, Cadence, and Mentor Graphics—working hard to grow both their revenue and their net income.

"There's a steady drive by Moore's Law to design more and more into the chips, and the design grows more and more complex," says Gary Smith, chief analyst at Gary Smith EDA, a market intelligence and advisory services firm in Santa Clara, California. To accommodate this relentless change, EDA vendors are constantly in an upgrade cycle. And yet, their biggest customers expect more functionality and better performance for the same price, which leads to lower profit margins. "The whole basis of the electronics industry is on the back of this industry. But the EDA companies are not compensated well," Smith says.

To succeed in these challenging conditions, market leader Synopsys decided that the best way to attract more customers, keep existing ones, and improve its margins was to bond ever more closely with its customers. The tighter its relationship with the engineers and Ph.D.s that make up its customer base, the more it would learn about their constantly changing needs.

Commitment to Customer Success

With fiscal 2010 revenues of almost $1.38 billion, Synopsys has fought hard in the past few years to reach the top spot in EDA, and the Mountain View, California–based company is determined to stay there. It has grown from a $500 million firm through a flurry of acquisitions, strong investment in R&D, and competitor weaknesses over the course of the last 10 of its 25 years in business.

Synopsys's chosen differentiator is a commitment to enabling its customers' success by anticipating their needs through every stage of the chip design life cycle. It delivers on that commitment by offering reliable, relevant, and responsive support resources. Thriving customers, after all, have little reason to move to a competitor. This is especially true in EDA, because chip design projects often involve millions of dollars and months if not years of time.

CE PILLARS

- *Operational excellence.* A centralized CRM system serves as the "system of record" for all customer support issues and standardizes processes for all support technicians across Synopsys's business units. All support cases come through the central CRM system, and calls are routed globally to the support staff members with the right expertise.

- *Interaction excellence.* A self-service portal enables customers to initiate and check on service requests. Through a community forum, engineers can pose questions or converse with other customers who have faced similar design challenges. The idea is to encourage customers to ask for help—and for Synopsys to proactively offer help—at each step of the chip design journey.

For a full discussion of the CE Pillars, see Chapter 7.

"Our customers are using our tools to design every chip in your cell phone, your computer, the new Android, that TV you just purchased. We are used in everything from your gaming systems to your automotive electronics," says Vito Mazzarino, vice president of field support operations at Synopsys. The world's top chip designers are among the company's customers.

Rather than getting an SOS call when a customer's project is running late, with big money at stake, Synopsys wanted to ensure customer success from the beginning. That meant making it easy—almost intuitive—for busy engineers to ask for and receive help in the way that was most valuable to them. And it could not succeed by providing generic levels of service; customers had to feel as though they were getting personalized support from staff members who understood their problem.

And so Synopsys went about infusing its organization with customer-centric systems, processes, and culture. An immediate hurdle, however, was its diverse collection of CRM systems. Thanks to Synopsys's dozens of acquisitions, customer information was spread across 17 different data repositories. This made it all but impossible to deliver a consistent experience across the company's multiple business units.

Synopsys was in good company. In a recent survey by Bloomberg Businessweek Research Services, a majority of respondents said that disconnected applications were a major obstacle to improving the customer experience (see Chapter 4, Figure 4.1, "Disconnections, Silos Are Biggest Barrier to Improving Customer Experience"). The EDA vendor realized that it needed to standardize on a single CRM system, which would also enable its engineering support staff to follow a consistent process for supporting customers, no matter where in the company they resided.

Synopsys chose a CRM system from its enterprise resource planning (ERP) system vendor, SAP, which enabled additional synergies between these two core business systems.

A second hurdle was the geographic and size distribution of its customer base. "We have customers in every part of the globe," Mazzarino says. "There are big companies producing semiconductors, but we also have small start-ups in garages in California and China." The challenge was to develop a service and support strategy that would address diverse customer needs while maintaining Synopsys's profitability in a difficult market.

Five-Pronged Approach Adds Up to Customer Success

After studying its different types of customers and gaining a better understanding of their needs, Mazzarino's field-support organization developed a layered customer-support and field-support strategy that is based on the various channels that customers use to get support. Different channels come into play at the different stages of the project life cycle.

The key to providing differentiated support was enabling both support techs and customers with the tools to access the right support and data at the right time. Synopsys's five-pronged strategy is as follows:

1. Customer Education   The starting point for all customers is education on Synopsys's tools and methodologies, ranging from traditional instructor-led classes to online offerings. Many of these options are free, such as self-paced video training on new software releases. Synopsys also offers training via archived WebEx presentations. With the notorious time pressure in the electronics industry, customers are always tempted to skip over the education step, Mazzarino says. But his organization sees these resources as a building block to later success. "This is a way of avoiding support and other problems down the road," he says.

2. Online Customer Portal   The second layer is an online portal called SolvNet. Membership in SolvNet—which is free with the maintenance contract—gives engineers access to a variety of assets, including best practices, a library of tool documentation, FAQs, and a knowledge base containing reusable code. Customers can use SolvNet to initiate and check on service requests, which flow into and out of the CRM system automatically. SolvNet is integrated with Synopsys's core systems. Through a community forum, engineers can pose questions or converse with other customers who have faced similar design challenges. The idea is to encourage customers to ask for help—and for Synopsys to proactively offer help—at each step of the chip design journey. "We really stress with the customer to get out there early. We don't want them to wait until the project is late and they are panicking," Mazzarino says. Currently, 35,000 to 38,000 engineers are registered on the portal, out of a total user base of about 50,000.

3. Support Centers   Located in the United States, India, and China, these centers are staffed not with traditional service representatives, but with 130 electronics engineers, most of them with master's degrees. "Most have done design work at other companies," Mazzarino says. "We look for designers who like the people side of the business and recruit them. It takes a special kind of person." If a customer runs into a problem, she can upload a test case to a support engineer over SolvNet. All support cases come through the central CRM system, creating one "system of record" for all customer issues. The central CRM system also routes calls globally to the person with the right expertise, providing a personalized experience and minimizing the time the customer might otherwise spend bouncing from one agent to the next.

4. Field Application Consultants   Engineers in local offices are also available to help customers get up and running with their design projects—once again, in the interest of encouraging success early to avoid bigger problems downstream. Consultants partner with salespeople, and, early in the sales cycle, they preview what type of help and support the customer is likely to need. They are also skilled in suggesting resources on SolvNet or elsewhere, with a view toward efficiency. "Often, we can move the customer to a different resource, where the issue can be handled more effectively," Mazzarino says. For example, when a new software release or patch comes out, the consultant will engage the affected customers directly, sharing tips and best practices. Working with sales reps, the consultants set up notifications and subscriptions in the CRM system, so that the rep in charge of the account will know if an issue comes in via a different channel. For example, if three individuals from one customer have open issues, the sales rep might call the field application consultant and share relevant information about the account. In this way, Synopsys customers from large global companies sometimes discover things that they did not know about what their own colleagues on the other side of the world are doing.

5. Professional Services Organization   The top tier of Synopsys's support structure is its professional services organization, the chief function of which is to offer design services on complex projects.

This team concentrates on helping customers structure their design environment and match the right resources, such as tools and methodologies, to the job at hand. The multitiered support approach also optimizes Synopsys's customer service costs.

"Customer support is a business of human touch, and we never lose sight of that," Mazzarino says. "But we have to do this in a way that allows us to maintain our profitability."

To that end, Synopsys attributes many cost efficiencies to its focus on the customer experience. The company estimates that it has reduced the amount of time application consultants spend on reactive support from 33 percent to 20 percent, enabling the company to shift support to more accessible channels and leverage a broader global talent pool.

Gary Smith is confident that Synopsys will succeed despite the EDA industry's ongoing fluctuations and transitions. "This industry is all about change," he says. "They are focused on their customers and on R&D." That is just what it takes to thrive in this historically challenging industry.

PART II

Making It Happen

CHAPTER 4

Throwing Out the Old Playbook

For almost three-quarters of companies, the top barriers to improving customer experience are related to disconnections in processes, applications, customer information and social media channels.
— BLOOMBERG BUSINESSWEEK
RESEARCH SERVICES SURVEY, 2010

A SUCCESSFUL AND PROFITABLE CUSTOMER experience does not happen at the margins of the organization; instead, these initiatives are holistic, involving the entire enterprise and transforming the corporate mindset. Stretching far beyond "customer service," the customer experience edge encompasses each and every customer interaction, whether it's through the call center, the supply chain, the website, social media, or the product or service itself.

Even more critical, it's the customer—not the product or service—who should be at the center of the corporate universe. This means tossing out old ways of doing business and gutting or transforming many of the systems, processes, and organizational structures under which you have been accustomed to operating. The new playbook—the one leading to the customer experience edge—is based on enabling deeper, richer, and ultimately more fulfilling customer interactions. Essentially, "business as usual" has been flipped on its head. For instance:

- Product centricity is out; customer centricity is in.

- Processes need to be designed from the customer's perspective, not just for internal efficiencies.

- Your purpose is to provide customers with relevant value, not to sell products and services.

- Customers don't need to listen to you; you need to listen to customers *and* incorporate those new insights into your processes.

- You no longer call the shots. Customers will choose to interact and engage with their social network and the companies they purchase from wherever, whenever, and however they want.

- Employees at all levels need to be empowered to provide a great and economical customer experience.

Does this sound radical? It is. But this is what it takes to create a customer experience that translates into profits and differentiation for your company. Otherwise, as Strativity Group's Lior Arussy says, "You're just sitting at the children's table, playing with toys."

Two types of companies engage in customer experience initiatives, Arussy explains: those who pursue the customer experience as a full-company effort and embed the initiative in their business strategy, and those who are forced into dealing with the customer experience as a reaction to an event, such as poor customer satisfaction scores or an embarrassing social media fiasco. In the first case, the customer experience is a total value proposition, not just a customer service, marketing, or PR concern. These companies are designing a value proposition across multiple business divisions: product design, marketing, billing, fulfillment, customer care, and company-generated communications.

"The ones who 'get it' are trying to create new and relevant value for customers, and the more relevant they are, the better their chance of retaining customers, upselling products and services, and lowering their cost of doing business," Arussy tells us.

Changing Roles, Changing Rules

This new way of doing business will change the rules and roles for everyone in the corporate ecosystem, including the customers themselves. For instance, consider the following areas.

Leadership

Company leaders now need to be engaged with and even passionate about customers. Too often, businesses throw money at customer experience initiatives. But without passion at a high level—and clear direction as to how to turn that passion into long-term customer loyalty and profitability—these efforts don't always pay off. Top executives and customer experience leaders need to motivate people in business units throughout the organization to rally around the customers, getting to know them and their needs. "There has to be a love for people and a core belief that serving them well will drive desired business outcomes," says Leigh Durst, principal of Live Path, a customer experience consultancy. "For too long, we've been focused on other aims first."

According to Forrester Research, Inc., one vital ingredient of high-performing customer experience organizations is inspiring leaders. "Because the customer experience organization gets most of its work done through others, the ability of its leaders to influence people across the business is critical to long-term success," Forrester says in its report, "Three Secrets of Success for Customer Experience Organizations."[1] To permanently shift the corporate culture, customer experience (CE) leaders must make employees at all levels of the company want to change themselves, Forrester concludes.

Employees

Organizations can no longer limit employee authority. The old "that isn't my department" just doesn't fly anymore, as it leaves customers frustrated and angry, and then what happens? They flame you on their favorite social channel. Today, employees need to be "agents of experience," which requires enabling them to access information to answer customers' questions and empowering them with tools to fulfill unexpected needs. All employees (and particularly frontline employees) should also be seen as prime sources of insights that can be fed back into product development, marketing, and customer service. "We all deliver experience, and in some way, we shape that experience with what we do," says Frank Eliason, who famously helped move Comcast's customer service operations onto social media and is now senior vice president of social media at Citi.

Employee empowerment often requires cultural change within the company, as the environment itself needs to foster customer experience–focused behavior. There may be no better example of this than Zappos, whose CEO, Tony Hsieh, goes so far as to say that his company's culture is its brand. The Zappos culture is laid out in its 10 core values, which include an "obsession" with customer service and bringing passion, fun, and a sense of adventure to the job.[2]

Customer service reps at Zappos are given the freedom to offer all customers the highest levels of personalized service, including delivering flowers to a customer whose mother had recently died.[3] When employees are hired, they take an intensive four-week training course that immerses them in the company's culture and processes. At the end of the training, they are offered a $3,000 bonus to quit that day, with the idea being that only those who are truly passionate about the company's approach will stay. According to Hsieh, only about 2 or 3 percent of people take the offer, on average.[4]

"It may sound like our top priority is customer service, but it's about the culture," says Aaron Magness, senior director of brand marketing and business development at Zappos. Instead of weighing employees down with bureaucracy and policies, "We just allow employees to do what they do best," he says. "They are naturally empowered—you can't do that if you have a policy in place for every interaction."

Zappos also experiments with employee performance measurement. Eschewing traditional call center metrics such as average call-handling time, it has developed an employee dashboard to show people how they're doing from a cultural perspective and in terms of living up to the company's 10 core values. All companies can learn from this variation on performance measurement. True customer centricity requires that employees be compensated on driving outcomes, not just carrying out a set of prescribed tasks. This requires new types of performance measurement, as we'll discuss in Chapter 11, "Measures of Success."

Customers

Customers themselves are in a new role. There's been a shift in the balance of power between customer and company, as digitally engaged and always-connected customers rely on their peers and social media commentary to conduct research and make buying decisions. According to a 2009 Nielsen Global Online Consumer Survey, the forms of advertising most trusted by respondents were recommendations from personal acquaintances (90 percent of respondents) and opinions posted online by consumers (70 percent).[5]

Customers are increasingly using mobile devices and the Web as a primary source of product and pricing information, as well as for opinions on which products and services to choose. And they increasingly expect to contact the company, obtain information, and make transactions through any channel they desire, whether that is the phone, the Web, in person, tweets, instant messaging, or something else. No longer is the customer-company relationship a one-way street, with the company broadcasting marketing messages and product and pricing information; the new relationship is two-way, with customers expecting to make their personal preferences known and have them fulfilled. With so much information available at any given time—through search engines, social media commentary, online forums, and shopping comparison websites—there is a new transparency of price and product information that puts the customer in the driver's seat.

What's more, customers are no longer simply consumers of products and services; companies will increasingly work to involve customers more directly in co-creating new products and services. The aim is to co-innovate on more successful offerings and encourage word-of-mouth advertising, as engaged customers become natural advocates of the products and services they helped develop.

Breaking Down Organizational Barriers

Amid all this change, organizations also need to undergo a transformation: they need to break down the corporate silos that served companies well in industrial times but cause big problems today. Traditionally, business departments have operated as separate fiefdoms, with their own performance goals, processes, programs, and information, and with little meaningful connection or communication among them. Rather than being accountable to one enterprisewide set of goals and values, each often marched to its own set of orders. Structuring business activities by specialty might have worked well in the Industrial Age, when efficiency was the goal, but this approach doesn't lend itself to fulfilling the needs of people—both customers and employees—and that's what customer centricity is all about.

Customer centricity cannot be achieved by one business department or even several departments acting independently. The company needs to act as one organization, presenting a single face to customers and employees. There needs to be consistency across all customer touch points and all channels of communication, so that when customers call for support, for instance, they get the same treatment and information as they would get if they opted for self-service or visited the company's corporate Facebook page.

Goals and strategies also need to be aligned and synchronized among all business functions. There needs to be one organizationwide sense of purpose, mission, and values, and it needs to be embraced by everyone. This cannot happen when business functions perceive themselves as separate from one another and are not accountable for something bigger than performing their own individual tasks and showing how their performance meets the overall business purpose.

A classic example is when, say, the purchasing department opts for less expensive and thus lower-quality components in an attempt to meet cost-cutting goals. The downstream impact on manufacturing and customer support is, of course, detrimental, as both have to deal with the increased costs that result from customer complaints or products not passing quality assurance tests. The same is true for customer service and eventually every customer interaction. The bottom line is, pursuing efficiency gains (or any other goal) without awareness of how these actions fit into the larger picture will backfire.

When business functions are aligned and synchronized, they are better able to collaborate with each other, as well. An example is the common disconnect between the call center, which is dealing directly with customers, and the marketing department, which tends to gain an understanding of customers in more indirect ways. "Marketing is doing focus groups and obtaining customer research, while the frontline [call center] employees are gathering this data in real time," Durst says. This sort of fragmentation does not have the best interests of the customer at heart; indeed, these groups often work at cross-purposes because they are measured based on different metrics.

TIP

To encourage intercompany collaboration, some companies locate product development adjacent to the call center so that input from customers can be applied to product design more rapidly.

Unfortunately, these types of fragmentation seem to be the rule; in the Bloomberg Businessweek Research Services (BBRS) survey, the top barriers to improving customer experience all relate to disconnections and silos in processes, applications, customer information, and social media channels (see Figure 4.1).

FIGURE 4.1: **Disconnections, Silos Are Biggest Barrier to Improving Customer Experience**

Which of the following are obstacles to your company improving the experience customers encounter when doing business with you?

Organizational and process silos in our company

73%

Lack of coordination across channels to ensure consistency

72%

Large number of disconnected tools, technologies, and applications

71%

Lack of a complete view of the customer to better understand their needs and make interactions more relevant and customized

66%

Base: 307 director-level and above executives at midsize and large companies.
Source: Bloomberg Businessweek Research Services, 2010.

Removing these obstacles and smoothing the way to better communication and collaboration is an essential requirement of moving to the new customer-centered paradigm. For instance, Eliason was integral in Comcast's current practice of using Twitter to monitor and resolve customer problems.[6] Adopting Twitter as a window into customer issues ultimately led to a cultural shift and other transformational events at the company, such as a corporate restructuring that broke down departmental silos. "It created a whole new company," he says. Today, Comcast sees customer experience reaching far beyond fixing customer issues and extending into how consumers behave and how that translates into new services. "We are focused on providing a great experience end-to-end—it's not just phone calls and truck rolls, but our brand image and how we design our product suite," says Rick Germano, senior vice president of national customer operations.

In addition to introducing the Comcast Customer Guarantee, the company recently hired a senior vice president of customer experience and has invested almost $2 billion in the customer experience over the last few years, Germano says. These investments include improvements to its network infrastructure, online self-help, ongoing enhancements to its products and services, and even creating a dedicated digital care team. According to Germano, the number of customer problems has dropped by more than 20 percent, the company's "get it right the first time" commitment has improved by more than 33 percent, and technicians' on-time arrival is now at 95 percent.[7]

At Zappos, customer service and the customer experience are not relegated to one part of the company, but "are part of what everyone in the company does," Magness says. In marketing, that translates into communicating the company's service-level commitments to customers. In the Customer Loyalty Team (or call center), it's the freedom to lavish customers with extra service. In merchandising, it's a focus on supplying the products that customers want. "It's not one department—everyone is measured on their ability to enhance the customer experience," Magness says.

And at Cardinal Health, the $99 billion health-care services company, the implementation of a problem tracking and resolution system was instrumental in helping to break down the barriers across its business units, support teams, operations staff, and distribution centers. Previously, Cardinal Health had had "a patchwork of systems" across its pharmaceutical and medical departments, according to Deborah Dexter, director of customer service for business operating systems. "We heard some concerns from our customer service reps that it was challenging to work across multiple applications," she says. Now with a system that holds all customer data and "the foundational capabilities for our organization," employees gets a 360-degree view of customers from all of Cardinal Health's customer service, operations, and inventory support teams. (For a full report on Cardinal Health's customer experience edge, see the case study on page 67.)

Redefining Processes from the Customer's Perspective

Business processes often need to be redesigned to reflect customer centricity, as well. In the past, the main idea behind process design was to maximize efficiency and reduce costs. And certainly efficient operations, as well as balancing the impact of costs on revenues, continue to be important, even in a business that stresses customer centricity. But in the end, efficiency cannot get in the way of doing the right things from a customer perspective.

To strike the right balance between efficiency and customer centricity, we like to juxtapose efficiency and effectiveness. Think of it as needing to use a ladder to fix a hole in the wall that's beyond arm's reach. You can climb the ladder as quickly as you can, and you can have all the right tools in your toolbelt, but none of that matters if you put the ladder against the wrong wall. Similarly, if your processes are not designed to fulfill customer needs, it doesn't matter how well you tune them or how efficiently they run. Making a bad process run faster doesn't help anyone. You've got to put the ladder against the right wall, and then start thinking about efficiency.

When you're reengineering processes for customer centricity, you need to look at your processes from the outside looking in rather than the converse. What would make most sense for the customer? For many companies, the customer is seen as an unwelcome disruption that interferes with their otherwise smooth-running processes. After all, it's easy to define an order-processing system if the customer never changes his mind and never needs to return or exchange something. But in a customer-centric approach, not only do processes need to take these types of events into account, but flexibility needs to be designed in from the beginning, with the expectation that exceptions will occur at any point during the process, from start to finish. If the process cannot accommodate a disruption, then the process is not designed correctly. Business processes (and the underlying technology that automates these processes) need to treat customers and the unexpected actions they might take not as a problem, but as an expected disruption.

Companies that deliver a great customer experience have thought through the many ways in which customers behave and realize that customers do not behave in predetermined ways. They've analyzed their processes from the customer's perspective and redefined them with the customer in mind. They realize that they cannot train customers to take certain actions. For instance, even though they've developed a self-service component on their website, they still invest in their phone-based customer support. And the experience that customers get on the one is reflected on the other, even if they start on the website, move to chat, and end up with a representative on the phone. That is the difference between an organization with the customer experience edge and one without it.

So, how do you begin to see your business processes through the eyes of customers? For most companies, this means creating mechanisms to listen to actual customers, analyzing this feedback, and then acting on it. These programs—often referred to as "voice of the customer" programs—can use a number of "listening" mechanisms that capture both solicited and unsolicited feedback, including surveys, social media monitoring, customer e-mails, calls into the call center, comments on company blogs, and feedback on third-party sites, according to Temkin Group's Bruce Temkin.

Most important, you need to create feedback loops so that you can take action on the input you receive. The insights you collect from customers through these various mechanisms are valuable only to the degree that you act on those insights, either by redefining your processes or by improving or redesigning the products and services that you offer.

An example is Sony Canada, which in 2010 revamped its customer feedback system as part of its effort to differentiate itself through the customer experience.[8] It began surveying customers, through an automated function in its customer relationship management (CRM) system, after customers had called into its call center. The survey includes five questions that focus on touch points that Sony determined are important to customers, as well as an opportunity for open comments. The questions are: Was the employee knowledgeable? Friendly? Patient? Did the employee get a resolution for you? How likely are you to recommend Sony Canada to someone else?

Sony acts on the responses in several ways. Customer support agents call every customer who scores low (0 to 6 on a 10-point scale) on whether she would recommend the company. High-scoring customers receive a coupon toward future purchases. In addition, company presidents receive daily feedback reports, and the marketing department can track results on the CRM home page. Sony is clearly a company that meets the CE essential of "responsiveness."

Letting Customers Have Their Way

Customer centricity also breaks down traditional boundaries between customers and organizational processes, as companies invite customers to provide input directly into their processes, such as in the practices of real-time demand planning and product co-creation. This idea of directly involving customers in personalizing products and services based on their preferences and even helping to co-innovate new ones has historically been called *mass customization*. Although it's not a new concept, the idea of providing personalization and customization—what we might today call "engaging the segment of 'one,'"—is now exploding in industries from apparel to retail to communications to financial services. It is a vibrant example of how some companies have become hyperresponsive and hyperrelevant to their customers, fulfilling the "relevance" and "responsiveness" customer experience essentials.

TIP

It's one thing to monitor social media; it's another to incorporate those insights into improving the customer experience. Citi's Frank Eliason encourages companies to create feedback loops to take action on what they hear from customers. "Ninety percent of companies that are listening to social media aren't doing anything with that information," Eliason says. "They're usually listening within their own silos. What's the point of listening if you're doing nothing with it?"

Personalization and customization require an organization's underlying systems and processes to be integrated and flexible in a whole new way. Companies that can pull this off are functioning at a high level of customer experience, and their reward for this achievement is higher market share and more engaged, loyal customers.

In the early days of mass customization, McDonald's, Burger King, and other fast-food purveyors encouraged customized food, adding and subtracting pickles on burgers and the like at will. Levi's caused a stir in the mid-1990s when it offered its Personal Pair customized jeans (not that consumers adopted this first venture en masse). The key factor to be learned from these examples is that allowing customization does not bankrupt the company. Early on, these quick-serve restaurants were able to reengineer their systems and processes to allow efficient flexibility, within reason.

Now, personalization and customization have really taken off, including in the business-to-business (B2B) market, but particularly in consumer goods. For instance, while it's been possible for automobile buyers to order the options they wanted if they were willing to wait months for the custom car, now they can receive alerts to key moments of the assembly process and watch footage of the car being built.[9] Customers can "curate" their own clothing collection with items culled from millions of Web clothing stores and share their taste with the world in their own "boutique" on Google-backed Boutiques.com.[10] And Nike and Reebok are pushing customized shoes as the next wave of cool.

In configuring your own special ZigSlash basketball sneakers, you can choose from dozens of colors for each component of the shoe—everything from the laces to the sole and each part of the Reebok "slash" logo.[11] (The freedom to create an eye-burning pair of sneakers combining pink, olive, and teal blue patent leather with accents of acid yellow is apparently now the consumer's inalienable right.) Customers who are not ready to take the plunge can order models designed by other customers or by their favorite basketball player instead. Browsing others' creations lends a nice social media touch to the Reebok store, with the feeling of belonging to an exclusive group.

Customized ZigSlash sneakers sell for nearly $140 and take six to seven weeks from configuration to production to package delivery. The fact that at least a certain segment of the market accepts the comparatively long lead times and high price is an indication of just how powerful the lure of customization is.

WHAT IS: The Segment of 'One'?

Mass customization, or what today we might call "engaging the segment of 'one,'" is the principle of enabling customers to decide the exact specifications or personal attributes of a product or service, at or after the time of purchase, and to have that product or service supplied to them at a price close to that for an ordinary mass-produced alternative. Alternatively, they can have this exact requirement supplied using the vendor's knowledge of the individual customer's needs.

Source: MadeForOne.com.

According to Cognizant Technology Services, financial services customers are also increasingly interested in designing their own products and services, from putting their photo on a credit card and designing the layout of their mobile banking graphical user interface (GUI) to tailoring their retirement investment portfolios.[12] Going further, Progressive Insurance offers customers the option to pick their own monthly premium cost and coverage. And in the hospitality industry, Marriott International, Inc., now emphasizes personalized experiences for its Rewards members. When a frequent customer calls to make a reservation, call center agents have at their fingertips enough information about that person's preferences that they can deliver a personalized, and therefore more satisfying, experience. Much hinges on the 360-degree visibility afforded by integrated systems.

For example, if the call center gets a call from a frequent business traveler who often stays at Marriott properties at a prenegotiated corporate rate, the system immediately recognizes the person (and therefore his status and preferences) by his phone number or Rewards number. That customer is then routed to the right service desk, where he will receive personalized service. There, the agent can see in the customer's file that this no-nonsense road warrior wants nothing more than confirmation of dates at the agreed-upon rate and then to get off the phone. If that person has opted in his customer profile to receive an e-mail confirmation, one will be dispatched. If he hasn't, it won't be. Electronic communication is cheap for the communicator, but in our world of information overload, companies need to be judicious about how they use this tool.

Traditional service industries, such as cable television, are coming around to the idea that customers call the shots. Mass customization expert David Gardner points out that consumers should be able to choose from a menu of channels to create their own bundles, allowing them to focus on a few preset channels (as you would have in a car radio, for example). This would be a major improvement over the inflexible approach today, under which consumers have to accept and *pay for* providers' "platinum deluxe" packages, which give them dozens, if not hundreds, of channels that they will never watch.

These companies and others have every reason to move toward customer centricity; the problem is that their legacy systems and processes (the old playbook) do not allow customers freedom of choice. Customization requires complex order management capabilities that most established companies do not currently have, including seamless cross-channel ordering, simplified ordering of complex products and bundles, better collaboration with internal/third-party partners, order fulfillment across multiple enterprises, and process/systems integration. This might seem to be a daunting task, but changing the organizational mindset is even more challenging. Once employees begin to view the world from the customer's point of view, things can begin to change.

B2B: Engaging the Segment of One

Personalization and customization are an equally critical capability in the B2B world. Smaller, younger B2Bs often have the advantage of being nimbler than their larger, more established counterparts. Take Interior Concepts of Spring Lake, Michigan. A small manufacturer of furniture used in call centers and schools, the company not only custom-makes every product, but also *custom-designs* every product. Customers choose the colors and materials that they prefer, typically requesting and configuring a completely different product with each order. This degree of individualized service is the core of Interior Concepts's value proposition to its customers, and it would have been impossible without implementing an engineer-to-order solution.[13] This type of software is invaluable in helping manufacturers cope with customers' increasing appetite for customization.

As markets continue to shift to being demand (a.k.a. customer)-driven, as opposed to supply (a.k.a. company)-driven, other types of innovative software will become increasingly important. Product configuration and customer ordering software have progressed to the point where companies can provide customized goods for consumers and businesses. On the web you can order shirts, shoes, and other clothes exactly as you would want them.

There are organizational implications as well. The product engineers enter approximately 500 to 600 business rules at the beginning of the process of building a furniture model, reusing sections from one model in another. The business rules reside in the system so that nothing can be lost in translation from one engineer to another.

That was the rub. The engineers had a lot of reservations. They thought their jobs might be taken away, especially given the clouded economy at the time of the implementation of the process in 2003. Rather than displacing human expertise, however, automating Interior Concepts's quoting and engineering process allowed the engineers to fully utilize their knowledge by moving into value-added tasks such as product development, which had previously been outsourced. Postimplementation, engineers no longer functioned as order processors. They created and modified models—a much more valuable use of their time.

Being able to deliver custom-designed and custom-made office furniture at a reasonable cost allowed Interior Concepts to differentiate itself from offshore contract manufacturers, back when offshore was viewed as the only game in town. Given that today, high energy and logistics costs have weakened the benefits of producing in low-labor-cost regions, especially for heavy goods like office furniture, Interior Concepts is now in a rather enviable position.

Increasingly, developing the customer experience edge will include some ability to personalize products, services, or the delivery of the experience itself. And that will require operating from a new playbook, with new processes and rules that enable deeper and richer customer engagement and collaboration.

CASE STUDY: CARDINAL HEALTH, INC.

Cardinal Health Transforms Customer Experience with a Cross-Company Service System

Cardinal Health, Inc., has long recognized the importance of delivering "an exceptional customer experience"—in fact, it's one of the company's top priorities, says Deborah Dexter, director of customer service for business operating systems at the Dublin, Ohio–based health-care services company. Cardinal Health is one of the largest companies in the United States, with $99 billion in revenue. While the company has operations in Asia, Canada, and South America, the vast majority of its revenues come from domestic organizations.

Cardinal Health's customers include pharmacies, physicians' offices, hospitals, and ambulatory care sites. "We touch just about every part of the health-care industry with our products and services," Dexter says. "We are shipping products to all those points of care and more."

CE ESSENTIALS

- **Reliability.** Cardinal Health's Interaction Center measures key performance indicators, such as service level agreements, to ensure that requests are serviced in a timely manner. The system also tracks trends and makes needed modifications quickly.

- **Convenience.** When a customer calls with a problem or question, customer service reps across the company can access a complete record of that customer's interactions with Cardinal Health and service her needs.

- **Relevance.** Cardinal Health relies on feedback from voice of the customer (VoC) surveys and advisory council meetings with customers and continuously improves its processes to meet the changing demands of all customers (pharmacies, physicians, hospitals, and others).

- **Responsiveness.** Customers with shipment inquiries get a quick response, as the CRM system allows service reps to route inquiries to the right distribution center.

Delivering exceptional customer service was a challenge. Cardinal Health had "a patchwork of systems" across its pharmaceutical and medical departments, Dexter says. The pharmaceutical segment acts as a wholesaler to retail independent and chain pharmacies, while the medical unit provides supplies to hospitals, physicians' offices, laboratories, and ambulatory care sites.

"We heard some concerns from our customer service reps that it was challenging to work across multiple applications," says Dexter. "We wanted to be able to streamline to one tool across the business."

Since 2009, Cardinal Health has been working on a phased implementation across its business units of a problem-tracking and resolution tool it has dubbed SAP CRM Interaction Center. The system contains customer data and "the foundational capabilities for our organization," says Dexter. It also provides a 360-degree view of our customers from all of Cardinal Health's customer service, operations, and inventory support teams. Incoming requests may include inquiries about customer orders, products, or delivery status. "We work very hard to solve these requests very quickly," she says.

The tool also has a tracking mechanism that Dexter's group can use to see how long it took to service the request. "We wanted to make sure we can document the interaction with the customer," she explains.

The Interaction Center provides automation to record each inquiry, noting which agent received the inquiry and who else was involved in responding to it, enabling everyone involved to track a customer's request. That way, whoever receives a follow-up can see all service requests and inquiries from the customer by pulling up the interaction record. "The tool provides the automation we need for visibility on customer requests and enhanced automation to make the process very seamless for the customer," Dexter says.

CE PILLARS

- **Operational excellence.** Cardinal Health's problem resolution system breaks down the barriers across its business units, support teams, operations staff, and distribution centers.

- **Interaction excellence.** Through the Interaction Center, any customer service rep can access a customer's relevant history to help resolve a problem.

- **Decision-making excellence.** Because the CRM system incorporates knowledge management and analytics, decisions are based on relevant, real-time data.

For a full discussion of the CE Pillars, see Chapter 7.

If the inquiry is related to a shipment, a customer service rep can create a service ticket and route it to one of Cardinal Health's distribution centers across the country. Based on the system's routing capabilities, customer service reps can document the customer's inquiry and account information, allowing the tool to route the inquiry to the appropriate distribution center automatically. The company has established minimum response times for responding to service requests, which enables the company to be more responsive to customer needs very quickly, Dexter says.

While the Interaction Center has not been completely rolled out to the entire company, the implementation of the first two phases has already delivered important improvements in the customer experience. By mid-2011, about 1,400 customer support reps were using the interaction tool. This included employees in the operations organization and distribution centers, as well. Dexter notes that the company has already exceeded its service-level goals by more than 10 percent.

Employee feedback on the Interaction Center has been very positive. "We are receiving rave reviews around case management and the accountability that the tool drives across all of the teams," says Dexter. "Our employees are saying it is definitely benefiting our customers."

That feedback is based on voice of the customer surveys and advisory council meetings with customers. These are the channels that let us know that "we are moving the needle in the right direction," says Dexter.

The metrics that Dexter's group has established are service-level agreements to ensure that customer requests are serviced by Cardinal Health in a timely manner. The goal is that when a customer calls, the customer service reps are armed with everything they need to ensure a positive customer experience, she says.

Lessons Learned

There were important lessons learned from this experience. Dexter says that three critical success factors for the Interaction Center are

1. The incorporation of knowledge management and analytics into the system. A superior customer experience for Cardinal Health customers was achieved in large part because the Inter-

action Center was able to provide real-time customer information, Dexter says.

2. Involvement of all stakeholders early in the development and deployment process. As with any project, some unexpected issues cropped up. But thanks to leadership buy-in and strong partnerships, the "decision points" were turned around in a very timely manner, Dexter says. "That happened by aligning our leaders ahead of time on plans and shared metrics" and determining roles and responsibilities at the outset.

3. Organizational change management techniques. When looking at new technologies and new processes, it is critical that the organization is prepared for the change. Also, all stakeholders must be working together to get a clear understanding of the needs of end users, Dexter says.

Overall, the Interaction Center has had a positive impact on the customer experience and on internal operations at Cardinal Health. Says Dexter, "We're pretty pleased."

CHAPTER 5

The New Customer Experience Recipe

Do not stint on the first step—identifying and understanding your customers. Without the "C," there is no customer experience.

COMPANIES DECIDE TO HONE their customer experience edge for many reasons: competitive threats, eroding customer loyalty, bad news in social media, or weak top-line or profitability performance, to name just a few. In many cases, companies that are in search of growth turn to a superior customer experience (CE) to differentiate themselves from their competitors in a commodity business. In still others, the interest in CE starts in the customer service or marketing department and percolates upward, eventually becoming a C-suite- or board-level agenda item.

Once a customer experience initiative reaches the executive suite agenda level, the next question is where to get started. In this chapter, we'll take a look at some of the key ingredients of the customer experience edge.

We should start by warning that there is no single recipe for customer experience initiatives that is the perfect answer for every company, and thus we can provide only guiding principles for the ingredients involved. This is not a one-size-fits-all situation. Just as companies enter into a CE initiative from different starting points, they will also use very different strategies, depending on their industry, the types of customers they have, and, in particular, their overall business strategy.

The real starting point is this: defining what you are as a business and then matching that with a customer experience strategy that aligns with and helps fulfill your business strategy, including profitability. For example, if your brand promise is to provide clean, comfortable lodging at an economy price, your customer experience strategy shouldn't include luxury perks—not if you want to remain profitable, that is.

While this sounds simple, it's easy to overlook this step and begin to equate "customer experience" with "customer extravagance." It's the Apple versus Costco argument—each offers a radically different experience, yet each inspires fiercely loyal customers, as Paul Hagan, an analyst at Forrester Research, Inc., points out in a blog post.[1] Costco customers don't expect an infinite variety of products or sleek surroundings, and Apple customers don't expect bargain-basement prices or a variety of brands; similarly, you need to figure out what your value proposition is and create a customer experience strategy to match.

In Forrester's report, "What Is the Right Customer Experience Strategy?" Hagan offers examples of a customer experience strategy for each of the "generic" company strategies, as defined by Michael Porter, Harvard professor and business management guru[2] (see Table 5.1).

TABLE 5.1

Company Strategy	Customer Experience Strategy
Cost leader	Self-service optimization that delivers simple and efficient experiences
Differentiator (offers consistently innovative products or services)	Proactive guidance that educates customers as they adopt your breakthrough products and services
Segmentor (offers products and services that fit a narrowly targeted market segment)	Tailored intimacy that creates deep connections with customers through personalized interactions

Source: Forrester Research, Inc.

The upshot: as long as you stay focused on your business strategy and design the right customer experience, supported by the right technology foundation, your customer experience will not bankrupt the company.

Customer Experience Ingredients

While customer experience strategies will differ from company to company, there are certain activities that all companies need to engage in when they embark on a CE initiative, no matter what their strategy (see Table 5.2).

TABLE 5.2

Customer Experience Recipe
Set up several ways of obtaining customer feedback, in both structured and unstructured formats
Use these "listening posts" and your own internal data to get to know your customers intimately
Create continuous feedback loops to use what you learn
Segment your customers according to their value to your business
Map the customer journey and define customer touch points
Determine customers' moments of truth
Develop consistent experiences through all customer channels

Let's take a closer look at these activities.

Get to Know Your Customers

With business as usual, the corporate perspective is formed by looking from inside the company out to customers. But in businesses with a customer-centric perspective, the company and its processes are seen from the viewpoint of the customer, looking from the outside in. By looking through the customer's eyes, you can begin to fathom the types of services and experiences you could offer that would fulfill the four essentials of customer experience: reliability, convenience, relevance, and responsiveness.

To gain that perspective, you need to define who your customers are and what they value, so that you can align your efforts with their needs and desires. This entails everything from who they are literally (such information as would be found in your customer database) to more profound truths, such as what makes them tick, what are their communication preferences, what unmet needs are lurking in their psyches, what they're good at, and what capabilities they lack. The key is to discover everything possible about your customers— psychographics as well as demographics—by several different means, including the following.

Analytics   Many companies have vast volumes of data about their customers in their own computing systems, but they are not able to turn this information into actionable insights. Analytics and business intelligence (BI) tools can help you develop those insights, either on a stand-alone basis or as an adjunct to your customer relationship management (CRM) system. Tools of this sort will turbocharge your ability to draw inferences from existing data, spot trends, and the like. In Chapter 8, we will go into more detail about the key analytics and BI technologies that can be used to build and strengthen the customer experience.

Social Media Monitoring   There is no better way to find out what is on your customers' and prospects' minds than to monitor social media sites, including both the obvious (Facebook, Twitter, industry forums, and other sites that provide company and product reviews and ratings, such as Amazon) and the nonobvious (special-interest groups aligned with your brand, as well as the multitude of others that spring up seemingly every day). Product review sites like Yelp, Epinions, Buzzilions, Blippy, and Swipely are increasingly becoming platforms for raves and rants, and you need to know about both. Smaller businesses may be able to monitor social media manually, but midsize and larger companies need to automate their monitoring processes by using a sentiment analysis tool. These tools can help you stay on top of online opinions, product ratings, reviews, and sentiments. Since they are automated, it is much easier to keep abreast of trends, allowing you to be proactive. (We will take a closer look at sentiment analysis tools in Chapter 8.) The main task here is to watch, listen, and learn, gaining knowledge and finding out what customers and prospects value. In some cases, it may also make sense to respond, especially when you detect specific problems or complaints that customers are having through Twitter. Companies such as Southwest and Comcast respond to tweeted complaints quickly, successfully resolving conflicts more quickly than they could have if they'd waited for customers to contact the call center or for the tweet to go viral.

Basic Research   Of course, you have the traditional research options open to you: focus groups, surveys, test groups, and direct dialogue with customers. Any of these should have a social media link, as well (for example, you target likely "influencers" from Facebook and then invite them to a focus group, staying in touch afterward).

Crowdsourcing   Traditional focus groups and test markets can be replaced by social media outreach. The Web and social channels provide entirely new ways of running "tests" of campaigns and new product ideas.

Firsthand Experience   There is no better way to learn about your customers' experience than to live what they do. David Neeleman, former CEO of JetBlue, regularly worked as a flight attendant on JetBlue flights to get a direct, real-time idea of what it was like to be a customer, as well as to collect ideas on how to offer innovative, relevant, and ultimately valued experiences.[3] Similarly, Ven Bontha, customer experience management director for CEMEX USA, tells us that he rides regularly with drivers on the company's truck routes to get a sense of the challenges involved in delivering cement to customers. Additionally, as part of their training, all customer care employees are required to visit customer job sites and ride along in the trucks to get a sense of what the experience is about, he says.

Developing Profiles   Companies that sell to the mass market may need to go to greater extents to forge one-on-one personal relationships with customers than their business-to-business (B2B) counterparts, whose major customers are well known. To put a face on otherwise anonymous customers, some companies, such as Best Buy and Microsoft, define and continually refine customer profiles, sometimes called personas. Best Buy creates detailed descriptions of customer "types," including their needs, attitudes, psyche, relationship with Best Buy, and, in some cases, value to the company. The giant electronics retailer even assigns these profiles names, such as "Maria Middle America" and "Empty Nesters Helen and Charlie," to help associates quickly understand the type of customer they are dealing with and treat them accordingly.[4] For instance, if a salesperson recognizes a customer as "Jane," a profile defined as an upscale suburban woman in her mid-forties who tends to purchase premium services, he won't give her a hard time when she tries to return a $12 power cord without a receipt. Sales agents are empowered to take action (for the right customer) rather than having to escalate a query up the food chain. "If we don't empower employees to serve people well, we're basically telling them that they—and the customer—don't matter," says Live Path's Leigh Durst. "We give them no reason to care or become vested as an agent of good experience."

Determine Your Differentiating Touch Points

Whether you are a business-to-consumer (B2C) or a B2B company, it is essential that you map your customer journey so that you can see your company the way customers do. What does a customer go through, from researching a hotel, through booking a room, checking in, and all the way through checkout? What happens when a customer lands on your website or enters your store and considers a purchase, all the way through checkout, delivery, after-sales services, or return?

There are hundreds of these interactions, sometimes called "touch points," that make up an entire customer journey.

At each of these points, you have the opportunity to leave the customer with either a negative or a positive impression. The goal, of course, is for each interaction to be a positive one—or for you to respond to negative interactions, which can leave an even more long-lasting positive impression. However, there are so many touch points along the customer journey, direct and indirect, that even if it were possible to make each one consistently and equally "delightful," doing so would not be sustainable, cost-wise.

WHAT IS: A Moment of Truth?

A moment of truth is an interaction that leaves a profoundly negative or positive long-standing impression. These are different from ordinary touch points because they last longer; whereas the half-life of a transaction could be measured in days, that of a moment of truth could be measured in months if not years, says Paul D'Alessandro, partner at Diamond Advisory Services at PricewaterhouseCoopers. He points to a respondent in a survey conducted by Diamond Advisory Services who told a story of flight attendants handing out pizza during a delay on JetBlue Airways. "This happened four years ago, and it was still a formative notion of this person's experience of JetBlue," D'Alessandro says. "You might forget a flight attendant topping off your drink, but you'd never forget this type of pizza event." What's more, he adds, for every two profoundly bad moments of truth, you need to outweigh them with three profoundly good ones.

Instead, you need to identify and focus on the most important touch points, sometimes called *moments of truth* or *trigger points*, which are the make-or-break interactions in which a customer is most likely to form a strong opinion about you. It is at these moments that you have the opportunity to reinforce that impression, for better or worse.

That's why, once you've determined your customers' moments of truth, you need to make an honest assessment of how well you perform at those key interactions and then lay out a plan to economically fill any gaps and strengthen any weak links. You also need an action plan to turn around a negative experience. Many times, a company's most loyal customers are those who had had a negative experience at some point in time, but the way the company responded and resolved the problem made all the difference. According to a blog post by Forrester Research, Inc., analyst Andrew McInnes, customers who have exemplary problem-resolution experiences are far more likely to become repeat customers and major advocates of their suppliers.[5]

CEMEX's Bontha can attest to that. The company launched a major effort to ensure on-time delivery, including computer systems that enable visibility into delays. "When we immediately inform the customer about a delay, we are acknowledging our interest in their business," Bontha says. Ginger Conlon, editor of *1to1 Magazine*, agrees. "If you resolve a problem, you wind up having more loyalty than if there never was a problem to begin with," Conlon says. (For a full report on CEMEX's customer experience edge, see the case study in Chapter 8, page 157.)

For a B2B company, there are much more complex customer journeys and many more touch points. The customer journey for an enterprise software company, for instance, includes the licensing agreement, application installation, implementation and configuration, after-sales support, license renewal, and so on. In this case, you could end up with 15 to 20 moments of truth that need to be optimized to deliver the experience that the company wants to deliver. The complexity of your business and how you interact with customers will define how many moments of truth you have and where you need to focus. When you've created and can consistently deliver a highly valuable, relevant, and cost-efficient experience at your high-impact touch points, you have achieved the customer experience edge.

Think of touch points as being like the reading on an EKG machine, where a flat line means that you're dead, suggests Shaun Smith of CE consultancy Smith+co. Similarly, if you measure your customer experience and customer satisfaction is the same across each touch point, it means either that you're mediocre and undifferentiated or that you're at an unsustainable level. "If you're flat but getting perfect scores, you'll go out of business—you can't afford to be excellent in every area," he says. "So you need a sine wave where the curve peaks at those touch points where you differentiate in the most distinctive way for your organization." The sweet spot is where two factors coincide: maximum value for the customer and maximum differentiation for the brand.

Durst recounts a hotel that determined through customer surveys and data analytics that a key moment of truth occurred within 30 minutes of guests entering their room. Within that time frame, they had determined whether they were happy with their room or whether it was too close to the elevator, for instance, or had a broken thermostat. Now, the hotel front desk calls each guest within a half-hour of his arrival to ask if everything is OK. "If I can change my room before I unpack my bag, how great is that?" Durst says.

Disney determined that for customers visiting its theme parks, leaving the park and entering the parking lot was a moment of truth. There were many things that could go wrong after a day of enjoyment that could ruin the experience of the entire day. Families could have difficulty finding their car, or they could discover that something had gone wrong with their car, like a flat tire or a dead battery. To take the hassle out of leaving the park, and thus creating a differentiating experience at a moment of truth, Disney began offering a jump-start service at all park locations. It also developed a system that enabled it to tell customers where they had parked, based on their arrival time.

Segment Your Customers

Just as not all touch points are created equal, not all customers are created equal, either. If you provide the same perks for your least-profitable customers as you do for your top ones, at best you force the elite to subsidize the malingerers. At worst, you go broke. You've already defined your customers in your "Get to Know Your

Customers" exercise. So now, take those data and classify your customers into segments, as many as make sense. Categories could include high-revenue or high-profit customers, those with high customer lifetime value, and those with the greatest amount of influence through social media, such as people with thousands of Twitter followers or a highly read or linked-to blog.

Once you have segmented your customers, you should start to design your customer experience strategy to meet the expectations of the different segments. It is critical that you go through this exercise of mapping the experience to each segment, both because customer expectations are very likely to be different for different segments and because you may not be able to afford the same level of experience delivery for all customers. Furthermore, some customers may not want the same experience that you offer some other customer groups.

With your customers segmented, you can then work to find ways to get closer to them by learning about them and anticipating their needs.

At Comcast, Rick Germano says that the company is in the very early stages of analyzing its different customer segments from a customer service perspective. The company is working to understand how to target various bundled services to these segments, whether at a demographic level (young families, retired people, or young singles) or from a value standpoint. "We're looking at ways the service hierarchy could be prioritized, but our overall focus remains on providing a great experience for each customer," Germano says.

We discussed Marriott's personalized service offerings to its top customers in Chapter 4, which are all based on customer segmentation. In fact, more than half of the hospitality giant's revenue is from its Rewards members, and a significant revenue base comes from a smaller subsegment of top-value customers. This subsegment consists of Platinum members, who stay in a Marriott brand hotel 75 nights or more per year, says Mike Keppler, senior vice president, Marriott sales, marketing, and revenue management systems. These most-valuable guests are offered more specialized services, using information the company gathers about them, says Ed French, senior vice president of Marriott Rewards. In addition, if Marriott sees a decline in a top-value customer's total revenue or number of reservations, an agent calls or e-mails that customer to see if there are issues to resolve. In 10 percent of the cases, there is an actual issue that Marriot can take action on to resolve, French says. "We found that even in the tough economy, our Rewards members continue to stay with us, and we saw their business stay strong worldwide," Keppler says.

SPOTLIGHT ON: *The LEGO Group*

The LEGO Group makes extensive use of customer segmentation, which enables every customer to enjoy the experience best suited to them, while the highest-value experience is reserved for the highest-value customers, according to Conny Kalcher, The LEGO Group vice president of consumer experiences. In this way, the company is clearly demonstrating the customer experience essential of "relevance."

For a full report on The LEGO Group's customer experience edge, see the case study on page 83.

Keep It Consistent across Channels

A dramatic shift for all companies has been the need to keep up not just with existing touch points, but also with the new ones that are continuously being created through digital channels. Whatever your customer experience strategy, you must implement it uniformly across all the channels in which you operate—physical stores, call center, website, e-mail, chat, physical, social media, and the like. These channels need to be synchronized with one another and be consistent with particulars such as pricing and product availability. (We understand that there can be good reasons for prices on the same item to be different in different channels, but consumers are not likely to see it that way.) When Marriott found that its customers were spending more than three million hours per year on the company's website, for instance, the company realized that it needed to extend its specialized services to top-value customers through that channel, as well as to maintain consistency across all points of inter-action. Marriott's system capabilities now allow all touch points to recognize these customers and tailor the service, including self-ser-vice, to the guest's value, history, and preferences.

That is not to say that you should put the same resources into each channel. Still, you can leverage the respective strengths of differ-ent channels to ensure that you offer the right products and services to the right customers at the right time. If you have a mobile con-sumer shopping application, for example, that will be a good venue for offering pop-up in-store coupons, whereas the website works well for showing shoppers purchases made by other buyers of that item.

As in any good recipe, the ingredients that we've laid out here can be used to a greater or a lesser degree, depending on your specific situation and your desired outcome. You might substitute other ele-ments, or you might merge some together. Whatever you do, do not stint on the first task: identifying and understanding your customer. Without the "C," there is no customer experience.

As we said at the outset, there is no one recipe for the customer experience edge. But following these general guidelines will set com-panies on the path to achieving the four customer experience essen-tials (reliability, convenience, responsiveness, and relevance) and, ultimately, the customer experience edge. Next, we will look at the results that companies have been able to achieve by honing their cus-tomer experience edge and how you can learn from these results to establish your own financial success criteria.

CASE STUDY: **THE LEGO GROUP**

Through Engagement and Interaction, The LEGO Group Plays Well with Customers

More than 50 years ago, The LEGO Group was founded by Ole Kirk Kristiansen, who named it after the Danish words leg gotd, meaning, "play well." Today, as the fourth largest toy company in the world, The LEGO Group not only helps adults and children do just that, but it also strives to play just as well with its own customers.

CE ESSENTIALS

- **Relevance.** By engaging with "lead users" and other consumers on a variety of channels, the company discovers which experiences and product features enthusiasts want to see and incorporates real-world demand into its new offerings.

- **Responsiveness.** The LEGO Group has formed an online community to interact with and respond to consumers and plans to begin using sentiment analysis tools to keep up with consumer conversations online.

As a company whose major product is its colorful building blocks, it's hardly surprising that The LEGO Group regards customer experience from a pyramid perspective. "We have a unique situation," observes Conny Kalcher, vice president of consumer experiences at The LEGO Group in Slough, U.K. "The people who buy the products are most often parents or grandparents, but the people who consume the products are kids. We work on consumer experience with both of these groups," Kalcher says.

In fact, The LEGO Group segments consumers into several categories, based on their affinity for the LEGO brand, Kalcher says. At the top of the pyramid are the lead users—the adults and children who engage most heavily with the company, to the extent of helping to co-create LEGO products.

The next segment down is the one-to-one layer, consisting of people with whom the company maintains an ongoing dialogue. The third layer is the connective community layer, or people who spend time on The LEGO Group's online collaboration platform, where they can share files and work with staff members in a secure environment, Kalcher says.

And finally, the base of the pyramid is the active household layer—people who have bought LEGO products at some point in time. All consumer types want something different from the LEGO brand, Kalcher says, so their relationships with the company are varied. And it is The LEGO Group's self-proclaimed job to move as many people up the pyramid as it can, changing the consumer relationship from a monologue to a dialogue.

For example, not long after The LEGO Group first developed its line of programmable robotics/construction toys, MindStorms NXT, in conjunction with the Massachusetts Institute of Technology, the software that enables the robots to perform different operations was hacked. Rather than condemn the people behind the system infiltration, the company decided to befriend them. "We had to make a decision about whether we would work with these people or sue them," recalls Kalcher. "We decided to work with them." The result: these consumers co-created the second generation of MindStorms with The LEGO Group, she says, since they knew even better than The LEGO Group's engineers what they wanted the robot to do.

CE PILLARS

- **Operational excellence.** The LEGO Group combined and centralized all the departments that interact with consumers, including consumer service, community, clubs, loyalty, and consumer insights.

- **Interaction excellence.** The LEGO Group engages with consumers through many channels, including its website, blogs, discussion forums, on-site meetings, loyalty program, online collaboration platform, and one-to-one dialogues.

- **Decision-making excellence.** The company incorporates what it learns from consumers into its offerings, resulting in profitable strategic decisions.

For a full discussion of the CE Pillars, see Chapter 7.

"By working with them, we [get to] know the lead users on a personal level," Kalcher says. Lead users are introduced to the company, and The LEGO Group involves them in special projects for which they have a passion, such as Web, game, and community development. "They can become part of the company and still be doing their day job," Kalcher says. Thanks to their input, the company's new offerings match real-world demand.

A segment of the lead users is known as the LEGO Certified Professionals. This subgroup is interested in turning their LEGO hobby into a part-time or full-time business, Kalcher says. Currently, there are about a dozen Certified Professionals worldwide. "They come to us with a business plan, and we grant them the right to use the logo, and then we stimulate the long tail," Kalcher says, referring to Chris Anderson's book, *The Long Tail: Why the Future of Business is Selling Less of More*. The long tail theory, according to Anderson, is that our culture and economy are increasingly shifting away from a focus on a relatively small number of mainstream products at the head of the demand curve to a larger number of niches in the "tail."

One Certified Professional is a former real estate lawyer from New York, whose business is now building LEGO models for clients using LEGO Architecture, a high-end series that is geared primarily for adults. "We think by involving consumers in the things they are really passionate about, they will become ambassadors for the brand," says Kalcher. "That is really powerful."

Lead users can demonstrate the brand's potential in a much stronger way than the company itself can, Kalcher says. In fact, another subsegment, known as LEGO Ambassadors, arranges LEGO events all over the world. "They are displaying their passion for LEGO products at these big shows," Kalcher says, as well as demonstrating to families what can be done with the products. Such shows draw 2.5 million visitors a year, according to Kalcher. In total, there are 70 LEGO Ambassadors from 24 different countries.

Other LEGO communities have also sprung up, such as the Kids' Inner Circle and adult LEGO User Groups (LUGs). They refer to themselves as AFOLs (Adult Fans of LEGO), and the company has developed relationships with more than 50 such groups, which have 55,000 registered members with their own websites, blogs, and discussion forums.

All of The LEGO Group's work to interact and engage with its consumers seems to be paying off. The company has approximately 9,000 employees globally, including more than 115 toy developers, and the LEGO Club has more than 4 million members worldwide. In spite of the worldwide recession, company revenue was up 37.3 percent in 2010.

Enabling Consumer Centricity

Getting to this high level of consumer interaction and engagement required organizational change. The LEGO Group started by combining all the departments that interact with consumers, Kalcher says. About three and a half years ago, all of the departments that had direct contact with consumers were centralized: consumer service, community, clubs, loyalty, and consumer insights. "It was a bold step, but it has given us space to develop that area much faster," Kalcher says.

To understand consumers even better—and even interact with them directly—The LEGO Group is looking into using sentiment analysis tools, which provide an automated way to "listen" to what people are saying about your company on the Web and alert you to whether things are going in a positive or a negative direction. The LEGO Group is also conducting an audit to determine the best way to leverage social media, and it plans to establish a Facebook page for consumers who are older than 13. The LEGO Group has also introduced a consumer loyalty program to manage loyalty rewards and points redemption, using SAP's CRM software to store the information. The global program is available in all of The LEGO Group's retail stores in 24 countries and online. "Our aim is to develop it going forward so it becomes an engagement program as well as a loyalty program," explains Kalcher. "The more consumers engage with us, the more we offer them things that are meaningful to them."

CHAPTER 6

A Fresh Look at the Top and Bottom Lines

For more than half of companies, cost and ROI are the top concerns with customer experience initiatives.

THERE IS A CENTRAL PARADOX of the customer experience edge: customer centricity needs to stem from a genuine desire—even a passion—to do right by the customer. At the same time, your customer experience efforts need to result in a positive impact on your company's top and bottom lines. Otherwise, as Strativity Group's Lior Arussy tells us, "We don't recommend companies do this." After all, if your company goes bust because it is giving away the store (those universal free shipping and free returns deals come to mind), that is not going to be a good experience for your customers in the long run.

So, how do you focus on these two seemingly competing imperatives at the same time: revenues and profits, on the one hand, and putting customers first, on the other?

Certainly, executives are wary of this very issue. According to the Bloomberg Businessweek Research Services (BBRS) survey, top concerns with customer experience initiatives are cost and ROI (see Figure 6.1).[1]

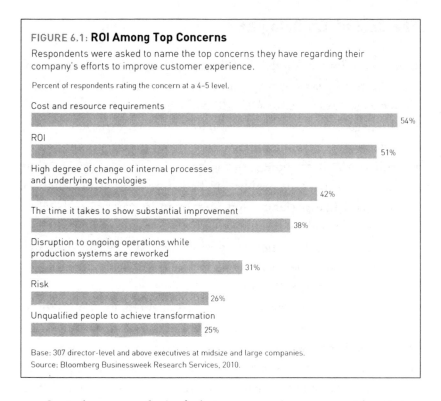

FIGURE 6.1: **ROI Among Top Concerns**

Respondents were asked to name the top concerns they have regarding their company's efforts to improve customer experience.

Percent of respondents rating the concern at a 4–5 level.

Cost and resource requirements

54%

ROI

51%

High degree of change of internal processes and underlying technologies

42%

The time it takes to show substantial improvement

38%

Disruption to ongoing operations while production systems are reworked

31%

Risk

26%

Unqualified people to achieve transformation

25%

Base: 307 director-level and above executives at midsize and large companies.
Source: Bloomberg Businessweek Research Services, 2010.

So, is there room for both the accountant's concerns with growing revenues and profits and the zealot's approach to (using customary customer experience parlance) being "obsessive" and "passionate" about customers? We believe there is. Done right, the customer experience (CE) involves creating wins for the customer, but behind those customer-focused wins are business and financial success for your company. Financial drivers can range from reducing customer churn, to acquiring new customers, to reducing the cost of sales, to decreasing the sales cycle. "It has to be something you can point to and say, 'We have moved the needle on either revenues or expenses,'" Arussy says.

For all the talk among CE advocates of passion, obsession, and devotion to customers, embarking on a CE program cannot be backed with the idea of "if you build it, they will come." There needs to be a clear sense of what your return is going to be, and you need to calculate the ROI.

The Cost of *Not* Doing CE

One way to look at the ROI of the customer experience is to analyze the cost of *not* focusing on the customer experience. What is the cost, for example, of a single bad experience? If you include all the negative impacts that resonate from that experience, costs include the lost revenue opportunities from that customer and all the others who hear about it through word of mouth, as well as the resource costs to fix the problem and possibly your own reputation, should that bad experience blow up into an Internet cause célèbre. Remember, the rule of thumb is that twice as many people will hear about a negative experience as a positive one, and on the Web, that increases to four times as many people who will hear about a negative experience than a positive one.

Many companies jeopardize their customer relationships by making decisions that don't take these types of costs into account. This is particularly true when companies look to cost cutting to improve their financial health instead of looking at the customer experience. "Say you're planning to launch a cost-reduction effort," Arussy tells us. "Your first question should be, how much will it affect customer loyalty and spending? What if your $300 million cost reduction costs $1 billion in revenue because customers find you're irrelevant to them?" Rather than focusing on cost alone (too much a habit during the downturn years), your mindset needs to encompass the cost of losing your relevance to customers.

Arussy cites the example of Starbucks introducing its Via instant coffee product in 2008, at the height of the financial crisis. Typical cost-cutting measures would probably have hurt Starbucks' customer experience (and therefore its bottom line), so instead it listened to its customers, discovered a new product to meet an unmet need, and now has new organic growth that would not otherwise have been possible. Because of the negative economic conditions, it took two years for this effort to pay off, but pay off it did. Had Starbucks focused solely on cutting costs, it would be much worse off now.

"You think [customer experience] is expensive?" says Arussy. "How much are you wasting by not doing it? That is the message companies don't have."

We can also approach this question mathematically. Let's say you're a company with 500,000 customers, and the average lifetime value of your customers is $1,000, just for simplicity's sake. Then, let's say you force customers to use a self-service capability as part of a cost-cutting move. And your customers hate it. What is the revenue impact if, as a result, your retention rate decreases by 1 percent? With 500,000 customers, that's 5,000 lost customers, or $5,000,000 in lost business.

What if you had 10 million customers, with an average annual purchase rate of $50, and the retention rate slips by 1 percent? If you do nothing to fix the issues, you will lose $5 million in revenues that your salespeople will have to make up just to stay on par with the previous year's revenues. Bear in mind that this does not include the lost revenue from future cross-selling and upselling opportunities or the future wallet share of these customers. And in many cases [for business-to-business (B2B) companies, in particular], the results can be even worse than what these calculations show.

On the other hand, what if you took one small step to improve the customer experience that resulted in a boost in first-call resolution or positive word-of-mouth impact? Let's say the result is a rise in retention rate from 85 percent to 87 percent. With 500,000 customers, that's $10 million more in revenues and 10,000 fewer customers your salespeople have to find in new business the following year.

Lesson learned: the cost of doing nothing, when it comes to the customer experience, can be significant. The worst possible stance for a company (of any size, in any industry, or with any customer base) is to do nothing with the customer experience because of the fear that the return is uncertain. Traditionally, it is difficult to prove a negative, but when it comes to the customer experience, this is relatively easy to fathom.

Passion and Profits

The idea of financial gain from the customer experience can get murky when, clearly, there is an emotional component at play. As we mentioned in Chapter 4, there needs to be a certain level of passion for customer centricity that fuels the customer experience edge. However, mixed with the passion and the drama, there also needs to be a focus on the business outcome.

Smith+co's Shaun Smith illustrates this in his recently published book, *Bold: How to Be Brave in Business and Win*. Smith uses words such as *zealous*, *infectious*, *dramatic*, *obsessive*, and even *cult-like* to describe the characteristics of companies that he considers to be customer experience leaders. From Virgin Galactic to Burberry, Smith sees these companies as being driven not by making money, but by making a difference—being distinctive by declaring their principles and then sticking to them. Even more important than focusing on profits, he says, is having a sense of purpose. He calls it "putting purpose before profit."

"They succeed because they have the courage, confidence, or just sheer chutzpah to pursue a purpose that is beyond profit, to engage, entertain, and educate their audiences," Smith says on his blog.[2] "They are not just different but dramatically different and push to the extremes the consequences of their desired positioning and strategy."

But even Smith acknowledges in his blog that "none of these practices are worthwhile unless they lead to successful business outcomes, such as increased revenues and sustainable profits. These companies believe that by focusing on customer value, they can become more profitable and sustain these profits longer than the competition," he says.

In fact, one company that he profiles, U.K. luxury retailer Burberry, reported a 50 percent rise in profit in the 2010–2011 fiscal half year ending September 30, 2010, as well as 21 percent revenue growth in that time period, a time when many retailers were reporting declines. Those results were followed by 31 percent revenue growth for the second half of the fiscal year. Smith attributes this to Burberry's focus on digital marketing, social media, and improving the in-store and online experience as opposed to cutting costs.

Among the many examples of Burberry's multichannel digital prowess is its Artofthetrench.com social networking/fashion blog site, designed by a top fashion influencer. The site displays hundreds of images of models and regular citizens wearing its signature coat in seemingly endless ways. Visitors listen to hip, mood-inducing music and are invited to click on the images to read more about the person wearing it, indicate which they "like" the most, leave a comment, or even write about their own trench coat experiences. Images are also sorted by categories, such as "highest volume of comments" or "most 'likes.'" People can upload their own photos of themselves or friends modeling a creatively worn Burberry trench coat. Burberry calls the site "a living celebration of the trench coat and the people who wear it."

Burberry established a Facebook presence early in the game, which it frequently updates with photos and albums of upcoming seasons, as well as videos of up-and-coming British acoustic artists, to further extend and strengthen its brand. In addition to its three million "friends," it also has more than 80,000 Twitter followers, to whom it provides updates of which celebrities were wearing which of its fashion pieces.

Burberry's ad campaigns are also cutting-edge, with three-dimensional images on its website that can be clicked, rotated, paused, and dragged 180 degrees. The company has live-streamed fashion shows to various websites, into stores, and even onto a digital billboard in London's Piccadilly Circus. It also launched a "runway to reality" initiative, enabling consumers to buy fashions that they see on the runway via their iPads or online, with delivery in seven weeks. Soon, Burberry will offer a made-to-order service, enabling customers to add details such as studs and initials to the iconic trench coat.

Clearly, this is a company that gets the idea that brands can no longer just "be"—they need to "do" something. It also understands the importance of delivering on the four CE essentials of reliability, convenience, responsiveness, and relevance.

Not All Customers Are Equal

In Chapter 5, we mentioned segmenting your customers as an ingredient in the customer experience recipe. We want to discuss this again here, as customer segmentation plays a strong role in enabling the balance between purpose and profit. Essentially, companies need to focus their products and services on the best segment they can serve, and within that segment, they need to focus on delivering what matters most to attract and keep customers. This means consciously eliminating customers who cost too much to serve and who might be better served by other product lines.

"It's about real passionate belief in making a difference for customers, but also creating a commercially minded business model that allows you to do that," Arussy says.

An example is Southwest Airlines. The company has received accolades for its customer centricity, even while refusing to offer amenities such as reserved seating, baggage transfer, and a hot food service. Does that sound like customer centricity to you? Actually, it is—Southwest keeps its eye focused on what it has determined that its customers really need from an airline: low fares, no fees for regular checked baggage, and on-time service. Anything else is a distraction. The chairman and cofounder of Southwest once asked a dinner companion, "Would customers pay $100 more for inter-airline baggage transfers? No, they wouldn't—they value on-time, low-cost flights."[3]

Customer segmentation also means concentrating your resources on high-worth customers who will repay the investment—now, or via an expanded lifetime value. "Customer lifetime value has come into all industries for the first time," says Diamond Advisory Services/ PricewaterhouseCoopers's Paul D'Alessandro. "The more you understand the overall profitability of the customer, the more you [should be] willing to invest in those customers or cut off others."

Sounds a bit harsh, right? But consider that failing to segment your customers means asking your best customers to subsidize your worst. Rather than continuing to enrich the experiences of your elite customers, you invest the premiums they pay in customers who probably don't have an iota of loyalty to your company. Not only is that not good business, but it's not fair, says Martha Rogers, one of the founding mothers of customer experience and one-to-one marketing and a cofounder of Peppers & Rogers Group. "Differentiating according to customer value [and potential value] doesn't mean you treat anyone badly," says Rogers. "It means you stop putting resources toward the people who are costing your best customers a lot of money."

If you don't distinguish between your most profitable and your least profitable customers, your return on investment (ROI) will be reduced. Customer segmentation is a driver of customer experience ROI.

TIP

> Zappos takes an unusual approach to customer segmentation, choosing to eschew the practice. "All of our customers are the best customers," says Aaron Magness, senior director of brand marketing and business development at the online retailer. "We have a level playing field where everyone enjoys this great experience." Magness points out that Zappos's most profitable customers are also the heaviest users of the store's free-returns policy, as they are willing to test new categories and buy higher-end goods. "The free marketing for us is the referrals," he says. "They may be sending things back and forth many times, but there is a high likelihood that they are telling friends how easy it is to be a Zappos customer." In this way, Zappos is fulfilling the CE essential of convenience.

Tesco PLC is a good example of a company that segments its customers to ensure a profitable customer experience. With $86 billion in revenue, Tesco is the U.K.'s largest retailer, as well as the fourth largest in the world. It matches tightly segmented product lines with its six distinctly different customer groups, according to Coriolis Research Ltd., a market research firm that worked with Tesco.[4] At the high end of the spectrum are the "Finer Foods" customers, who overlap somewhat with the "Healthy" consumers, representing about one-quarter of the total. These customers desire (and can pay for) the nicer things in life (not just organic strawberries and grass-fed beef, but high-end personal care products, wines, and housewares).

Solidly in the middle of the pack are the "Traditional," "Mainstream," and "Convenience" customers, who together make up about half of Tesco customers. These customers are aware of price and alert to product promotions, but are willing to spend on items that reflect their values (such as higher-priced foods for special occasions or prepared foods for weeknight dining). "Price Sensitive" customers are less affluent and make up nearly one-quarter of the total. Here, the focus is on everyday value.

A pioneer of supermarket loyalty programs in the late 1990s, through its Clubcard, Tesco offers benefits commensurate with customer spending levels (at a rate of one point per pound spent). Tesco's genius: it mines and slices the data from its 16 million–member loyalty card program to segment and more fully understand both its customers and its products, providing an entirely different experience for each customer segment. "Customer data is in the fabric of every decision we make in the company," says Mike McNamara, Tesco's CIO. "We know an awful lot about our shoppers."[5]

For example, at a cost of 21 pence, Tesco Value bath soap is as unadorned as soap can get, whereas Tesco brand liquid handwash costs just under £1. At the other end of the spectrum, priced at £5, is Tesco Finest creamy body soufflé—a whopping 2,000 percent higher than the Value offering. As you can see, Tesco serves its less well-heeled customers with effective and well-priced options, while extracting copious profit from those who can afford and want to pay for a higher-end experience.

At their worst, supermarket loyalty cards are just a different way for customers to get a discount, says Clive Humby, chairman of dunnhumby, a consulting firm that worked with Tesco, in a published interview.[6] But used effectively, "They open worlds of possibility when you mine the rich data they produce to add relevance to your customers' lives."

For instance, when Tesco mails out coupons, people in different customer segments receive personalized coupon variants, depending on their profile. And if Tesco cuts prices, it does so with the knowledge of which products, across which customer demographics, will have the most impact on its top and bottom lines. "You should only collect this information if it's going to do you some good," McNamara adds.

Before it introduced customer segmentation and analytics, Humby says, Tesco had been accustomed to monitoring top-line numbers to the exclusion of the bigger picture. "'What are my sales this week?' 'What were my sales last week?' and so on. That's the way they measured things. If you look at that level, you can't see the impact."

Now, however, Tesco mines both structured and unstructured data with an eye toward increasing customer satisfaction and retention, as well as its own growth. For instance, it has implemented technology in thousands of stores that allows customers to provide in-store feedback on their shopping experience by filling out a card, using their mobile devices to leave a voice message, or sending a text or an e-mail. It then turns these unstructured data into structured formats that can be fed back into stores, creating continuous improvement. For example, a disgruntled customer's voice mail is translated by language processing software, and the customer receives an instant response.

With all these efforts, Tesco is succeeding at the heart of "the new competitive battleground" of the retail industry—"shopper centricity," according to Pierre Lever, managing director at Planet Retail, an analyst firm that covers the retail industry.[7] This shopper centricity is paying off. In March 2011, in a European retail climate that is difficult at best, Tesco customers are buying up the more expensive goods in the retailer's Finest line, as well as the Value products that one would expect to thrive in a downturn.[8] According to *Bloomberg Businessweek*, sales growth at Tesco will outpace that of its global rivals, including Wal-Mart, through 2015.

Another good example of thoughtful customer segmentation is the *New York Times*. Until March 2011, anyone could read the newspaper's articles completely free of charge on the Web. However, the venerable publisher rolled out a new approach that provided advantages to its print subscribers, while fully acknowledging the new world of its digital readership.

In an e-mail to its readers, the *New York Times* explained the new segmentation:

- Home delivery subscribers would continue to have full and free access to content on the website through their PCs, smartphones, and tablets.

- Others would get free access to up to 20 articles, videos, or slide shows per month. When they exceeded that, they would be asked to become digital subscribers, with a choice of three digital subscription options.

- The "Top News" section would continue to be free on the *New York Times*'s smartphone and tablet apps.

- Readers who find *New York Times* articles through links from search engines, blogs, and social media will be able to read those articles, even if they have reached their monthly reading limit.

We consider this to be a good example of a company that has considered the needs of a wide range of customers and potential customers and how to offer an experience that can be beneficial not only to different segments, but also to its own top and bottom lines.

The Payoff

As you eliminate experiences that frustrate and irritate customers (endless customer service loops on the telephone, for example) or are able to turn negative experiences around, you may well find that you are actually taking cost out of the organization. A good example is

Progressive Insurance. The auto insurer continually changes its business processes and introduces innovations that are squarely aimed at customer needs, namely, taking the pain out of dealing with automobile insurance. It seems to recognize that customers not only do not enjoy paying for car insurance, but also don't enjoy dealing with the long-drawn-out process of filing a claim and repairing their car after the terrible experience of being in a car accident.

To start, Progressive initiated a transparent pricing policy on its website, on which prospective customers can see not only a policy quote for Progressive automobile insurance, but also the prices for its nearest competitors, even if those competitors are offering lower prices. This was a customer-friendly move that was a major differentiator at the time. After all, the Web introduces price transparency, so why not make it quicker for customers to see what they will inevitably find, anyway?

The company also began offering a "concierge" service that allows customers who have had an accident to drop off their cars at a designated location and let Progressive handle the repairs. This reduces the time each driver has to spend on the claims and repair process from about four days to about 15 minutes, according to the company.[9]

Another customer-centric move was to target what it determined was one of its customers' biggest sources of frustration—its claims settlement area. The process was cumbersome and time-intensive, with customers having to fill out a complex form and then deal with follow-up questions. It was not a customer-friendly process for a person who had just endured an accident.

Instead of tinkering around the edges, Progressive revamped the entire process by creating "roadside settlements." Now, customers can call a mobile claims assessor to come to the site within minutes. Assessors gather crucial details, check the customer's policy details via their mobile PCs, and, in some cases, submit the claim on the spot. A check can be automatically dispatched, and the claim is settled on the spot. Not only did this approach cut claims processing costs, but customers feel that they are being taken care of.[10]

Progressive's innovations continue. Today, in 30 states, the insurer allows customers to "name the price" that they're willing to pay for auto insurance, and the company will offer a package that comes closest to that price. The service is a Web-based offering in which prospective customers enter their personal information and how much they are willing to pay for insurance. After seeing what their named price will buy in terms of coverage and deductibles, they can also drag a "slider" bar to the right or left to see how their coverage and price can change.[11]

The company also offers Snapshot, a device that plugs into a car's on-board diagnostic port and tracks how and when you drive. The data are transmitted to Progressive and are also viewable by customers on the website. People who drive fewer miles and less aggressively can receive discounts of up to 30 percent.[12]

By focusing on customer wins, the company has lowered its costs, enjoys higher profits, and has increased its market share.[13] Progressive has risen from number 10 in market share in the early 2000s to number 4 today.

Financial Drivers

The impact that you want to see is, of course, financial. A better customer experience should have a positive effect on both your top line *and* your bottom line. In its report, "The Business Impact of Customer Experience, 2011," Forrester Research, Inc., shows a high correlation between the quality of a customer experience. Forrester calls this CxPi or Customer Experience Index. Three key elements of loyal behavior are

- Willingness to buy more

- Reluctance to switch

- Likelihood to recommend[14]

Sounds good, of course, but how do they affect a company's bottom line? As analyst Megan Burns writes in the report, customer experience leaders in 11 industries have a financial advantage over customer experience laggards across all three areas of loyalty. According to Burns, the potential annual benefits of excellent CE top $1 billion each for wireless providers ($1.5 billion) and hotels ($1 billion). She notes that, known for below-average customer experience, airlines could reap almost $800 million apiece by boosting their CxPi score.

In the financial services industry, according to a 2011 Forrester report, loyal customers are willing to buy more, borrow more, invest more, and stay longer with the firms they already use. According to Forrester analyst Bill Doyle, one trait above all drives loyalty, and that is (emphasis his) *the perception on the part of customers that the firm does what's best for them, not just what's best for the firm's own bottom line.*[15]

In most cases, the financial drivers of CE will come down to the following areas.

Increased Revenue

The revenue benefits of customer service improvements are well documented, according to TARP Worldwide's John Goodman, reaching 10 to 20 times the cost implications. When you can turn customers into extremely loyal customers, not only will they buy more from you, but they may also influence others to buy from you, as well. Additionally, trust and loyalty will drive them to buy your more value-added products at higher margins or become early adopters of your newest products and services.

This can be seen in a survey by the relationship management firm Convergys.[16] The study identified 15 percent of surveyed customers as "super-loyalists" or "advocates." This group was much more likely than other respondents to exhibit profit-inducing behaviors, such as recommending the company to friends (56 percent more likely), making more frequent purchases (185 percent more likely), not shopping at competitors (377 percent more likely), and responding to requests for feedback, special offers/discounts, and new products/upgrades (29 percent more likely).

These results are well illustrated at Akbank, one of the leading banks in Turkey. It launched a centralized customer relationship management (CRM) system to support its customer experience strategy, and within six months of the implementation, it had sold 500,000 new products, increased its customer base by 200,000, gained €2.2 million in gross profits, and cut €3.5 million in service costs. (For more on Akbank's customer experience initiative, see the case study on page 213.)

Premium Pricing

To truly optimize relevant, highly valued experiences, companies need to understand which experiences customers are actually willing to pay for, Diamond Advisory Services/PricewaterhouseCoopers's D'Alessandro says. This means knowing not only how highly customers value attributes such as accessibility, trust, and innovation, but also whether are they willing to pay for them. "Companies need to get to a point where they know the actionable things to tackle and the economic return," he says. According to a recent Strativity Group survey, 29 percent of loyal customers who feel that they're getting a superior experience are willing to pay premium prices of 10 percent or more, whereas 66 percent of dissatisfied customers expect discounts of 5 percent or more if they are to continue doing business with a company (see Figure 6.2).

Customer Retention

When a customer encounters a problem, there is an average 20 percent drop in loyalty, Goodman tells us, which varies depending on the type of problem. (For example, a torn package might be 2 percent, while infestation of a food item would be 70 percent.) In the average market, for every five customers with problems, you are likely to lose one of them—along with that customer's revenue. On the flip side,

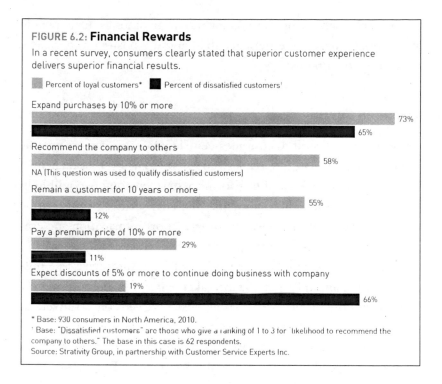

FIGURE 6.2: **Financial Rewards**

In a recent survey, consumers clearly stated that superior customer experience delivers superior financial results.

Percent of loyal customers*　　Percent of dissatisfied customers'

Expand purchases by 10% or more
73%
65%

Recommend the company to others
58%
NA (This question was used to qualify dissatisfied customers)

Remain a customer for 10 years or more
55%
12%

Pay a premium price of 10% or more
29%
11%

Expect discounts of 5% or more to continue doing business with company
19%
66%

* Base: 930 consumers in North America, 2010.
' Base: "Dissatisfied customers" are those who give a ranking of 1 to 3 for "likelihood to recommend the company to others." The base in this case is 62 respondents.
Source: Strativity Group, in partnership with Customer Service Experts Inc.

if you can prevent or fix five problems, you will retain one customer (and his revenue) that otherwise would have been lost, he says.

D'Alessandro cites similar statistics. In the insurance industry, normal churn is about 9 percent, he says. But according to a study that Diamond Advisory Services conducted, that jumps to 17 percent if a customer has one bad customer experience or, more specifically, a "moment of truth."

According to the Convergys study, there is a 57 percent attrition rate among customers who reported a bad experience and received no response vs. a 30 percent attrition rate among customers for whom the issue was resolved.

Improved Reputation

On average, twice as many people will hear about someone's bad experience as will hear about her good experience. This outcome is even more dramatic on the Web, where four times as many people hear about a negative experience than about a positive experience, according to Goodman.

Reduced Costs

In some cases, a shift to customer-centric processes can create efficiencies that translate into reduced costs. At Comcast, Eliason helped the company create an online forum where customers could help one another with troubleshooting. The cost savings of this can be extended if you take that peer-to-peer support information and create a knowledge base for your phone agents, he says.

"Typically each month, the Comcast help forums have 14.5 million visitors, and if 80 percent are taken care of in the forum, how many calls does that avoid?" Eliason tells us. "Even conservatively, at $8 per phone call, there are huge savings in just one month."

Twitter monitoring also pays off here: "We can predict what's going to happen before the call center has a clue," Eliason says. For instance, during a 2010 outage that affected several East Coast cities, people began tweeting about it immediately.[17] Comcast was able to respond instantaneously with a tweet providing followers with an estimated time when the outage would be fixed, as well as follow-up tweets reporting on its progress, says Rick Germano, senior vice president of national customer operations at Comcast. This significantly cut back on calls to the call center and long waits in queues. All told, as we mentioned in Chapter 2, Comcast reduced its service calls by four million in the first four months of 2010 vs. 2009 because of its social media monitoring and follow-up response, which has translated into reduced operating expenses, according to Germano.

Smith+co's Shaun Smith also points to Progressive's mobile claims assessors. This program cut the administrative cost of claims processing and reduced the amount of an average settlement because people are willing to accept less when they do not have to wait longer.

Another example is CEMEX USA. When CEMEX determined that on-time delivery was its customers' top priority, it revamped its processes and centralized its business applications to ensure that it could meet that expectation. This involved increasing the visibility of its delivery operations, streamlining its bill of lading process, installing cameras on its truck loading docks, and setting system alerts when delays were likely. The result: it has boosted order accuracy from 92 percent to 99.9 percent. Thanks to efficiency improvements and incremental sales as a result of the initiative, CEMEX has achieved an ROI of 30 percent. It has also lowered costs, as the customer care center now manages 29 percent more volume with the same headcount as before the implementation.[18] (For more on CEMEX USA's customer experience initiative, see the case study in Chapter 8, page 157.)

Meanwhile, Synopsys attributes many cost efficiencies to its focus on the customer experience, including a reduction in the amount of time its application consultants spend on reactive support from 33 percent to 20 percent. This enables the company to shift its support to more accessible channels and leverage a broader global talent pool. (For more on Synopsys's customer experience initiative, see the case study in Chapter 3, page 42).

Building a business case for customer experience initiatives is something that many companies overlook, as it is all too easy to get caught up in thinking that the end goal is simply "delivering a better customer experience," without the business goals baked in. In addition to establishing your financial drivers, developing a successful business case also requires taking a macro look at your business. Customer experience delivery affects every aspect of your business, from cost of sales and marketing, to returns and renewals, to upselling and cross-selling, to market share and the overall profitability of your company. So don't aim for the trees and miss the forest. Mistaking customer experience for a sales force automation initiative or an interactive voice response (IVR) or Web self-service implementation can turn out to be a very costly error that can seriously impede if not torpedo your customer experience edge.

PART III

Technology: The Core Ingredient

CHAPTER 7

The Underlying Foundation for the Customer Experience Edge

Companies with tightly integrated applications rate their customer experience offering at 4.34 on a scale of 1 to 5, while others rate their customer experience at a mediocre 3.62. That's a 20 percent difference in customer experience for respondents with tightly integrated applications.

—BLOOMBERG BUSINESSWEEK
RESEARCH SERVICES SURVEY, 2010

FOR MANY EXPERTS, improving the customer experience is just a matter of changing the corporate culture and adding passion for customers. And we agree that these are crucial for developing a strong customer experience.

However, there is another less discussed element that no amount of culture change or organizational transformation can replace: technology. Indeed, technology, done right, is the secret ingredient that enables companies to create the customer experience edge in a scalable, lower-cost way that works not just for 10 or 100 customers but for thousands of customers in a profitable and sustainable manner. More specifically, there are two broad categories of technology that are the basis of the customer experience: the foundational information systems that you use to run your business, and the more "disruptive" technologies that allow companies to meet or exceed customer expectations in the new world of networked consumers.

We believe that even if you have the best customer-centric culture and the highest levels of passion for customers, if your technology is working against you—if it's too complicated, too costly, or designed simply to build products more quickly rather than supporting the four essentials of the customer experience—it just might not allow you to hone the customer experience edge.

"The vast majority of technologies available today are amazing from a capability standpoint," says Strativity Group's Lior Arussy, such as customer relationship management (CRM), performance management, and business analytics. "However, the majority of clients have no idea how to maximize those capabilities. It's like driving a Rolls Royce at 10 miles per hour."

The business world seems to agree on the core role that technology plays in providing a strong customer experience. In a 2010 survey by Accenture,[1] the majority of CIOs (65 percent) and, importantly, chief marketing officers (50 percent) agreed that technology now underpins and shapes the entire customer experience.

That is what Part III of this book is all about: the role of technology in shaping and delivering a consistent, high-value, profitable customer experience—the customer experience edge. We will explore this from three different standpoints. In this chapter, we will look at the integrated applications that serve as the foundation for the customer experience, enabling your company to work in concert with its customers and supply chain partners, and to empower your customer-facing employees to be responsive to customer needs. As we'll discuss further, companies with a strong integrated foundation rank their customer experience significantly higher than those without one.

In Chapter 8, we will discuss the more leading-edge, or disruptive, technologies that you can integrate with the foundational systems to move up the customer experience curve, including mobile capabilities, Web channels, location awareness, social media, real-time marketing technologies, and new ways of capturing and analyzing customer data for actionable decisions.

WHAT IS: An Integrated Technology Foundation?

An integrated technology foundation consists of core business applications that enable back-office and front-office workers, as well as customers, to easily share up-to-date information about customer transactions and interactions across channels and across business functions (finance, manufacturing, sales, service, and so on).

The applications serve as a "system of record" instead of there being separate, disconnected repositories of information. So, when an event occurs (a problem is logged, an order is made, or some other operation takes place), those data are available to anyone who interacts with the customer. In this way, an integrated technology foundation makes even a large, diverse organization appear as "one" to the customer.

Finally, the third chapter in this section will cover the role of the CIO and the IT organization as change agents for customer centricity. As you'll read, CIOs who understand how to align technology and business strategy can become key players, even leaders, on the customer experience team, with the opportunity to help safeguard and even forge their companies' future.

Framework of Excellence

In Chapter 2, we defined the four essentials of customer experience (CE) as reliability, responsiveness, relevance, and convenience. We've discussed what these essentials look like and the strategies and techniques that enable you to deliver them. Now, we're ready to discuss how you go about delivering on those essentials through technology.

There are three key technology-related areas in which companies need to excel if they are to deliver on the four CE essentials: operations, customer interaction, and decision making. Companies have been engaged in these three activities for years, but all three need to undergo a transformation to become customer-centric. Let's further explore what we sometimes refer to as the *framework of excellence* or the *three pillars of customer experience* (see Table 7.1).

TABLE 7.1: **Three Pillars of Customer Experience**

Pillar	What it Looks Like	Why it's Important
Pillar 1: Operational excellence	Business processes are highly functional from start to finish, and employees can see a full view of all relevant customer data, resulting in well-tuned operations.	An important differentiator for any company today is the ability to achieve optimal levels of accuracy in ordering, billing, delivery, and other customer-facing activities. Orders need to be shipped as promised, field service technicians need to get spare parts in time, sales reps need information about unpaid bills or back orders, and retailers' shelves need to be stocked when a promotion hits the street. If you have too many broken promises, customers will no longer consider you to be reliable, the most important of the CE essentials. This is an area in which companies can no longer compromise on excellence.
Pillar 2: Customer interaction excellence	Companies engage with customers in the digital, "always-on" way that they increasingly prefer, providing interactions that are rich and consistent across channels.	The rubber meets the road with each customer interaction that you have. One negative experience can turn into a costly event as a result of lost revenue, missed opportunities to develop passionate advocates, expenditure of resources to fix the problem, and damaged reputation. No matter how customers want to engage and interact with you, it has to be consistent, convenient, enriching, and increasingly personalized, on an array of channels in any combination. You need to be where your customers are, whether that's social media, the call center, your website, or their mobile device. And the experience you offer has to meet and even anticipate their needs.
Pillar 3: Decision-making excellence	Companies collect customer information and then mine and analyze it for insights. They also integrate these insights with existing applications and processes to improve their decisions and create well-targeted product and service offerings and innovations.	Smart and strategic decision making has always required insight into customers, based on information that you already have or can acquire externally. However, companies need sharper insights into customers than ever before. With increasingly digital customers, there are more customer data available (internally and externally) to mine and analyze for actionable insights. The challenge is developing insights that go beyond the ordinary and lead to competitive advantage.

We believe these three pillars are at the core of any company's customer experience strategy. Each is important on its own, but all three combined elevate the customer experience to a level of excellence that is attainable and offers cost sustainability over time. See Figure 7.1.

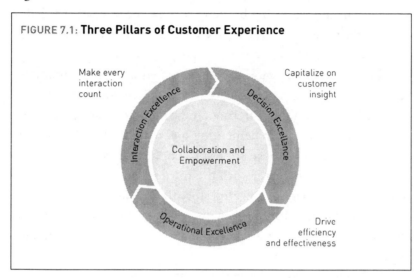

FIGURE 7.1: **Three Pillars of Customer Experience**

Here is an example of these pillars working together, enabled by technology:

- By using a sentiment analysis tool, you can monitor and listen in on social media "buzz." If you combine this with other customer data and apply business intelligence and text-mining capabilities, you gain valuable insight into what customers are thinking about your products and services, and you may become aware of negative experiences and can take action. This way, you enable decision-making excellence.

- Your sentiment analysis tool picks up on a negative tweet, which triggers an alert for you to contact the customer. By following up with the customer (either via Twitter or by responding through another channel, such as e-mail or even a phone call), you can react and address the problem; by doing so, you've enabled interaction excellence.

- The customer service representative can immediately create a service request in the CRM system, which then triggers the internal process to resolve the problem. A service ticket is created, spare parts are ordered, and a service person is dispatched. By following through with a solution to the problem and fixing any broken processes or policies that led to the problem, you've enabled operational excellence.

The three pillars can be your guide to choosing supporting technologies that enable you to create the customer experience edge. It's not just about offering a new mobile application (interaction excellence) or implementing a text-mining tool (decision-making excellence)—those are just the first steps. When you bring those capabilities together with the third pillar, operational excellence, you've got a more powerful story to tell. After all, if your basic operational processes are broken, increasing your customer interaction will just expose that weakness, and no amount of decision making can make up for that.

"Job one is getting the basics right," agrees Smith+co's Shaun Smith. Companies need a greater level of awareness of what their customers' biggest issues are, and they need to resolve these issues. Smith likens the situation to trying to fill a bucket with a hole in it. "If you're losing customers because the bucket is broken, the first thing you need to do is fix the hole," he says. "Only then can you top up with new customers and keep them."

The Right Foundation

Now, we realize that you can provide a strong customer experience without technology. Think of your favorite small business—your lawn mower repair person, for example—whom you appreciate for his beyond-the-call-of-duty personalized service in which technology does not play a part. From the dawn of commerce, small businesses have thrived on their ability to forge personal connections with their customers. However, these organizations are of a size where the proprietor knows your name without being prompted by a CRM system. He can make a check-in phone call to see how that expensive lawn mower repair worked out without a technology-based reminder. And he might offer to sell you a refurbished riding mower when he hears that you've moved to a new house with two acres of property without an event-based marketing system.

TIP

According to the global Bloomberg Businessweek Research Services survey, a majority of respondents (86 percent) associate improved net income with the timely and accurate insights they could achieve through a connected technology backbone. Those with tight integration also said that it was easy to obtain a consolidated view of enterprise data, and more than half reported a substantial positive impact on net income.

But what happens when the small business owner goes on vacation, and someone else is left to manage the store? With no information technology to enable the new person to access customers' history of interactions, it is very likely that a loyal longtime customer may not get her usual level of service. Now, imagine that problem multiplied many times over in large organizations, which serve thousands or millions of customers through an ever-increasing array of channels, including the corporate website, the call center, and social media. No matter how customers contact the business, it needs to track orders, respond to requests and complaints, keep its promises, and ensure that information such as pricing and availability is consistent across all channels.

Of course, most large businesses have implemented technology that automates basic business functions and helps sales and service people do their jobs. However, with customer behavior and competitive threats being in an increasing state of flux, it is much more difficult for some of these existing business systems to fulfill the three pillars of customer experience and enable the four customer experience essentials.

An example is a simple price change that needs to be implemented across multiple systems, including the retail outlet, the website, the invoicing department, collections, the field sales force, the call center, and so on. This is an everyday occurrence that can be paralyzing to companies that are unable to make changes quickly because their systems cannot support the changes. For others, it takes too long, resulting in missed opportunity and lost revenues.

The fact is, most businesses, small or large, need a technology foundation that enables them to deliver a consistent, personalized, high-value customer experience profitably in the multichannel, increasingly digitized world that we live in today. This foundation is necessary for keeping records on all customer activity, making relevant information available to the right people when they need it, and alerting people to exceptions so that prompt action can be taken.

We call this the *integrated technology foundation*. To be honest, we're not big fans of the term *integrated applications*. It's one of the most overused and misused phrases in the ranks of computer industry jargon. But rather than make matters worse by creating more confusion, we've decided to use the term in this book, with the understanding that we mean something very specific when we use it.

To us, an integrated technology foundation—or integrated applications—is a platform that delivers all the core systems that are key to the customer experience and connects the different pieces of your business processes, from start to finish. This integrated foundation serves as the connective tissue that pulls together the many disparate parts of the organization, enabling people throughout the company to serve customers across geographies, channels, and business functions. When a customer interaction triggers a process, such as placing an order, there's a centralized way to orchestrate the many pieces of the process, including product selection, purchasing, fulfillment, logistics, distribution, billing, payment, product return, aftersales support, and so on. In summary, an integrated foundation is the secret sauce that enables a large, potentially complex organization to seem harmonious and appear as "one" company in the eyes of the customer, not a collection of departments and functions.

The rich interactions, data-based decisions, and excellent operational capabilities that have come to exemplify the modern customer experience are built on a technology foundation that enables cost-effective, reliable, and consistent delivery of personalized, high-value customer experiences. We believe that you can't profitably deliver on the four essentials of customer experience without it.

The Importance of Agility

When selecting the right integrated technology foundation to support your customer-centric journey, it is important to keep in mind the huge importance of supporting business agility. One of the most difficult business realities today is the constant and continuous change in customer behavior. When you adopt a customer-centric strategy, your company will be challenged to constantly listen, analyze, and respond by quickly adapting its business processes to meet ever-changing customer needs. For instance, with customers flocking to alternative channels like Facebook or Twitter for transactions, service, product recommendations, payments, and other needs, it's important for you to stay current in your support of these new channels *now*—not months or years from now—in order to stay relevant. After all, there will always be a next "Twitter-like" trend or disruption, and your organization needs to be prepared to take advantage of it.

However, introducing new channels of customer engagement doesn't mean that the traditional channels will go away. As has been proven recently, the growth of Facebook and Twitter has not eliminated the need to support your website or call center. So, to ensure consistency of customer engagement, you need an agile technology platform that will let you modify or expand your business processes to handle new channels and business needs. And you need to be able to do this quickly and easily, without fiddling with the underlying "plumbing" for too long. The choice of an agile integrated technology foundation is, therefore, critical to ensure responsiveness.

A Clear Advantage

Of course, a generous percentage of large companies do not have an integrated technology foundation—far from it.[2] In the BBRS global survey, most respondents reported a moderate level of integration among their core business applications, including financial, human resources, talent management, customer relationship management, supply chain management, supplier relationship management, and product life-cycle management. Only a very small group (11 percent) said that they had achieved "tight integration." Most (89 percent) wanted to change this, however, with the intent of increasing their application integration in the next year.

It's no wonder. A majority of the respondents (86 percent) associate improved profits with the timely and accurate insights that they could achieve through a connected technology backbone. While less than half of the respondents currently have enterprisewide views of data (45 percent), those with tight integration said that it was easy to obtain a consolidated view. More than half of this tightly integrated group (51 percent) also reported a substantial positive impact on profitability.

In terms of customer experience, the survey findings were even more significant. When respondents were asked to rate the level of the customer experience that they provided, the difference between those with moderate and those with tight integration was remarkable. Those with tightly integrated applications ranked their customer experience 20 percent higher than other respondents (see Figure 7.2). Essentially, most organizations rate their customer experience as mediocre, while those with a tightly integrated application foundation said that their customers had a very good experience. (For more detail on this survey, see Appendix B.)

Another recent survey by BBRS revealed that a strong customer experience simply cannot be delivered without an integrated founda-

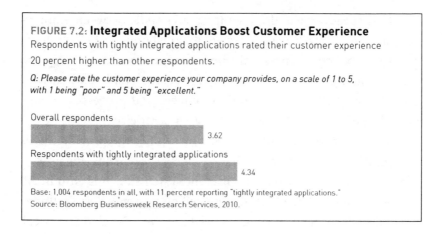

FIGURE 7.2: **Integrated Applications Boost Customer Experience**
Respondents with tightly integrated applications rated their customer experience 20 percent higher than other respondents.

Q: Please rate the customer experience your company provides, on a scale of 1 to 5, with 1 being "poor" and 5 being "excellent."

Overall respondents

3.62

Respondents with tightly integrated applications

4.34

Base: 1,004 respondents in all, with 11 percent reporting "tightly integrated applications."
Source: Bloomberg Businessweek Research Services, 2010.

tion. When asked to name the top obstacles to delivering customer experience, a majority (71 percent) of respondents named disconnected tools, technologies, and applications (see Figure 4.1). Respondents also named "lack of a complete view of the customer to better understand their needs" (66 percent), which, as noted in the previous survey, is directly tied to integrated applications.

Shaking Off the Past

It's easy to see why an integrated technology foundation is such a rarity. Companies acquire other companies (sometimes dozens of other companies) and very often don't take the time to standardize their systems as they go. Or, divisions get into the habit of building or buying technology that helps their individual needs, but without thinking of how it affects the organization.

Then, on top of this jumble of business applications, some organizations often add additional systems with specific capabilities, such as an isolated sales force automation system. The result is a classic mishmash of complex systems with a slew of departmental applications that are somehow connected to the main systems using highly complex and expensive technologies.

This type of technology setup creates walls between employees, making it very difficult for them to collaborate or help customers. You could come up with the best customer-centric strategy and exhibit the highest level of passion for customers, but when your business applications keep your employees and processes disconnected, you'll never achieve true customer centricity.

A large global networking company typifies the problem. This company had one department that was in charge of managing its warranty services, with dozens of different systems feeding into it. All of the systems had been interconnected and extended to do things beyond their original capabilities. Making even the slightest tweak in functionality meant that every one of these systems had to be changed. Just to analyze the impact of a potential change took weeks, and it took the company 18 months to make a significant system overhaul. Since warranties are such a crucial operation for the customer experience, this was clearly no way to operate.

This situation is not uncommon. It might seem like a good idea at the time to just keep adding functionality, such as a self-service application that could be justified on the basis that it would decrease the cost of service. What is missing, though, is the bigger picture. There is certainly a place for single-function applications, such as social media monitoring tools, customer feedback management systems, and sales force automation tools. But they can create strife down the road if they are bought and implemented without the ability to tie them into an integrated foundation that brings all the systems and processes together.

Here's what a customer experience might look like without an integrated technology foundation. A customer is shopping for a new washing machine at an appliance store. Using his mobile device, he checks out his favorite "social shopping" site to see what others think of a particular model. Encouraged by the recommendations, he visits the store's website as well to get further information on product specifications. He notices, however, that the listed price online is lower than that in the store. He could purchase the washing machine online, but the shipping costs and delivery times are a showstopper.

Tracking down a knowledgeable employee proves impossible, so he stands in the customer service line. When he finally gets to talk with a service rep, he asks if it's possible to either get the online price in the store or buy online and pick up the washing machine in the store, thus avoiding both the shipping charge and the delivery delay. Since neither is possible, he leaves the store a disgruntled customer, making sure to check back with his favorite social shopping site to remark on his negative experience.

Of course, with an integrated technology foundation, all of this could have been avoided. Pricing would be consistent across the website and the physical store, and multichannel combinations of purchasing and delivery would be available. And even if there were discrepancies in pricing or availability, frontline employees would be empowered to correct any errors or otherwise turn the negative customer experience into a positive one by accommodating an unexpected customer request.

Another example: a major customer is awaiting shipment on crucial material for its manufacturing process. To optimize its own operations, the customer calls the supplier to determine a window of time within which it can expect delivery. The field rep is unavailable, so the customer gets bounced around to various service agents, none of whom can provide an adequate response. When the field agent finally contacts the customer, she has no idea that the customer has already had several unsuccessful interactions, so the conversation that ensues is unpleasant, to say the least. Worse, it takes the field rep several hours to track down the requested information.

If the supplier had had integrated applications, the customer might have been able to quickly verify the delivery time frame through a self-service portal that collected information from the company's operational processes. Even if that were unavailable, call agents would have been armed with the customer's information as soon as the call came in. Any agent would have known that this was an important customer and would have had the delivery window information at his fingertips. The field agent would have been notified that all of this had taken place, so her follow-up call would have been seen as an extra sign of the supplier's taking good care of the customer.

Bringing It All Together

As these examples illustrate, the customer experience is more than what happens in front of the customer—it's more than productive sales teams, effective marketing campaigns, and efficient call centers. Behind the scenes, orders need to be shipped as promised, field service technicians need to get spare parts in time, sales reps need information about unpaid bills or back orders, and retailers' shelves need to be stocked when a promotion hits the street. And if you want to know who your most profitable customers are, you will need information from your financial system.

Clearly, organizations can no longer afford to view their front-office, back-office, and supply chain applications as separate functions. Bringing these activities together—marketing, sales, service, finance, human resources, product development, and supply chain management—will help attract and retain customers, fulfill demand, and deliver on service promises. Simply bringing the front and back office together for start-to-finish order management, for example, will shorten order cycle times, increase order accuracy, reduce the number of incomplete orders, decrease billing disputes, reduce order status calls, and lower inventory costs.

Every day, organizations lose revenue and incur unnecessary costs simply because they have failed to connect their front and back offices to close the loop on business processes. Products aren't available at the times and places needed. Service technicians don't have the right spare parts. Returns aren't correctly passed through to accounts payable. Service requests can't be resolved on the first call. All of these cause customer satisfaction to decline and customer attrition to rise. Furthermore, without an accurate and complete view of customers across the organization, companies may miss important opportunities to increase product quality, improve business processes, and spur product innovation. In addition, they can miss important revenue opportunities that would otherwise become apparent through the connection and analysis of back-office and front-office data.

Avoiding these missed opportunities, costly missteps, and broken processes means breaking down the walls between employees and redefining business processes to span front and back offices, channels, and customer touch points. You want customers to see one company, not a collection of departments or channels.

An integrated technology foundation is also crucial for learning more about your customers. These data need to be brought together from all touch points, departments, and divisions and combined with data from other sources so that they can be connected, consolidated, analyzed, and converted into useful customer knowledge. These insights then need to be embedded into critical planning and decision-making processes such as sales planning, new product development, and marketing investments, as well as resource alignment and supply chain planning.

Increasingly, these insights are needed by employees across all functions before they can even interact with customers, says Ray Wang, CEO of Constellation Research. "For every customer interaction, every worker needs to answer a few key questions," he says. "Who are you—do we know your identity? What other relationships do you have that I should know about? What have you bought? Are there credit risks? What entitlements do you have—maybe you're a VIP customer? How did we treat you the last time?" These questions need to be asked for all interactions, not just customers who come through the front door, but also those who interact through customer support or back-end functions like finance.

Furthermore, the answers to these questions need to be served up on whatever device the worker is on, Wang says, whether it's a cell phone, a tablet PC, or a point-of-sale (POS) device. "Companies have to move from a world of being reactive to being proactive, and that's a big thing," he says.

A Multichannel World

In today's multichannel business world, organizations also need to harmonize the many means of customer interaction (such as telephone, e-mail, fax, voice mail, text messages, Web self-service, Facebook pages, Twitter communiqués, QR bar codes, mobile applications, online requests, and physical presence). Customers use many channels to communicate with companies, and these interaction channels need to share a similar look and feel, offer consistent information capture, and share customer information. Customers should be able to start an interaction over one communication channel (say the phone) and complete it over a different one, such as a follow-up e-mail, according to Forrester Research, Inc.[3]

Here are a few examples of what multichannel harmonization looks like:

- Customer inquiries are intelligently routed in real time to the people with the right skills to best address the questions, no matter which channel the customer is using and no matter where in the world those experts might be.

- Companies provide customers with a rich choice of touch points that are targeted specifically to their needs. For instance, highly relevant information can be found on the corporate website. A social community can provide a customer network of other people with similar interests and concerns. The social media presence can also include chats with well-known experts in the field. Virtual "tryout" capabilities enable customers to better understand how a product would fit their needs. Phone or text updates can provide order status information. Mobile capabilities can be used for coupons, product information, price lookup, and reaching out to social media sources for recommendations and advice.

- When customers take action in one channel, the information on this action is carried over into other channels. For instance, they can buy online or via their mobile device, request delivery to their home or office, and return either online or at the store. After purchasing an airline ticket, they can check in online and use their phone as a boarding pass. They can also buy in the store using digital discounts and digital offer codes that are delivered to their mobile device, obtain accurate product or pricing information via their mobile, or use any other combination of channels that they prefer. The key is that no matter what they do, they get a consistent experience.

Clearly, offering hybrid models and catering to customer preferences require flexible and integrated systems. For instance, ordering systems need to ensure that inventory is allocated correctly. Customer service representatives need a cross-channel view of customer purchases that includes their catalog, online, and in-store purchase history. Management needs to see the relationships between cross-channel activities to see how these transactions impact key

TIP

Multichannel harmonization is something that customers today increasingly expect. According to a 2010 survey by Cognizant Technology Solutions and *Retail Info Systems News* ("2010 Shopper Experience Survey"), 63 percent of respondents favor the flexibility of purchasing a product online, having it delivered to their home, and, if needed, returning it to the store. Overall, respondents said that they are interested in emerging hybrid models like "order online and pick up in-store," "purchase in-store for home delivery," or "order in one store for pickup at another store." Preferences shift among different demographic groups. Women prefer free home delivery for out-of-stock items, while men and the millennial population want to make returns at the store and receive a discount voucher for a future purchase.

performance indicators (KPIs). To provide the level of service that customers expect and demand, according to a recent article by Cognizant Technology Solutions, retailers need a single view of inventory, as well as visibility into orders and how best to fulfill them.[4] This requires tight connections between order management, warehouse management, customer relationship management, sourcing, logistics, and other supply chain functions.

Getting to "Connected"

To achieve an integrated technology foundation, most companies first develop an application portfolio management strategy. Application portfolio management is a topic that's too complex to fully treat here, but briefly, your portfolio strategy should give you a picture of your future-state technical architecture, along with a road map for how to get there. This includes an inventory and analysis of your current applications—the good, the bad, and the ugly—and plans to consolidate and retire the systems that are too complex to manage. It may be worthwhile to upgrade your core platform to obtain new capabilities.

Application portfolio management not only reduces your total cost of ownership for technology but also greatly increases your ability to respond quickly to changing customer requirements. And, once you are operating from a somewhat normalized base, you can direct your focus toward using advanced technologies to move ahead in the game, which we'll explore further in the next chapter.

The complexity of your application portfolio is relevant if you are trying to operate as a company that is unified around the goal of customer centricity. When your core systems are working in concert, you can afford to venture into new technology areas, piecing in new solutions where they make sense as part of your application portfolio.

There are many good examples of companies that are doing just this. One is Colmobil Corp., an automobile importer in Israel. In light of the changing global economy and new types of digitally engaged customers, Colmobil decided that in order to sustain its healthy growth, it needed to shift its focus from the cars it sold to the people who were driving them off the lot. To make this transformation from product centricity to customer centricity, it decided that it was necessary for the company to overhaul its organizational structure and its legacy technical environment, both of which were designed to support more traditional business processes.

"After many years of working this way, we started realizing the customer may touch the company in each and every division, and even in different divisions at the same time," says Gil Katz, CIO at Colmobil. The company wanted to provide a consistent, personalized experience across all of these interactions.

To make this possible, Colmobil decided that the system should consist of fully integrated components, including enterprise resource planning (ERP), CRM, and industry-specific applications, with a CRM-based front end. Through this front end, sales and service employees record and access all customer transactions and interactions, in addition to following standardized CRM policies and processes when they talk with customers. Because the systems are connected, all customer interactions are recorded through the CRM system and flow to operational systems, enabling sales and service agents to access the entire customer record and history of transactions, across divisions. The result: employees see a complete, unified picture of the customer, for the first time in the company's history.

Today, returning customers are offered personalized service, including special offers and discounts, based on their transaction history and preferences. Vehicles are also delivered and processed more quickly, thanks to radio frequency ID (RFID)-enhanced streamlined movement of vehicles from warehouse to dealer. (For a detailed description of Colmobil's transformation, see the Colmobil case study on page 129.)

Another example is Synopsys. When it decided to differentiate through the customer experience, it first needed to consolidate its 17 different CRM systems—the result of multiple acquisitions—into a "single system of record." With customer data separated into multiple systems, it was all but impossible for the company to deliver a consistent experience across its multiple business units. It standardized on a single CRM system offered by its ERP vendor, which enabled additional synergies between these two core business systems. Today, its online portal offers customers a range of self-service options, including access to an online community. All support cases also come through the central CRM system, which routes calls globally to the person with the right expertise. This provides a personalized experience and minimizes the time that customers would otherwise spend being bounced from one agent to the next.

Because all issues are centralized, the system can notify sales reps when an issue comes in via a different channel. If three individuals from one customer have open issues, the sales rep can call the field application consultant and share relevant information about the account. In this way, Synopsys customers from large global companies sometimes discover things that they did not know about what their own colleagues on the other side of the world are doing. Additionally, customers can use Synopsys's portal to initiate and check on service requests, which automatically flow into and out of the CRM system. (For a full report on the Synopsys customer experience edge, see the case study in Chapter 3, page 42.)

These examples bolster our belief that the customer experience is not a technology but a customer-centric business strategy. However, an integrated technology foundation and other, more advanced technologies are a mission-critical element of Colmobil's and Synopsys's success, as they are integral to any company's customer experience edge. Not only do integrated applications provide the foundation on which companies can begin to understand each customer's needs, but they are also at the core of reshaping business processes to meet customer expectations, empower employees to best serve the customer, and determine how to most efficiently and effectively deliver on those needs.

As increased competition drives companies to become more customer-centric, they are realizing that their underlying technologies are an inhibitor. If your company has disparate systems and broken processes, you are not well positioned to take advantage of the emerging technologies we will cover in the next chapter, which are designed to increase customer centricity. Until you get your house IT systems in order, you won't have the necessary agility to embrace these new technologies. Adding ever more isolated applications on top increases complexity and decreases flexibility. Meanwhile, your competitors will be busily thinking up new ways to make customers happy and implementing them the same day—or, at least, a lot more quickly than you can do.

CASE STUDY: COLMOBIL

Customers, Not Cars, Now Drive Auto Importer's Strategy

As part of its growth strategy, Colmobil transformed its business from product-facing to people-facing.

The automobile industry tends to be highly traditional, with a decidedly product and service focus. So when Colmobil Corp.—one of Israel's leading importers and distributors of cars, trucks, and buses—decided to reorganize its business around the customer rather than the vehicle, it was a radical decision.

Colmobil is a 70-year-old family-owned company with an almost 20 percent share of Israel's automobile market. In 2007, when the global recession hit, Colmobil was facing a range of challenges, including increasing government regulations, a changing retail market, and a technology infrastructure that was highly dependent on older, legacy systems. The company was confident that it was doing a good job of importing, warehousing, selling, delivering, and servicing vehicles for consumers and commercial clients. To continue growing, however, it needed to explore additional opportunities, such as expanding its business interests in other countries (including Eastern Europe) and in other business areas (including the trade-in market).

These realities—combined with a changing retail market, thanks to increasingly knowledgeable customers who were adept at using online resources and social media—drove Colmobil to change its entire organizational structure and business processes. As part of the transformation, it overhauled its legacy technology infrastructure, as well. No longer could Colmobil focus on the cars it sold; it needed to focus on the people who were driving those vehicles off the lot.

CE ESSENTIALS

- **Reliability.** Colmobil sales and service employees record all customer transactions and interactions in a centralized system and follow standardized policies and processes.

- **Convenience.** The automobile importer fitted new cars with RFID tags and placed tag scanners at its entrance gates. When a customer arrives, reception agents can offer a personal greeting rather than a request for identification. When the customer leaves, the exit gate opens automatically. Vehicles are delivered and processed more quickly, thanks to streamlined movement of vehicles from warehouse to dealer.

- **Relevance.** Business systems and processes focus on individual customers rather than on vehicles purchased. As a result, sales and service agents can access the entire customer record and history of transactions, across divisions. Returning customers are offered personalized service, including special offers and discounts, based on their transaction history and preferences.

"The way we were structured, we were always leaning toward the vehicle and were never able to understand who the customer was behind the vehicle or the relationship between one customer and many vehicles," says Gil Katz, CIO at Colmobil, which is headquartered in Rosh Ha'ayin. So, if a customer purchased vehicles or services from more than one of Colmobil's divisions—in some cases, simultaneously—it had no way to know that, because the systems were not integrated. The divisions focused on vehicle brand—Mercedes-Benz, Mitsubishi Motors, and Hyundai Motors—and after-sales service.

For instance, a business-to-business (B2B) customer might buy dozens of trucks from the Mercedes-Benz unit, but if he bought his daughter a Hyundai or services for his own personal vehicle, "no one knew he was a valued customer of the company," Katz says. As a result, the customer's experience as a business client was inconsistent with his experience as a consumer, and agents had no opportunity to individualize his experience based on his preferences or on issues that had arisen during his last few transactions.

CE PILLARS

- **Operational excellence.** Colmobil implemented a new technology system that consists of fully integrated components, including ERP, CRM, and industry-specific applications, and that revolves around customers, not vehicles.

- **Interaction excellence.** Colmobil is currently creating business processes to enable sales agents to recognize high-value customers and offer them special discounts.

- **Decision-making excellence.** In the future, Colmobil will use data analytics to segment customers, enabling the company to better understand the needs of high value customers and support them using relevant data.

Revolving Around the Customer

To address this issue, Colmobil made the strategic decision to replace the legacy systems that had been built to support the old organizational structure with a new system that revolves around customers, not vehicles. It decided that the system should consist of fully integrated components, including ERP, CRM, and industry-specific applications, with a CRM-based front end. Through this front end, sales and service employees record and access all customer transactions and interactions, in addition to following standardized CRM policies and processes when they talk with customers. Because the systems are integrated, all customer interactions are recorded through the CRM system and flow to operational systems. The result: employees see a complete, unified picture of the customer, for the first time in the company's history.

"Through the process of replacing our information systems, we laid down the infrastructure for changing from product-centric processes to customer-centric," Katz says. Tightly integrated applications are a key component of how highly companies rate their ability to provide a strong customer experience, according to a recent survey by Bloomberg Businessweek Research Services (see Figure 7.2).

Colmobil also restructured its formerly brand-centric divisions to a structure that is now focused on how customers view the vehicles, in addition to doubling the size of its service division. A year and a half since going live, "we're built to face the market and the customers rather than what we're selling," Katz says.

The next step, he says, will be to fully capitalize on all the opportunities this new infrastructure presents, in terms of seeing the life

COLMOBIL AT A GLANCE

- **Business description:** Family-owned importer and distributor of passenger cars, commercial vehicles, trucks, and buses, representing Mercedes-Benz, Mitsubishi Motors, and Hyundai Motors

- **Location:** Rosh Ha'ayin, Israel

- **Products and services:** Vehicle sales, service, trade-ins, finance, insurance

- **Annual revenues:** Over $1 billion (private company)

- **Number of employees:** 790

- **Number of customers:** Over 350,000 customer records in the corporate database

- **Vehicle sales (2010):** 42,500—a new record for the company

- **Vehicles serviced:** 700 daily

cycle of customer interactions. In doing so, Colmobil has overcome some of the most common obstacles to the customer experience, named by respondents in a recent survey by Bloomberg Businessweek Research Services (see Figure 4.1). Katz notes, "It's a different approach to customers, where it's not just a financial relationship."

Phil Reed, an analyst at automotive information website Edmunds.com, says that Colmobil's approach is targeted at the right goals. Reed states, "Dealerships are known for endless consultant studies that advise them to add parking spaces or valet parking, but it's pretty clear it starts with respect for the customer," he says. "People like to be known and remembered." And with customers increasingly using the Internet to research prices and profit margins, Reed says, the relationship becomes even more important.

Importance of Technology

Customer segmentation through data analytics also will play a role at Colmobil, Katz says. "We want to really focus on those customers who are doing business with us by understanding their needs and better supporting them using relevant data rather than wasting energy on those who are less high-value." Customer segmentation of this sort is a core principle of customer experience management.

Colmobil also is using RFID to expedite the movement of automobiles as they are brought to port. New cars are fitted with RFID tags as they are being unloaded, and the tag information is combined with the vehicle identification number in Colmobil's back-end systems. In addition, RFID scanners will be placed at the entrance gates of the service centers, so that when a customer arrives at the gate, his information appears on the monitor at the reception desk. There, the reception agent can offer a personal greeting rather than a request for identification. After the car has been serviced and accounts settled, the exit gate will open automatically without further inquiry. In the future, Colmobil has its sights set on the Web and extending the customer experience to online channels.

Culture Change

The biggest challenge to implementing these processes, Katz says, is changing the organizational culture. "The system can support that already, but we're working on educating the different lines of business to use what we've created and capitalize on it," he says. "They're used to taking care of the vehicle, and now they need to take care of how the customer feels, and that when he walks out, he's satisfied. It's a different way of thinking, and it takes time to embrace that change."

Katz is walking a fine line between providing employees with sufficient customer information, but not so much as to overwhelm them. He is also sensitive to customer concerns about privacy. "We don't want the customer to feel a person he doesn't know knows too much about him," Katz says. This insight shows that Colmobil is truly imagining each interaction from the customer's point of view.

The organizational restructuring has gone a long way toward showing employees that there is a strong commitment to Colmobil's transformation. Katz says, "People who used to work under one manager now work under another." He notes further, "People changed assignments of what they do, and they're now expected to do things that may not come naturally." Employees were very involved in the process redesign, he says, which has increased the overall level of cooperation.

Employees also are well aware that the experience Colmobil is now able to offer customers is what they themselves—as customers of other businesses—would like to receive and what is often lacking. "It's part of the cultural change in the world that puts the customer at the center," Katz says. "They feel we're doing the right thing."

It is too early, Katz says, to measure benefits in terms of revenues, profits, and customer retention, but he expects the improved customer experience to lead to profitable outcomes. "When you build a better customer experience, the word gets around, and your reputation gets better," he says.

The technology infrastructure, Katz says, was crucial to the overall success of the effort, as was a strong level of collaboration between

IT and other business functions, such as marketing. Katz is not just CIO but also part of the executive board at Colmobil. In his role as CIO, he says, his job was to pave the road, so that when the company drove down it, it was a smooth ride. "In IT, we have to be one step ahead of the company's strategy, so that when it wanted to change from product-centric to customer-centric, we had a plan and were able to implement the technology to support it."

CHAPTER 8

Adding Disruptive Technologies to Advance the Game

In 2009, there were 174 million smartphone users worldwide; there will be one billion by 2015.
—IN-STAT, 2010

Mobility will be the top business/technology trend impacting customer experience in the next three years, according to more than half of businesses surveyed.
—BLOOMBERG BUSINESSWEEK
RESEARCH SERVICES, 2010

ALL BUSINESSES ARE COMING TO GRIPS with "the new consumer." Customers simply don't behave the way they used to. In their personal and professional lives, the way people expect to consume information, interact with suppliers, make purchase decisions, and conduct transactions are all in a continual state of flux, thanks to the Web, pervasive use of mobile devices and social media, and other emerging technologies.

Via their mobile devices, consumers today can engage in a wide variety of activities. They can read product reviews and receive receipts and coupons; check in for a flight and use their smartphone as a boarding pass; receive shipping updates and mobile coupons via short messaging service (SMS); make feature and price comparisons; get recommendations and advice from online forums and social shopping sites; check the latest deals offered by websites that offer discounts through collective buying; and tweet about bad experiences as soon as they happen or share them on Facebook.

You need only look at the numbers to get a clearer view of today's customer. In 2009, there were 174 million smartphone users worldwide, and that number is forecast to grow to one billion by 2015, according to In-Stat.[1] And according to Insight Express, 82 percent of adult mobile users used their device in the store, while shopping.

Meanwhile, the social networking scene is booming: as of early 2011, there were 200 million Twitter users and 500 million active Facebook users, with half of the latter logging onto the site on any given day and all of them accounting for 700 billion minutes per month spent on the site. Even e-mail is becoming old-fashioned, as Twitter, social media messaging, SMS, and other forms of messaging continue to ramp up in popularity. According to ABI Research, consumers worldwide will send more than seven trillion SMS messages in 2011, inspiring companies to use this channel for marketing messages, such as coupons and product promotions.

The mentality of consumers has infiltrated the workplace as well. Young professionals have grown up with the Web, mobile devices, and social media and see these technologies as essential for doing their jobs effectively. Sometimes referred to as "millennials," younger workers may not be drawn to employers who do not make innovative use of mobile applications, social networking, and other emerging technologies, and they will grow frustrated when their workplace technology lags behind the tools they use at home.

And so, while companies cannot abandon traditional channels such as the call center, television programming, and newspapers, they can no longer rely on these venues to reach customers, as customers have moved online, taking their attention—and their wallets—with them. Increasingly, customers expect a rich choice of technology capabilities that are targeted specifically at their needs. For instance:

- Rich Internet applications (RIAs) that enable personalization, Amazon-like navigation and cart capabilities, multiple search and display options, and product-comparison tools

- An online community for troubleshooting problems, sharing advice, and networking with people who have similar concerns

- Information delivery to mobile devices, such as catalogs, receipts, and order status

- Integration with social media tools, such as blogs, forums, and chats, to help with buying decisions

- Real-time marketing and location-based services that deliver information or special offers at the exact time the customer needs them

In this chapter, we turn to what we think of as game-changing technologies—social media monitoring and engagement, mobile applications, rich Internet applications, and unified communications, to name a few. These technologies are often considered "disruptive" because they can launch companies into unfamiliar, and ultimately highly valuable, terrain, allowing you to move up the curve of customer experience and meet or exceed the expectations of increasingly networked customers.

Meet the New Consumer

Best Buy exemplifies a retailer that is striving to provide the type of multichannel customer experience that the "new consumer" is looking for, with the aid of disruptive technologies. The consumer electronics retailer plans to double its current $2 billion in annual online sales within five years by introducing a broader selection of merchandise on the Web and adding more Web-based services and digital content.

Best Buy customers will be able to get more product information, customer reviews, and ratings through their mobile devices, as well as in-store pickup for mobile orders. The retailer is increasing its SMS initiatives and has made its weekly circular interactive by incorporating SMS "calls to action" and mobile scannable QR (quick response) codes, which are two-dimensional codes intended to be scanned by the camera in a mobile device that is equipped with a specialized reader application. The code can transfer information to the mobile device, including rich product information, recommendations, reviews, and URLs for mobile websites. Best Buy is also incorporating QR codes into the product fact tags in its stores to provide shoppers with more product information in the aisle via their mobile devices. The company also uses SMS as an opt-in service, sending subscribers such information as the "deal of the day."

WHAT IS: QR Code?

> QR codes are two-dimensional codes that are intended to be scanned by the camera in a mobile device that is equipped with a specialized reader application. The code can transfer information to the mobile device, including rich product information, recommendations, reviews, and URLs for mobile websites. The codes can be placed on a product tag, in advertising text, on store signs, and in numerous other places.

Best Buy is also rolling out a multichannel network, called Best Buy On, that is intended to inform and entertain. It will feature how-to videos and information on a new technology topic every month. The messages will also be broadcast on screens throughout its stores.[2]

These moves are in response to what consumers today want from retailers. "There's a new definition of convenience: the ability to interact with a company on your terms," Shari Ballard, executive vice president at Best Buy, told analysts at the corporate announcement of the plan.[3]

Under the Hood

We should note that while emerging technologies are essential to the customer experience, they are ultimately most effective once the basics are in place. The integrated technology foundation discussed in the previous chapter provides you with a simple, robust, and cost-effective way to consistently and reliably deliver orders as promised, send out invoices, take customer calls, fulfill service requisitions, and carry out other basic business processes. It enables all four customer experience (CE) essentials (reliability, relevance, consistency, and responsiveness) and all three CE pillars (operational, interaction, and decision excellence). The addition of emerging technologies heightens effectiveness in all these areas, changing the game and allowing you to obtain the much-sought-after customer experience edge.

To see why, let's take another look at the Swiss grocery retailer Coop, first mentioned in Chapter 2. Like many large companies, Coop ran its back-office operations on an enterprise resource planning (ERP) system, which it integrated with its customer relationship management (CRM) front-office application. Coop's @home division had launched a successful online store based on cutting-edge Web technology, but it did not stop there. The company quickly realized that it could leverage its e-commerce platform to add an iPhone shopping app that the time-pressed, tech-savvy Swiss would love.

Coop was able to do this quickly, effectively, and affordably only because it had a solid foundation upon which to build. The shopping application was up and running in two months, well before the grocer's biggest competitor was able to launch a mobile app. What is more, because Coop's application connects to its integrated core, shoppers can see a real-time view of product availability, reserve 60-minute delivery windows while shopping, and get consistent pricing across the physical and virtual channels. These capabilities provide Coop with a competitive advantage and eliminate the source of much frustration for customers. The shopping app also enables Coop to fulfill all four of the customer experience essentials, as well as the pillars of interaction and operational excellence. (For a full description of Coop's iPhone application and the benefits the company is realizing, see the case study in Chapter 2, page 26.)

Being Selective

Which technologies you ultimately choose to leverage for the customer experience edge, and how you do so, will depend on your customers and their preferences and needs. For instance, Forrester Research data show that customers still generally prefer to contact vendors by phone, closely followed by e-mail and Web self-service. The younger generation, however, is showing us the way of the future as it leans toward peer-to-peer communication, social networking, and instant service channels such as chat.[4]

This is why companies that are doing a good job with the customer experience first work to understand what channels of communication their customers are using, whether they're interacting via phone, online chat, social media, or e-mail. Then they design the experience based on that. For instance, a customer who makes a phone call has different expectations from one who engages in chat or e-mail, and, often, the same person expects a different response when interacting by phone rather than by chat or e-mail. Denis Pombriant, founder of CRM consultancy Beagle Research Group, LLC, in Stoughton, Massachusetts, explains this further. Someone who is calling the call center may have first tried and failed with other channels, and so when he makes the call, he's feeling frazzled and maybe not very friendly. Simpler issues tend to be resolved through other channels, so you get a higher percentage of complex or difficult problems coming in to the call center. The callers' experience reaching you has changed, and the experience that they're expecting is different, as there's more frustration and thus urgency. "Designing the customer experience comes with the understanding that the ideal experience in one channel is not ideal in another channel," Pombriant says.

As you consider the range of disruptive technologies available in the marketplace, your investment decision should also be guided by the CE pillars: How does this technology turn data into actionable insights and better decisions? How does it make every interaction count? Does it make my operations run more smoothly?

With all of this in mind, here are a few of the key technologies and capabilities that can help you achieve the four essentials and the three pillars of customer experience.

Rich Web Capabilities

Nearly every company today has a Web presence, but many companies' websites are based on custom-built, outdated, and ultimately costly technologies.[5] The mother of all disruptive technologies, the Web is a low-cost, high-impact channel through which you can market, sell, and provide services to customers. Customers today expect to be able to interact with vendors online 24/7, and they increasingly desire the rich and personalized experience they have with many retail websites. Vendor websites provide real opportunity for innovation, as the possibilities for creating a closer, more intimate relationship with customers are endless: interactive catalogs, enhanced product galleries, embedded product ratings and reviews, and user-focused online self-services. As in the Coop example, the richest online customer experience is one that leverages integrated back-end systems and processes.

The central role of the Internet for future growth is as pertinent for business-to-business (B2B) companies as it is for business-to-consumer (B2C) companies. In ThomasNet's September 2010 *Industry Market Barometer*, respondents named "increased online marketing" as one of their top four strategies for continued success. They also cited developing business in new U.S. geographies, creating innovative products and services, and pursuing business in new industries. In all, 60 percent of the 3,243 manufacturers, distributors, and service companies surveyed said that having an online strategy was either critical or important to their growth in the second half of 2010. As one survey respondent said, "Our sales are up 37 percent over the same period last year, and we've set four successive months of sales records. More attention to online marketing and sales has allowed us to penetrate new markets and seed demand for new products."[6]

The ThomasNet survey also points to Keats Manufacturing Co. as an example of a company that is fueling growth through its online strategy. This custom job shop manufactures metal parts used in such products as automotive fuel injection systems, hearing aids, and appliance timer controls. To make up for losses incurred during the recession, Keats pursued an online strategy to showcase its capabilities, equipment, and projects to help market its business and expand worldwide. The result: a 30 percent increase in the company's net income.

Cognizant Technology Solutions is also looking at the Internet as a huge opportunity for industrial manufacturers, even though adoption has so far been slow.[7] Cognizant sees this changing as manufacturers realize that they can increase sales through functions such as online product recommendations and customer-specific promotions. To do this, the consulting firm says, industrial manufacturers will need to revamp their websites with rich Internet application technologies, provide easy access to data to help with buying decisions, and enable ample online postpurchase support. Among other things, RIA technologies provide customers with a more visually guided experience as they perform actions such as product comparison and product search.

Industrial manufacturers need to shift from websites that rely on multiple stand-alone applications catering to functions such as "search," "order," and "cart processing" to a single RIA technology–based portal, according to Cognizant. One manufacturer that did this increased parts sales by 150 percent and online order volume by 300 percent within a year, according to Cognizant.

Mobility

Combined with the Web, mobility is far and away the world's most prominent and influential megatrend. The rapid adoption and dissemination of mobile phones and other mobile computing devices (including tablets and smartphones) to even the most remote places on earth is without precedent in the history of technology.

Consider that in the first 74 days after its launch in 2007, Apple sold one million iPhones.[8] Less than three years later, when the iPad was introduced, it took just 80 days to sell three million units.[9] Beyond Apple's devices, there were as many as 174 million smartphones worldwide by 2009; that number is forecast to grow to one billion by 2015, according to In-Stat.[10] With this ongoing revolution, mobility, connectivity, and the democratization of information have reached entirely new levels that organizations must leverage in order to gain a competitive advantage.

It is not surprising, then, that in the Bloomberg Businessweek Research Services (BBRS) survey, mobility was named as the top business/technology trend affecting the customer experience in the next three years (see Figure 8.1).

Additionally, according to a Yankee Group survey, the number one reason that CIOs are investing in mobility solutions is to improve responsiveness to customers and foster collaboration with customers and partners.[11] To that end, as mentioned in Chapter 3, companies are increasing plans to provide key applications and data to employees via their handheld devices in the next two years, including customer order status, inventory levels, and other operational data. This can be seen as moving one step closer to providing this information directly to end customers. With more customers holding what they consider to be a world of information in the palms of their hands, it will become increasingly intolerable to them that they cannot get real-time data on orders, inventory, pricing, deliveries, and more whenever and however they choose.

From a service standpoint, the increase in mobility emphasizes the importance of enabling a consistent multichannel approach for customers. Many times, customers choose many channels for one transaction. A service request may start via a smartphone and then go to an online chat or e-mail. We see more transactions being conducted via smartphone. The proliferation of channels adds to the

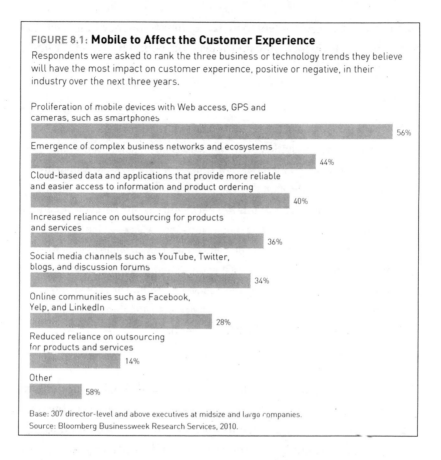

FIGURE 8.1: Mobile to Affect the Customer Experience

Respondents were asked to rank the three business or technology trends they believe will have the most impact on customer experience, positive or negative, in their industry over the next three years.

Proliferation of mobile devices with Web access, GPS and cameras, such as smartphones — 56%

Emergence of complex business networks and ecosystems — 44%

Cloud-based data and applications that provide more reliable and easier access to information and product ordering — 40%

Increased reliance on outsourcing for products and services — 36%

Social media channels such as YouTube, Twitter, blogs, and discussion forums — 34%

Online communities such as Facebook, Yelp, and LinkedIn — 28%

Reduced reliance on outsourcing for products and services — 14%

Other — 58%

Base: 307 director-level and above executives at midsize and large companies.
Source: Bloomberg Businessweek Research Services, 2010.

complexity. Companies need to establish a mobile platform that can accommodate applications for any device and integrate those applications with their back-office systems.

Companies need to get even more creative about how they think of mobility, according to Diamond Advisory Services' Paul D'Alessandro. In addition to thinking of mobile devices in "communications" and "application" terms, he says, consider their ability to act as a sensing platform. For instance, mobile devices can sense and transmit real-time information, such as your geographic location and medical information (heart rate, glucose levels, and the like). When you combine these three capabilities (communications, applications, and sensing), he says, you can create a customer experience around mobile that will motivate customers to increase their frequency of interaction with you, one for which they might even be willing to pay a premium.

TIP

Mobile coupons are taking off. According to Burrell Associates, a research and consulting firm that tracks advertising, redemption rates of mobile coupons are 10 times those of coupons distributed by mail or through newspapers.[12] And according to a Mobile Marketing Association/Luth Research survey, 10 percent of cell phone owners surveyed use mobile location services at least once a week, and nearly half of people who noticed an ad while using location-based services took at least some action, a significantly higher rate than for those who noticed ads while sending or receiving text messages (37 percent) and almost twice the rate of those who saw an ad while browsing the Web (28 percent).[13]

For instance, D'Alessandro is working with health-care clients that are embedding biometric sensors in smartphones to enable physicians to better manage patients with chronic diseases such as diabetes, helping them take prescription medications properly and monitor health indicators captured by medical devices.

Another example is combining real-time marketing with location-based services, so that you can leverage the location-sensing technology inside a smartphone in order to push out specific offers like discounts and coupons. So, for instance, a shopper arriving in a retailer's parking lot could receive a text message about special offers that are available just as she walks through the door. With some real-time offer management systems, these services can grow more and more personalized over time, with the ability to learn from customers' responses to offers. For instance, if a customer refuses an offer, the engine learns from the rejection for subsequent offers. As a result, customers get a more personalized experience, because the vendor avoids sending offers that they are not likely to accept.

Online Communities and Social Media Sites

As we said earlier, it's one thing to put up a Facebook page or start a Twitter account and quite another to strategically engage in social networking. Social networking technologies and online communities are now mainstream, and companies are seriously investing in these means of customer engagement. In a recent survey by the CMO Council and Deloitte, respondents named social media and online communities as the top investment for their digital marketing dollars (see Figure 8.2).[14]

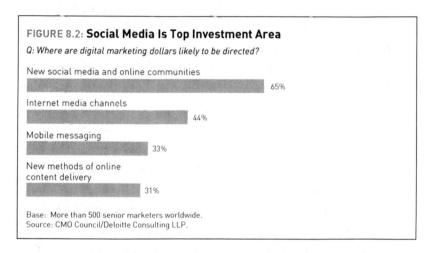

FIGURE 8.2: **Social Media Is Top Investment Area**

Q: Where are digital marketing dollars likely to be directed?

New social media and online communities — 65%

Internet media channels — 44%

Mobile messaging — 33%

New methods of online content delivery — 31%

Base: More than 500 senior marketers worldwide.
Source: CMO Council/Deloitte Consulting LLP.

It's important to heed the distinction between social media sites and online communities. With the former, a key is to listen more than you engage in order to learn about your customers and how they interact on the various channels. Beagle's Pombriant offers the 80/20 rule, where you listen 80 percent of the time and engage the other 20 percent. "Then you can respond with a rifle shot instead of with buckshot," he says.

Frank Eliason, who famously helped move Comcast's customer service operations onto social media and is now senior vice president of social media at Citi, agrees. In 2007, Eliason started calling customers on the phone when he noticed them mentioning problems with Comcast in their blogs. This led to Eliason's moving into a new role for the firm as director of digital care. In this capacity, he began monitoring customers' tweets on Twitter and eventually began tweeting back, providing his phone number and encouraging people to call him directly for help.

Soon, Eliason had a staff of people who were monitoring and responding to customer tweets and even discovering and resolving widespread problems before the call center received a deluge of complaints. Still, Eliason contends that social media should be viewed not as a marketing channel or even as a service channel, but as a communication channel owned by the customer: "A lot of companies don't respect that the customer owns the community, and if they want to, they can turn you off in a second. They don't need to listen to you."

In fact, when Eliason started responding to tweets, he would propose solutions right away, but he could see that this was a turn-off for the Twitter customer community: "From their reaction, I sensed they saw that as intrusive and presumptuous." He quickly switched to responding simply, "Can I help?"

Comcast, Eliason says, created a well-rounded approach to social media by defining its goals. "We didn't want to go out selling," he says. "We needed to improve our customer experience, and one of the keys was listening to customers, no matter where they were."

Once you begin to understand the various communities' motivations and quirks, you can enter discussions, lobbing a few salvos to see what you get back. In the B2C environment, many customers will be sensitive about and even hostile to vendor involvement in online communities. You will need to show ultimate respect for the participants before you will be accepted into the group. Even then, tread lightly. Eliason says, "You're there to listen, not preach or even answer questions."

When it's your own Facebook page or your own branded online community, the dynamics are different. Talbots, for instance, strikes a playful note with its Facebook page, encouraging fans to post stories about their favorite outfits or the worst present they ever received. Since shoppers seek out the site, there is no danger that they will perceive Talbots as intruding when company agents make suggestions about chic new outfits or alert the group to a flash sale that is available only for the next hour.

Online communities can be particularly useful in the B2B space. For example, the SAP Community Network (SCN) is a community of more than 2 million members. SCN is where SAP developers, analysts, consultants, integrators, and administrators connect and co-innovate with their peers, using a combination of active discussion forums, blogs, and wikis. SCN provides an environment in which members can collaborate, find answers to technical questions, get expert advice on handling day-to-day technical issues, follow up on business opportunities, and learn about leading-edge technologies. Members have access to a technical library of articles, white papers, and documentation, as well as software downloads and code samples. They can help themselves to relevant education via an extensive e-learning catalog and participate in active, moderated forums and Web logs. SCN is an invaluable resource for customers, while at the same time driving value to SAP by reducing incoming support requests and support costs. It is also much faster than SAP's support organization in responding to and resolving many issues, with complex technical questions being answered by community members in a matter of minutes. Think about the power of two million support people compared with the service and support team of a company like SAP.

Just-in-Time Information

A variety of technologies are converging to provide customers with information or offers that not only are valuable to them but are valuable to them at a very specific point in time. An example is real-time marketing. Seen mostly in the B2C world, real-time marketing involves harvesting unique, specialized information on consumers, allowing companies to present them with tailored offers while interacting with them in real time. Amazon is a prominent example of this technique, with its "customers who bought this also bought that" functionality at the point of purchase. The field is open for B2Bs to leverage real-time marketing technology; as long as the offers are relevant and engaging, customers will respond.[15]

In both B2B and B2C, companies are becoming more attuned to offering customers just-in-time information through text messaging, with the idea that they're delivering valuable information before customers even know they need it. The concept is what TARP's John Goodman calls the "psychic pizza." It refers to anticipating and delivering education and/or service to customers "just in time," or even before they know they need it, as in a pizza deliveryman saying as he approaches your door, "This is the pizza you were about to order."[16]

One client that Goodman has worked with, a chemical terminal company, offers customers updates on delivery time, which can fluctuate as a result of congestion in the Houston Ship Channel. "The minute they get an update, they send that to the customer to say it's on time or late or going to show up early," Goodman says. "We're finding just-in-time information transfer works especially well in the B2B environment."

Another example is CEMEX USA. It installed cameras in its loading docks so that people located at headquarters could see (literally) if there were any backups that would cause cement deliveries to be delayed. CEMEX has discovered that customers can deal with almost any contingency—even delays in their shipments—as long as they are notified early and told the truth. (For a full report on CEMEX's customer experience edge, see the case study on page 157.)

Companies are also engaging in just-in-time marketing, which PricewaterhouseCoopers/Diamond Advisory Services' D'Alessandro says increases the value of the services because they are seen within a framework of need. He cites the example of Southwest Airlines' "early-bird check-in" offering, where customers can pay extra to move to the front of the check-in line. The company framed this offering in such a way that customers could understand its value, in addition to offering it at strategic moments, he says. So, while traditional ticket purchasers would automatically go for the lowest-price offering, the system now looks for certain behaviors, demographics, or situations—tickets purchased close to departure time, complex routes, business travelers—and pops up the offering in the moment.

Unified Communications

Unified communications (UC) is the convergence of communication channels—phone, cell phone, e-mail, instant messaging, text—so that the call (or other type of communication) "follows" the intended recipient no matter where he is. For instance, if you call your cable provider or satellite TV company, it often has different call centers, with different phone numbers, depending on whether you have a technology, billing, or program issue. If it's discovered that you dialed the wrong number (after 15 minutes on hold and after providing your name, your account number, and a description of your problem), you will be transferred to the correct call center, at which point you'll need to go through the entire process again.

With UC, that frustrating experience is eliminated. No matter which number the customer calls, the information is passed to the correct service representative who can help. If an engineer is needed for a more complex support scenario, this resource is available, as well. Even if the engineer isn't in the call center and is working remotely, UC enables a virtual customer support center. The more specialized resource might be working at her desk checking e-mail, and she can get an alert that her expertise is needed for second-level support. If she's working on a mission-critical project, she can suppress alerts so that the request is sent to someone else.

With skills-based routing and presence information, companies can make every employee in the organization a technology support person. This is particularly helpful when customers call with two issues—say, their cable doesn't work and their last month's bill was too high. With two separate support centers, it's difficult to handle such a scenario. But with a virtual call center, companies can be prepared, since all the context and customer data can be passed on to another resource.

Another example is CEMEX, which uses the incoming number to route customer calls to the person in the support organization who is most suited to handle the call. Customers who are known to speak Spanish, for instance, are seamlessly routed to bilingual agents, which is much more satisfying than having to "Marque dos por Español."

With unified communication, the call has a much higher chance of reaching the target agent, even if that person is on the go. This can be significant in B2B environments, where customers require help from someone with specialized expertise.

Voice Analytics

Call centers are now using voice analytics technology to monitor customer phone conversations, both recorded and in real time. The purpose is to analyze the discussion to spot particular words and phrases, and also to detect nuances and levels of emotion that indicate a need for escalation or closer attention. For instance, the system might alert a more experienced service representative if it detects a customer becoming frustrated concerning the resolution on a problem. Mining of recorded calls can pick up on repeated references to a competitor's offering or a particular process problem that many customers are experiencing.

Further analysis could help companies train employees to help customers more effectively. For instance, searching all conversations for the words "thank you" could reveal the type of service that is particularly helpful to customers. Conversely, analyzing calls for negative words and phrases ("close my account") or pejoratives could help companies identify broken processes, poor-quality products, or service representatives who need more training.

Voice analytics can also help companies identify the speech patterns of high-value customers, so that reps can be alerted to offer these customers special offers and bonuses.

Collaborative Technologies

In their personal lives, many people (particularly the millennial gen-eration) have grown accustomed to having continual access to tech-nologies that enable them to communicate and collaborate with one another, including Twitter, instant messaging through social media, SMS texting, blogging, and data feeds. This expectation of natural and easy collaboration has now entered the workplace as well, where both employees and customers expect collaborative capabilities to be built into any interface or application with which they interact.

In fact, according to a global survey by Accenture, millennials today consider e-mail—the traditional mode of office collabora-tion—to be archaic. Younger employees today favor more real-time and interactive ways of communicating, such as text messages, social networks, and blogs.[17]

When businesses incorporate collaborative capabilities into their business and customer-facing systems, there are three key capabilities that they need to build in: helping people identify whom they need to contact (who has the information they are seeking and his avail-ability); enabling people to come together to keep one another up to date, understand what each is responsible for, when they need to deliver on what, and so on; and providing a way to disseminate criti cal information to everyone who needs it, on a timely basis.

Although this may happen today through e-mail, document management systems, one-to-one conversations, and the like, these modes are all quite disconnected. Now, technologies are available that make collaboration more efficient and effective. For instance, Facebook-like platforms bring people together in a dynamic way that helps them collaborate and share content in a by-now-familiar con-text, enabling communities to be defined and relevant news to be communicated rapidly.

Imagine a semiconductor company, for instance, embedding collaborative capabilities into its core development processes to enable quick and easy collaboration among its design engineers, the customer's engineers, the sales team, and the distributor. Or think of an insurer embedding collaborative capabilities into its business transactions and processes, enabling salespeople to collaborate with the claims department, customer support, and the repair shops and share any information that's relevant to a customer's claim to enable speedy resolution.

These types of collaborative capabilities can also be extended to customers. Typically, when customers need support, they might visit the vendor's website and search the FAQs, support documentation, or some other knowledge base for help. Alternatively, they might call the call center or use a live chat feature to get an answer to their question. But today, there are also online support communities that can offer fast, real-time advice on solving problems. Companies such as giffgaff are taking this concept to a whole new level, bringing the concept of collaboration into the context of the call center, leveraging the many-to-many model for customer support and service. Rather than one company supporting thousands of customers, the model is thousands of customers supporting thousands of other customers.

Social Media Monitoring

We talked already about listening to and engaging with social media, and now we'll talk more specifically about social media monitoring tools, also called *sentiment analysis*. This technology tracks online customer sentiment in an automated fashion. Although some companies start by assigning a team to keep tabs on public opinion, realistically, there is too much information available today for manual monitoring to be effective. There are so many places for your customers and prospects to talk about you (and to talk about themselves) that there is no way to keep up without using a tool.

An automated sentiment analysis tool will read tweets and postings in online forums and on social media, analyze them, and formulate a sentiment (positive, negative, or neutral) based on business rules. These tools can provide information on the ratio of positive to negative sentiments, trends in keyword mentions, number of views, number of brand mentions, and so on. When you integrate these results with CRM and other core applications, you can reach goals such as finding new market opportunities, developing more relevant and highly valued products and services, and responding quickly to negative trends.

These tools will alert you immediately if the tide has turned (in either direction), so that you can be much more proactive in your response. As companies from Nestlé to Wendy's have discovered, this can be particularly helpful in getting ahead of a brewing public relations crisis.

For many companies, the Web can be the beginning and end of all customer-related business processes. For example, let's say one of your customers has an issue with your product. She tweets about the problem. One of your customer service representatives spots the tweet and turns it into a service request. The affected department researches the problem and comes back with an answer for the customer. The agent then posts the answer on Twitter, on relevant blogs, and on the company's own e-community. A process that started on the Web thus ends there. The process starts where the customer is and thus can finish where the customer is.

Predictive Analytics and Business Intelligence

Generally speaking, analytics is software that combines a high-speed database capable of storing lots of data with software and algorithms that detect patterns in the data.[18] This is how Amazon is able to recommend other books to buy when someone buys a book—it tracks what other buyers have bought and uses that history to predict the future. Leveraging analytics is one of the quickest and most effective ways to gain a deep understanding of your customers, their different permutations, and their propensity to act in a certain way.

Predictive analytics can leverage sophisticated algorithms that yield critical insights concerning not only which are your most profitable customers today, but also which customers have the greatest lifetime value—and what is likely to keep them happy and in the fold. Analytics can also point to the best times to make an offer to a specific customer. For example, a financial services company might use analytics to determine the best time to offer a new credit line to a customer, such as just after the customer secures mortgage financing, as many purchases are associated with buying a new home. Analytics can also be used for real-time decision support, such as granting credit on the spot (in a store, for example) to someone who passes some basic tests.

Done properly, the use of analytics results in faster decision making. Organizations can achieve fast results by leveraging the transactional data that they most likely already have but rarely analyze. By doing this, they can obtain insights into customer needs and wants and turn these insights into action. An example is operational dashboards for frontline employees who need to access information in real time. With a dashboard, the call center operators, telesales teams, and other customer-facing representatives can better serve customers by making decisions in real time.

You can also analyze data from customer interactions on your website to discover new insights into the customer experience. "Sometimes the information you get from sentiment analysis is not intuitive—you discover what you didn't know," says Beagle Research's Pombriant. For instance, Pombriant tells of a vice president of global analytics and optimization who discovered a glitch in the company's website navigation that was causing a loss of revenue from a subset of high-revenue-potential customers. These customers had filled out all the forms required to buy the company's services, but before they hit the purchase button, a field popped up, asking one last question that these customers misunderstood. As a consequence, the purchase wasn't consummated, even though the customers believed it was.

This problem would have been invisible to the company if it had not used analytics to find out which customers were falling out of the purchase process and where. When the company discovered what was wrong, it could easily fix the problematic field; in fact, it determined that the field was unimportant and removed it. According to Pombriant, that one deletion was worth $12 million in revenue per year, all thanks to using analytics to analyze the customer experience. He adds, "You only know what you know—you can't predict how the customer is going to use your website."

There are many other technologies that companies are using—or that are just emerging—to enable operational, interaction, and decision excellence. Companies that are working to enrich their customer experience would do well to stay abreast of these technologies, try them on a small scale, develop new skill sets around them, and craft a strategy for enterprisewide implementation.

However, it's also important to understand that while some of these systems and tools can work without the existence of an integrated application foundation, their transformative power is apparent when it all comes together. It is when you establish your foundational core capabilities and then select disruptive technologies that enable all three of the CE pillars—operational, interaction, and decision excellence—that you can realize the customer experience edge.

CASE STUDY: CEMEX

Cementing Customer Bonds

Leading building materials maker CEMEX USA uses an award-winning customer experience to overcome the pitfalls of commoditization.

It is often said that cement is the most widely used substance on earth, after water. Without cement (the basis of concrete), there would be no tall buildings or interstate highways. Given its ubiquity, cement is the ultimate commodity. So when Houston-based CEMEX USA Inc. took stock of its business in 2003, executives realized that simply providing a good product at a fair price was not enough to yield differentiation in the marketplace.

"Anyone can make cement or concrete. Any of our competitors can do that," says Ven Bontha, customer experience management director for CEMEX USA, a business unit of CEMEX S.A.B. de C.V. of Monterrey, Mexico. "We were looking for a differentiating factor. In the end, cement is a commodity. We wondered, How can we

---

CE ESSENTIALS

- **Reliability.** CEMEX boosted order accuracy from 92 percent to 99.9 percent.

- **Convenience.** Customers who prefer self-service via the Web can see exactly the same information that customer care agents see.

- **Relevance.** Agents can identify incoming customer calls by their cell phone, home phone, and work phone. Customers are routed automatically to the same agent that they spoke with in their last call.

- **Responsiveness.** CEMEX notifies customers proactively of delays and how it intends to resolve them.

---

decommoditize this? How can we make it easier for our customers to do business with us?"

Long before "customer experience" became an imperative, or even a formal concept, CEMEX USA reorganized its operations and customer service, implementing a state-of-the-art CRM system to better focus on customers. The multiyear effort paid off handsomely in terms of better order accuracy and shipment visibility, leading to improved customer satisfaction. In March 2011, CEMEX USA won a Gartner and 1to1 Media CRM Excellence Award in the category of Customer Experience. Ginger Conlon, editor of *1to1 Magazine* and a judge for the CRM Excellence Awards, says that CEMEX was ahead of the curve.

"CEMEX USA was able to get buy-in in an industry that is not known for customer-centricity. The CEMEX team asked what their customers wanted and then aligned around that," she says.

The customer experience team at CEMEX USA achieved more than just order accuracy and customer satisfaction with the new system. Integrated with financial, operational, and other applications, it enables a host of other business benefits, according to company officials.

Multimillion-dollar paybacks from an integrated enterprise application suite supporting customer experience like that of CEMEX USA are not unusual. A Bloomberg Businessweek Research Services global survey of 1,004 respondents in late 2010 found a host of benefits (see Figure 8.3).

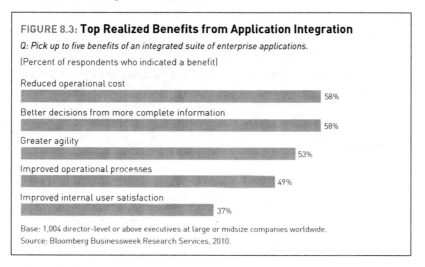

FIGURE 8.3: **Top Realized Benefits from Application Integration**

Q: Pick up to five benefits of an integrated suite of enterprise applications.

(Percent of respondents who indicated a benefit)

Reduced operational cost
58%

Better decisions from more complete information
58%

Greater agility
53%

Improved operational processes
49%

Improved internal user satisfaction
37%

Base: 1,004 director-level or above executives at large or midsize companies worldwide.
Source: Bloomberg Businessweek Research Services, 2010.

Getting to Know You

CEMEX USA's journey to a better customer experience begins in 2003, when its customer experience initiative was little more than a brainstorming session within CEMEX USA's management team. When Bontha joined CEMEX USA in 1995, the company had one cement plant. Over the next decade or so, the company's operations grew to 14 plants through acquisitions. CEMEX USA was able to consolidate its acquisitions' back-office systems rapidly, enabling aggressive growth. This was good for business, of course, but it also led to a sense of disconnection from customers. Frank Craddock, executive vice president of CEMEX USA's commercial operations, and Bontha decided in 2003 to call in a marketing research firm to interview its customers—on the phone and in person—to discover what really motivated their cement purchasing practices.

The research identified 41 attributes that were important to customers. At the top of the list was quality. On-time delivery was number two. The top 20 most important attributes fell into two general categories: service delivery and administrative functions.

"Our primary challenge to overcome was limited visibility into our delivery operations," says Bontha. "We relied on a third party to deliver most of our products, so obtaining accurate and timely information was an ongoing obstacle." Another priority was reducing the time it took for employees to locate a bill of lading, which is created when a customer places an order. The bill of lading includes many critical details about the order, including its destination and delivery times. So, streamlining that process was also a top goal.

CE PILLARS

- **Operational excellence.** CEMEX has made on-time delivery a number one priority by increasing the visibility of its delivery operations, streamlining its bill of lading process, installing cameras on its truck loading docks, and setting system alerts when delays are likely.

- **Interaction excellence.** Employees and customers have visibility into on-time delivery rates and other data, and CEMEX immediately communicates if a delay occurs. The contact center gives agents a 360-degree view of customers, and customers often speak to the same agent each time they call.

Supply Chain Challenges

In this industry, there is more to on-time delivery than meets the eye. Cement is a gray powder. As such, it has an indefinite shelf life. Once the additives and the cement are mixed with water to form concrete, however, the shelf life of the compound is less than two hours. You can accelerate or slow the setting time a bit, says Bontha, but the manufacturing process occurs on the road in the trucks. Time is of the essence.

When a project is launched and the concrete begins to flow, it must be poured continuously until no more is needed. This quickly turns into a supply chain challenge. Much depends on how far the customer is from CEMEX's cement terminals. Delivery times must be calculated with precision if the project is to go as planned. "We have to make sure we don't run our customers out of cement while they are pouring," Bontha says.

At the time the company launched its customer experience initiative, CEMEX USA did not track metrics like on-time delivery, as this information largely resided with third-party logistics providers. However, in 2009, the company implemented ERP and CRM systems from SAP, which created visibility into all of its processes. The company installed video cameras at its largest cement terminals, letting members of the CEMEX USA customer service team literally see in real time how things are going. "We can see the loading facilities. That is important because it takes about eight minutes to load a cement truck," says Bontha. If there are 10 trucks in line, it will take 80 minutes or more for the last one to be loaded and ready to go. If, for example, that last truck needs to deliver at 10:00 a.m., the system

CEMEX USA AT A GLANCE

- Business description: A unit of $14.1 billion CEMEX S.A.B. de C.V., CEMEX USA supplies building materials

- Location: Houston

- Annual revenues: $2.8 billion (2010)

- Number of employees: 8,000

- Number of cement plants: 13

- Number of cement distribution terminals: 46

- Number of aggregate quarries: 100+

- Number of ready-mix concrete plants: 320

will dictate that it should be loaded by 7:00 a.m., based on historical transit times and other data.

"If 7:00 a.m. arrives and no ticket has been issued, the SAP system immediately sends alerts saying this load has not been loaded yet. In the next 15 minutes, we make calls to the customer and to dispatch. We may make the decision to divert a load to this customer or whatever is the best choice at the time," says Bontha.

As much as customers hate delays, they hate lack of information even more. "When we immediately inform the customer about a delay, they acknowledge our interest in their business," says Bontha. This immediate alert works for other glitches, too. He recalls a recent incident in which the system flagged an error almost in real time, and the customer was notified of the error and how and when it would be fixed. "If we make a mistake, we own up to it," says Bontha.

That's key, says Conlon. The irony is, she explains, that "if you resolve a problem, you wind up having more loyalty than if there never was a problem to begin with." The experience of being notified proactively of an issue and its resolution creates a more memorable customer experience than if all had gone smoothly. Customers feel that the provider is on their side, working with them in their best interest. This drives real loyalty.

A survey by Forrester Research validates Conlon's point. According to a blog posted by Forrester analyst Andrew McInnes on December 6, 2010, "Customers' Problems Are Companies' Loyalty-Building Opportunities," customers who had an exemplary problem resolution experience were far more likely to become repeat customers and major advocates of their suppliers (see Figure 8.4).[19]

Broader Vision

Gaining insights about customers' unspoken wants requires more than a consultant's survey and discussions with existing clients. Innovation in any field frequently occurs when an idea in one industry is transplanted into another. CEMEX USA is a proponent of borrowing innovative and successful ideas about customer experience wher-

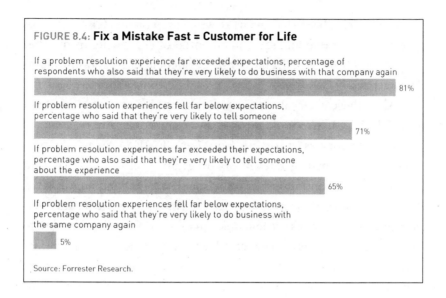

FIGURE 8.4: **Fix a Mistake Fast = Customer for Life**

If a problem resolution experience far exceeded expectations, percentage of respondents who also said that they're very likely to do business with that company again

81%

If problem resolution experiences fell far below expectations, percentage who said that they're very likely to tell someone

71%

If problem resolution experiences far exceeded their expectations, percentage who also said that they're very likely to tell someone about the experience

65%

If problem resolution experiences fell far below expectations, percentage who said that they're very likely to do business with the same company again

5%

Source: Forrester Research.

ever they may be found. One early model of excellence came from a local branch of Bank of Texas in 2004, where Bontha and his wife applied for a loan.

A few days after completing the loan application, he was stunned to find the money sitting in his bank account without any fanfare. He went back to the bank and asked to speak to the manager to thank him for the hassle-free borrowing experience. "He said, 'You're a Bank of Texas preferred customer; we have to give you what you want,'" Bontha recalls. Then the bank manager shocked Bontha. "On his screen was my history with the bank for the last 15 years," Bontha exclaims. "They knew everything about me. I'm so integrated with the bank, even if I get mad at them, I won't change banks. The entanglement is for a lifetime."

Using the bank experience as a springboard, CEMEX USA decided to cast the net wider and look at companies in other industries that were considered standouts in customer experience: Continental Airlines, Fidelity, and Mellon Bank.

This outreach effort is also a best practice, according to Conlon. "You need not just to stand out in your industry but to stand out as a company that is good at customer experience, period. A lot of companies have been shaken awake with social media. CEMEX USA got in ahead of that and saw the potential of borrowing from other industries. CEMEX USA notes how it can benefit by adopting similar practices."

All of these external experiences triggered a wave of ideas about how CEMEX USA should develop and use an extensive reservoir of knowledge about its customers. Consider CEMEX's Smart Silo program, a vendor-managed inventory program for customers that want a seamless and continuous supply of cement by relying on CEMEX USA to monitor their inventory in real time. CEMEX installs sensors in each customer's silo and links them to the CEMEX network to track consumption and dispatch additional supplies when inventory levels reach a reordering point. In addition, customers can view their current stock levels and orders received in the CEMEX Connect customer self-service online portal. The Smart Silo initiative also helps CEMEX USA optimize its fleet and asset utilization by dispersing demand outside the peak time.

The Foundation of Excellence

Another step in enhancing the CEMEX customer experience was the implementation of a new Customer Care Center at Houston headquarters in 2006. There is always a live operator to answer the call—no automated voice response system—since the personal touch is crucial. The customer care system brought to life the vision of complete customer information (the proverbial 360-degree view) on one screen.

CEMEX USA agents can identify an incoming customer call by any number: cell phone, home phone, or work phone. For each interaction, the system records the conversation and the screens for quality assurance. Reviewing the order at the end of the call is crucial. "It is very important to recap the call; otherwise that's where mistakes happen," says Bontha. Before implementing the system, order accuracy ran about 92 percent. Today, that key metric of the customer experience is over 99 percent.

Customers who prefer self-service via the Web see exactly the same information that the customer care agents see, including order status, invoice status, tickets issued, last 15 interactions, and pending support issues. "Continental Airlines was our model there," says Bontha. "We bill every night, and the information is available to the customer in the morning." If the data ever fail to be updated, customers will call to see what happened. They rely on CEMEX USA data to do their own planning.

The system tracks abandoned calls, automatically generating a report that is routed to supervisors, who call the person who hung up to see if they can help. "We don't like to see abandoned calls," says Bontha. "At the beginning they used to say, 'How did you know it was me?' Now they are used to it."

The state-of-the-art customer care infrastructure has enabled CEMEX USA to launch other programs. Last year, for example, a small balances collection subgroup of agents started making outbound calls, checking in on overdue accounts. The agent asks if everything is OK, or whether there is a piece of paperwork missing. "We have collected $30 million on that program," says Bontha. Today, that subgroup has spawned a permanent accounts receivable initiative. CEMEX USA initiated a lead generation program that gathers rich customer and prospect information and makes informed (as opposed to cold) calls. "Without the platform, we wouldn't be able to do any of this," he says.

The CRM system also helps CEMEX USA provide customized service. Customers are often routed automatically to the same agent they spoke with in their last call. Known Spanish speakers are routed to Spanish-speaking agents, rather than being asked to press 2 for Spanish. This makes customers feel that the experience is about and for them on a personal level, says Bontha. "We want them to feel, 'CEMEX is doing this for me.'"

At the same time, CEMEX's CRM deployment goes beyond traditional service center processes, as it easily connects with back-end processes, such as order management, the supply chain, dispatch, and truck management.

That Personal Touch

Technology is surely an enabler of the customer experience, but it takes a person to connect with another person. Employees play a major role in creating that sense of connection. Everyone is appraised and compensated on her degree of customer focus. Toward that end, it helps to start with people-oriented resources. Recently, the customer care team interviewed 200 candidates before hiring two new people. "We're looking for that service attitude," says Bontha.

Of course, just being personable is not enough. Candidates are evaluated based on their résumés and proven skill sets, but also on less tangible things, such as curiosity and tenacity. "Not everyone can survive eight hours on the phone. It's a tough job," says Bontha. "We put a pencil and paper in front of the person and then watch—are they taking notes? If they are smart, they will write things down and ask questions." With the raw materials in place, the CEMEX USA team pours as much knowledge as possible into its new hires. It takes three months of training before they are allowed to handle their first customer call.

Meanwhile, he and his staff work hard to create an enjoyable work environment. It seems to be paying off: the retention rate for customer care agents (notoriously a high-turnover group) is higher than average, with some employees on board from more than four years ago.

When Bontha received word that CEMEX USA had received the Gartner and 1to1 Media CRM Excellence award, he went to each person in the Customer Care Center and thanked them individually. "I could thank them in a group, but that's not personal. Our people are very proud of this award. It belongs to them," he says.

With a major award in hand and key customer experience indicators looking good, CEMEX USA is nonetheless not resting on its laurels. It understands, better than most, that customer experience is an expedition rather than a destination. Says Bontha, "We are still on the journey."

CHAPTER 9

IT as the Catalyst of CE Transformation

High-performing IT organizations are 44 percent more likely to recognize the strategic role IT plays in increasing customer satisfaction.
—ACCENTURE, 2010

A s we've seen in the last two chapters, technology is at the heart of delivering the customer experience edge consistently and profitably. Because of this, customer experience (CE) offers CIOs the opportunity (and the challenge) to secure a spot at the table when the company's business leaders are setting the customer experience strategy.

The CIO is in a prime position to be a key player in making the customer experience initiative successful. Such an initiative is a cross-organizational pursuit that depends on connected processes and unified goals and strategies. Many IT organizations have already been involved with enterprisewide efforts, such as business process management and application integration, that required coordinating people from multiple departments. As a result, many have acquired the skills, know-how, and cross-organization visibility that are needed for customer experience initiatives.

Business departments all have their own objectives and their own internal processes. IT has the overview perspective that can bring these individual perspectives together, balance their various needs, and bring them into alignment. In the customer service organization, for example, reducing the cost of service is still a big concern. IT is often asked to help with technology projects that enable self-service. When this happens, IT can play an important role in helping the organization keep the bigger customer experience picture in mind by emphasizing the danger of sacrificing customer centricity to achieve short-term efficiency.

A second example is IT's ability to unify departmental processes. A marketing organization, for instance, might generate high volumes of customer leads, but what if these are not the right leads from a customer profile perspective? Or what if there is no follow-through because of broken processes or disconnected tools? Very often, marketing is using a lead-generation tool that is disconnected from the sales force's sales force automation system. The IT organization can bring the two departments together by communicating the benefits to both parties of having a connected and unified solution.

As the organization that manages the business's systems, applications, and databases, IT owns the data across the organization. Through business intelligence initiatives, it is IT that provides critical insights into data across the enterprise. IT enables process automation and efficiency, as well as rapid change and agility. All that said, IT is in a prime position to also enable the four pillars of customer experience: reliability, convenience, responsiveness, and relevance.

The CIO Challenge

The challenge for CIOs is to adopt behaviors that enable their departments to live up to this type of role. If they don't, the job may be filled by someone from the business side who has an interest in technology. In a recent *Harvard Business Review* blog post,[1] Constellation Research's Wang defines four personas of next-generation CIOs (see Table 9.1).

TABLE 9.1: **The Four Personas of the Next-Generation CIO**

Persona	Focus
Chief Infrastructure Officers	Cost reduction, "keeping the lights on," managing legacy environments
Chief Integration Officers	Bringing together a hodgepodge of business processes, data, systems, and connection points with legacy systems and newer cloud-based approaches
Chief "Intelligence" Officers	Empowering the business with actionable insights, getting the right data to the right person at the right time, with the right interface
Chief Innovation Officers	Identify disruptive technologies for pilot projects, driving innovation

Source: Constellation Research.

Wang points out that most CIOs today fit squarely into the first category, chief infrastructure officer. It would be fairly easy for many of them to make the transition to the chief integration officer role; however, it would take strong business acumen to evolve into the two higher-level roles, he says. It is these two higher levels of CIO that can look across organizational boundaries, align IT strategy with the business, and use IT as a catalyst for business transformation.

A second challenge is that with software as a service and other cloud-based computing technologies, it's easy for leaders of business departments to make technology decisions that deal with their immediate needs without involving IT at all. If the head of the sales organization determines that he needs a better view into his weekly pipeline or a better way for sales reps to track their activities, for instance, he can subscribe to a sales force automation tool for his staff, using his credit card. If he went to IT with this request, he might be told to wait until next year's enterprise resource planning (ERP) upgrade. In some cases, business heads find it easier to go around IT.

Overcoming these challenges means that CIOs need to get out in front of the customer experience initiative and align it with the lines of business. In order to get business leaders on board, IT needs to balance immediate business needs with the fact that customer experience is not something that you achieve overnight, and certainly not through a sales force automation tool that's totally disconnected from all the other systems that manage all the other processes that ultimately serve the customer.

In order to be a catalyst for change, IT needs to show the lines of business that it can respond to their immediate and tactical needs, but at the same time, show them the path to grow strategically, which at the end of the day offers much more value.

According to a recent survey by Yankee Group, more CIOs are ready for the challenge. In the survey, CIO and CTO respondents agreed that business objectives, rather than the latest and greatest technology offerings, are driving their decisions.[2] The vast majority (91 percent) of large-enterprise respondents (those with more than 10,000 employees) rank "improving customer experience" as their number one corporate goal, according to Yankee Group's "2010 CIO FastView Survey: CIOs Make Business the Priority." While reducing costs and increasing employee productivity are important to enterprise CIOs, strategic growth and business goals take top billing among CIO priorities.

And according to a recent Accenture study, high-performing large-company IT organizations not only manage IT like a business, but also run IT for the business and with the business.[3] CIOs at these organizations are engaged in their company's business strategies—including CE initiatives—and are able to map out how IT supports those strategies. According to the survey, high-performing IT organizations are also 44 percent more likely to recognize the strategic role that IT plays in increasing customer satisfaction. Accenture defines high performers in IT as those that achieve "excellence in IT execution, IT agility and IT innovation."

Business executives also appear to recognize that just as technology is essential for the customer experience, so is the IT organization itself. In a recent Cognizant Technology Solutions survey, nearly three-quarters (71 percent) of U.S. business and technology executives and 57 percent of those in Europe said that they expected IT to play a greater role in enhancing the customer experience. Nearly half of all respondents said that IT will help enhance the business's revenue-generating capabilities.[4]

CIOs in Action

A case in point is the Verizon Wireless CIO, Ajay Waghray. For Waghray, "Everything and anything we do is all about the customer. That is really the backbone of our thinking." There are two drivers behind any technology implementation, he says: to provide customer value and to create enablers to move the business forward.

An example that he cites is creating an online experience that could scale to the levels required following the launch of the Apple iPhone. With more than 60 percent of the company's orders coming over the Web, Waghray knew that online volumes would explode after the iPhone introduction. With scalability in mind, he simplified the steps required for conducting online transactions and ensured that customers would get consistent information across channels when checking on phone upgrade pricing and eligibility. It was key, he says, for them to get the same answer regardless of the channel they used.

As it turned out, in the first two hours of the launch, between 3:00 and 5:00 a.m., he says, "We had higher volumes than any of our previous launches. It was historic, and IT enabled it—we handled it in a flawless way."

Despite its many acquisitions, Verizon Wireless had previously consolidated its billing systems, from 30 different systems down to 1, over a period of seven years. This provides numerous benefits, such as consistent customer processes and procedures. "The customer benefits tremendously," Waghray says. "Whether you walk into our store in Orlando, Chicago, or California, you will get the same service results consistently at all times." Customers can also view balances, change plans, upgrade devices, or change their address from either their phone, their PC, or an in-store kiosk. "They all have the exact same look, feel, and flow," he says.

Collaboration and teamwork across business departments, he says, is key. "We bring forth the ideas, and we have a partnership with the marketing arm and the operations arm. This is a journey, and it takes a lot of time to build."

As for business drivers, while self-service capabilities do save costs, that is not the main focus, Waghray says. "Saving costs is just a byproduct," he says. "If you improve the customer experience, it generally is a win-win all the way around."

Gil Katz is another CIO who has played a key role in leading the customer experience initiative of his employer, Israeli automobile importer Colmobil Corp. When Colmobil made the strategic decision to transform itself from a product-centric to a customer-centric company, Katz not only helped drive the decision-making process, but also felt that it was his duty to present the various strategy and technology options to the business leaders. "When management decided to take this road, it was my assignment to fulfill the promise," he says. "You first need to have the right infrastructure and tools, and only then go through the additional organizational changes." (For the full story of Colmobil's customer experience transformation, see the case study in Chapter 7, page 129.)

IT's Role in a Profitable CE

As part of the CE leadership team or centralized CE organization, CIOs and their staffs will need to be involved in building a lot of bridges internally. Traditionally, this may not have been a big part of the IT organization's portfolio of skills. But CIOs need to ensure that the IT organization forms collaborative, strategic relationships with enterprise departments to help the company develop effective and measurable ways to target, acquire, and stay intimately connected with its customers. Partnerships need to be formed with product development, marketing, sales, customer service and support, brand management, and customer-facing roles. Employee empowerment is also an IT/business collaborative concern. New metrics need to be developed, in tandem with the business, to measure the right things, using the right data. (For a fuller discussion of the new metrics of customer experience, see Chapter 11, "Measures of Success.")

According to Forrester Research, Inc., the leaders of a centralized customer experience organization need to have a strong network of relationships with other groups in the company from the start, as well as a natural ability to read people, sense resistance, and encourage collaboration across multiple groups. These abilities will play a big role in the CE initiative's success.[5]

Looking outward, CIOs have a major role to play in ensuring a high-value customer experience via technology. The customer experience involves the entire enterprise, and therefore it is an initiative that many people in many departments will want to be involved with. We're not advocating that CE become yet another political battlefield in which the winner gets to "own" the initiative. What we do know is that if customer experience is to be profitable, it needs to be guided by a centralized cross-organizational team. And who is better positioned to provide guidance on the technology decisions that could make or break CE success than IT?

PART IV

Sustaining the "Wow"

Ten On-Ramps to the Customer Experience Freeway

Good customer experience should just be the way you do business.
— PATRICIA SEYBOLD, PRESIDENT AND CEO
OF THE PATRICIA SEYBOLD GROUP,
AUTHOR OF MANY BOOKS
ON CUSTOMER EXPERIENCE

CREATING THE CUSTOMER EXPERIENCE EDGE is most definitely a journey, not a destination. In fact, you should think of the customer experience (CE) not as an end goal, but as a moving target, driven by changing customer behaviors and needs, constant technological improvements, and ever-improving insights culled from analysis of information.

Particularly in today's economy, however, time and money are short. In the North American Bloomberg Businessweek Research Services (BBRS) survey, the top concerns that respondents had regarding their company's efforts to improve the customer experience were financial in nature. More than half rated "cost and resource requirements" (54 percent) and ROI (51 percent) at a level of 4 or 5 on a scale of 1 to 5, with 5 being "very high concern" (see Figure 6.1).

Although your company may be looking for profitable new areas of investment as economic conditions improve, your senior managers also need to see rapid results.

The good news is, there are short-term actions that you can take now and see benefits in the near term. Not only can these quick hits move the customer satisfaction needle, but they can also motivate employees, who will see the swift improvements, and satisfy executives, who need to see results. It is important, however, to keep the long-term goal and bigger picture in mind; short-term fixes and purely tactical decisions can mean additional costs later on or be counterproductive in the long run.

Here are 10 "quick wins" that you can score early in your customer experience journey.

1. Kill a Stupid Rule

Most large companies have at least one process that they know hurts their customers (at least, the people in the trenches know that the rules hurt customers). Getting rid of one or more of these rules can quickly and cost-efficiently increase satisfaction immeasurably. "Usually there is no strong sense of customer input when rules are created, so rules or decisions often veer away from being good for customers," says Temkin Group's Bruce Temkin. "Stupid rules always exist." The bigger the organization, the more stupid rules you can expect to see.

Missouri's Commerce Bank of St. Louis killed a number of stupid rules a few years ago. It started with something as simple as getting rid of the annoying chains on the pens provided for customers, making it more convenient for them to fill out deposit and withdrawal slips. It continued by allowing customers to bring their dogs into its bank branches and then by not only removing the fee that most organizations charge for the use of their coin-counting machines, but also offering a reward for guessing correctly how much change you insert. Commerce, which has had a customer focus since opening its doors in 1973, strives to create a fun atmosphere, complete with free lolli-pops and dog biscuits in its branches. Customers seem to approve—Commerce has had the highest customer satisfaction ranking in retail banking in the Midwest region for three years in a row, according to J.D. Power & Associates.

2. Inject the Unexpected

Adding whimsy is a simple and inexpensive way to give your customer experience a positive vibe. Marketing guru Seth Godin made waves in 2003 with his seminal *Purple Cow* book and concept.[1] The idea was that your product or service offering needs to be distinctive and remarkable in order to stand out in an ever-more-crowded market-place. (Interesting side note: purple cow sightings are less unusual in Europe, as Kraft Foods markets its Milka brand of chocolate using this symbol in its advertising.) Godin's message is that the era of selling average products to average people is over. Having an imaginatively differentiated product or service that people want to recommend to their friends is the way to success, and this in and of itself can be the basis of the customer experience if your offering fills the bill.

For example, Godin cites Ian Schrager's quirky but luxurious boutique hotels as standing out in a very crowded market. The race to be the best hotel for business travelers had already been won by the likes of Hilton and Marriott, so the former owner of Studio 54 in New York did something different. He created buzz by placing his tiny, exclusive hotels in locations that were off the beaten path, without the benefit of signs signifying their existence—one has to be in the know to enter them. The interior of these hotels is dark and mysterious, more about assignations than about assignments, entirely divorced from the workaday world and family life. Flying in the face of much standard hotel doctrine, these hotels are nonetheless suc-cessful and sought after by celebrities and commoners alike.

You may have to go out on a limb to arrive at something delight-ful and different, according to Godin. His mantra is: in these times, avoiding risk is risky, and taking the safe path is unsafe, so don't be afraid to be different.

It's not necessary to look exclusively at your actual product offering to add whimsy, however; you can just as easily apply the concept of surprise to your business processes or other elements of the customer experience. In *Bold*, Shaun Smith's new book, a key principle is to "dramatize the customer experience." For example, computer support is not typically viewed as a glamorous business. But the Geek Squad jazzes things up by dressing its employees as "agents" and giving them Geek Squad cars that look like police vehicles, Smith points out on his blog.[2]

3. Make a Connection

Nothing creates an emotional bond like a personal connection. This is true no matter which channel your customer is using. On the Web and in printed collateral, your tone should be welcoming and not off-putting; in direct customer and client interactions, sales staff should be knowledgeable and attentive without being pushy. "Get in the habit of asking yourself, 'Would our target customers fully understand this?'" Temkin says.

An example of a company that does this is Sports Authority, which trained its employees to greet the customer within 15 seconds and, if the customer seems open to it, engage in a dialog about the customer's area of interest. "I walked into Sports Authority and got into a conversation with the sales guy about sand consistency on the golf course," says Andy Main, principal, customer transformation, for Deloitte Consulting. "He recommended a wedge based on the type of sand I am likely to encounter. This guy knew what he was talking about. He got the sale because he treated me like a serious buyer."

TARP Worldwide's John Goodman offers other examples. Procter & Gamble's Iams brand of pet food, for instance, offers a toll-free number for customers to call a pet loss counselor when their beloved cat or dog dies. "They spend lots of time holding your hand over the phone," he says. "That can form lifetime Iams customers."

The human touch is also applicable in the business-to-business world, Goodman says. In his work with a chemical terminal company, he has advised terminal operators to strike up conversations with truck drivers who are waiting to load their tanks. In some cases, the same drivers would return a couple of times per week. "The drivers would likely provide feedback on the company to whomever they're driving the chemical to," Goodman says. "This is a heavy industrial environment, with guys in hard hats, but it's still important to create an emotional connection."

Another very simple way to reinforce an emotional connection is to have employees who interact on social media sites use their real names. When Marriott recently made some changes in its Rewards program, for instance, the senior vice president of Marriott Rewards, Ed French, responded to customer queries via video. Afterward, he noticed that participants on Marriott's customer forums were referring to him by his first name, a sure sign of feeling connected.

We've already discussed Frank Eliason's early experiences at Comcast, where he started the company's Twitter-based customer service. Eliason says that he was hesitant at first to have his team members use their names to tweet with customers, although he himself used the Twitter identifier "@comcastfrank."

Now senior vice president of social media at Citi, Eliason says that a personal experience during his time at Comcast changed his mind about the impact of employees using their real names on social media. After being available nearly every day and night on Twitter for seven days a week for four straight months, he told his followers that he was taking a day off, as it was his daughter's birthday. "They ended up researching me and found my family website, where they learned that it was the anniversary of the death of another one of my daughters," he says. At the end of the emotional day, he says, he was going through his Twitter messages and saw that people had decided among themselves to "give Frank a break" and try to help each other with their service problems. "They did that for me, not Comcast," he says. "That's one of the reasons I use my picture and my name—trust is developed by individuals."

According to a recent Strativity Group survey, respondents said that the behavior of employees goes a long way in creating a superior customer experience (see Figure 10.1).

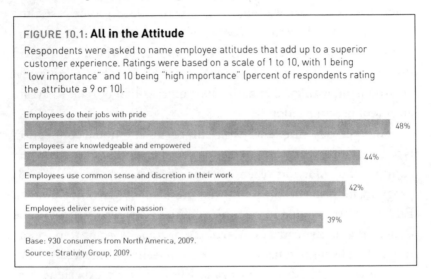

FIGURE 10.1: **All in the Attitude**

Respondents were asked to name employee attitudes that add up to a superior customer experience. Ratings were based on a scale of 1 to 10, with 1 being "low importance" and 10 being "high importance" (percent of respondents rating the attribute a 9 or 10).

Employees do their jobs with pride — 48%

Employees are knowledgeable and empowered — 44%

Employees use common sense and discretion in their work — 42%

Employees deliver service with passion — 39%

Base: 930 consumers from North America, 2009.
Source: Strativity Group, 2009.

4. Monitor Online Sentiment—and Respond

Whether you know it or not, customers are talking about you on the Web, and you need to know what they're saying. Employ a platform, tool, or service that enables you to monitor and analyze the reams of unstructured data on the Internet and in social media. These systems, called sentiment analysis tools, social media analysis platforms, or even "listening platforms," mine online and social sources to deliver insights into how a company or brand is being perceived.

You're going to need a system like this to harness all those data eventually anyway, and assigning people in the organization the task of doing this by hand can quickly become arduous, if not impossible. When you discover an unhappy customer (tweeting a less-than-stellar experience with your company, for example), help him as speedily as possible. This will go far toward staving off a groundswell of negative opinion.

Southwest Airlines is a great example. On a Saturday evening in February 2010, award-winning film director Kevin Smith complained to his more than one million followers on Twitter that he had been ejected from a Southwest flight for being too fat. The airline, which also has more than one million Twitter followers, responded within minutes and continued to tweet through the night, calling Smith on the phone, apologizing to him, offering to refund his airline ticket, and keeping the Twitter community aware of each action it was taking. By Sunday, it tweeted a link to its blog, where Linda Rutherford, Southwest's vice president of communications and strategic outreach, explained the specifics of the occurrence.

Essentially, she explained, Smith was boarded as a standby passenger, and when employees realized that he might have needed more than one seat, they made the decision to remove him. Although Rutherford said that Southwest stood behind its policy of assisting passengers who need two seats on board an aircraft, she also acknowledged that the communication among Southwest employees "was not as sharp as it should have been, and it's apparent that Southwest could have handled this situation differently," she said on the blog post.[3]

Although the incident went viral, it had all but completely died down by Monday, a testament to Southwest's quick response.

There are many examples of companies that have had to respond to unflattering videos, tweets, and blog posts (some more successfully than others), and, unfortunately, there is no surefire way to defuse these situations. (Think United Breaks Guitars, Comcast Must Die, or Dell Hell.) The sooner a company reacts (in minutes, not hours), the better.

5. Think "Community"

In many industries, online community forums or groups have sprung up around a particular company or product. Companies are strengthening their customer experience by working with these community forums. A good example is The LEGO Group, for whom aficionados the world over maintain a myriad of websites—tributes to their devotion to the brand. (For a full report on The LEGO Group's customer experience work, see the case study in Chapter 5, page 83.)

When this happens, companies should not ignore these communities; instead, they should watch them and listen to them. Understand the tenor of the group. Then make a cautious foray into the community. Ask if you can help, especially if the group is providing useful peer-to-peer support that would otherwise fall to you. Be prepared to pull back if the group does not welcome corporate participation, which may be viewed as being commercially motivated. If your participation is not welcome (and it will be clear if that is the case), you can still lurk and gather insights.

Of course, companies are also starting up their own communities. While it does take time to form a community, some rewards, like quick insights, can be garnered right away. Dell engages with customers within every type of social online community possible, while also creating branded communities for its different customer groups. The company gains insights and handles support in any and all of these forums, according to Manish Mehta, vice president of social media and community for the computer maker. "Listen, trust, participate" is a slogan of Mehta's group, he tells us. Dell has even gone so far as to create a Social Media and Community University for its employees. After an employee has successfully passed four courses, she is considered "certified" and may speak for Dell and engage with customers in any social Web forum. Currently, 8,000 out of 100,000 Dell employees worldwide have received this training; that number will increase exponentially in a rapid time frame, according to Mehta.

6. Source Passion Internally

Although customer experience initiatives are likely to result in business process transformation, this is not the time to seek the advice of an army of experts. Instead, mine the organization itself for customer champions rather than relying on outside experts.

The best data and the insights that you need to carry out customer experience activities are right within your own organization. Many employees in all business functions will have input into the full range of CE activities, including mapping the customer journey, identifying key moments that make or break loyalty, pinpointing gaps between expectations and current performance, and even creating innovative processes to fill these gaps.

To gather the needed insights and develop the processes to follow through on them, it is advisable that you choose a CE leader from within your organization and formally designate this person as the one who will form and lead a centralized CE team. According to Forrester, such a team can help enable cross-functional coordination, identify and share best practices, and support executives who need help understanding the role they play in CE.[4]

Ultimately, becoming customer-centric is something that needs to be baked into the DNA of all employees in the organization; it is not something that can be bolted on as "yet another corporate initiative" or accomplished by throwing money at it. "Good customer experience should just be the way you do business," says Patricia Seybold, president and CEO of the Patricia Seybold Group and author of many books on the customer experience, including her latest, *Outside Innovation*. "You should not have to add a lot of stuff to do this. Over time, it should become the way you operate," she told us.

7. Venture outside Your Industry

Call it benchmarking for CE. When Mike Bidwell, president of the Arizona Cardinals Football Club, wanted to step up the experience offered to sports fans in the Arizona Cardinals' new stadium, he and his executive team went to get an up-close-and-personal look at the organization that they considered the best in the world at entertainment park customer experience: they toured Disney World. "We toured their parks to get a better understanding of how they do things. The Disney customer experience is legendary," he says.

The team members liked what they saw so much that they engaged the Disney Institute to help teach management Disney best practices concerning leadership. Bidwell and the other executives saw a lot of value in importing hospitality techniques and principles from the worldwide entertainment leader, as sporting events are a form of entertainment.

"We learned a lot from them," says Bidwell. "It shouldn't just be the people who interact with the fans on game day [who are trained on customer experience]. All of us represent the organization and the team, at all times." To bring employees on board with the concept, all Arizona Cardinals employees are now called "team members," in much the same way that all Disney employees are called "cast members."

Some of the best innovations in one industry are inspired by ideas from completely different industries. CEMEX USA's customer experience management director, Ven Bontha, believes in borrowing ideas about customer experience wherever he finds them. For example, when he and his wife applied for a loan at a local Bank of Texas branch in 2004, he was struck that just a short time after he had completed the application, he found the money sitting in his bank account. When he thanked the manager for the quick turnaround, he was told that it was because of his status as a Bank of Texas preferred customer, Bontha recalls. "On his screen was my history with the bank for the last 15 years," Bontha says. "They knew everything about me. I'm so integrated with the bank, even if I get mad at them, I won't change banks. The entanglement is for a lifetime." Using that experience as a springboard, CEMEX USA decided to cast the net wider, looking at companies in other industries that were considered standouts in customer experience: Continental Airlines, Fidelity, and Mellon Bank.

"You need not just to stand out in your industry but to stand out as a company that is good at customer experience, period," agrees Ginger Conlon, editor of *1to1 Magazine*. (For a full report on CEMEX USA's customer experience initiative, see the case study in Chapter 8, page 157.)

8. Conduct Frequent Customer Surveys

Customer service surveys are everywhere you turn, it seems, but a way to get more targeted feedback from customers is to survey them right when they have finished a transaction with you, according to Seybold. These are called transactional, or event, surveys. After a call center conversation, an online chat, an e-mail exchange, or some other interaction, a short, automated survey is sent using the same channel as the event. If the customer is on the Web, the question will pop up in a window following the transaction. If the transaction was face to face, the survey invitation could be on the receipt.

A great time to ask for customer feedback is when a customer has just bought something from your website, says Seybold. This more specifically timed survey acts as a quality-control device, highlighting broken processes, moments of truth, and "make or break" moments. Indeed, these surveys are a superb tool for discovering a failed transaction. Customers who are happy with the service provided are likely to decline to participate in a transactional survey. Not so if they are unhappy—they will seize the opportunity to tell you just what the problem was. If you have lots of responses, Seybold says, you will get statistically valid results.

These surveys need to be accompanied by a closed-loop process with the customer service organization, so that if there is a problem, you can open or reopen a trouble ticket or otherwise get back to the customer quickly and fix it, Seybold says. If you are not ready, willing, and able to help customers with specific problems in real time, you are not ready to use transactional surveys. Indeed, if your company isn't ready to help customers with specific problems in real time, your company is on its way to oblivion.

For optimum results, transactional surveys should be short (no more than 12 questions) and not demand too much of respondents' time, says Fred Van Bennekom, principal at Great Brook Consulting, a customer support and survey consultancy.

Synopsys uses online transactional surveys as a quality-control device, to make sure that its support operation is on track. If a customer gives negative feedback regarding a just-completed transaction, the support staff will receive an alert that something is amiss. The agent will contact the customer the same day to offer help. In some cases, that means reopening a trouble ticket that the company had considered closed. "We might think it's closed, but this is the customer's perception; we have to follow up on it," says Vito Mazzarino, vice president of field support operations for Synopsys in Mountain View, California.

Starbucks, Home Depot, and others are also inviting customers to participate in transactional surveys at the bottom of their printed receipts in exchange for a discount. This extends the transactional survey from being a quality-control device to being a tool to gain deeper insights.

9. Don't Reinvent the Wheel

On the "if you can't beat 'em, join 'em" theme, companies are realizing that when it comes to the Web, social media, and mobile technologies, it's better to go where customers already are (that is, Facebook, iPhone, YouTube, or Twitter) rather than creating a new site for them to visit or a new interface for them to learn. This is particularly true when you are creating a community site or a mobile application.

Reliant Energy is a good example of this. One of the largest retail electricity providers in Texas, the company established a social media presence on Facebook, Twitter, YouTube, LinkedIn, and Flickr. Going even further, Reliant anchored these efforts on a centralized, comprehensive site that adds company-generated content and user-generated discussions on topics like energy innovation and energy-saving tips.

This way, consumer discussions across multiple social networks are centralized in a single searchable space. In practice, this means that a user-submitted comment or an article on Reliant's Facebook page or Twitter feed becomes available to Reliant users on the energyinyourlife.com site as well.

10. Leverage Analytics and Reporting Tools

Most companies have stockpiled a wealth of information in their customer relationship management (CRM) and other customer-related databases. A quick way to gain a strong lead in customer experience is to use analytics and reporting tools to look at these data. An analytics initiative can be done in a matter of months at reasonably low cost, and can have a real business impact.

Best Buy, for example, made speedy use of analytics during the early days of the downturn.[5] The retailer needed to understand why more customers were applying for financing on their purchases while the number of purchases over $1,000 was dropping. The company used an analytics tool to pinpoint the optimal level at which to offer financing—in this case, the magic number was $499. By deploying a rapid-results tool, Best Buy was able to glean insights that it could put to use right away.

Customer experience initiatives are truly an ongoing expedition. Along the way, the more CE "wins" you can score for a small amount of money in a short period of time, the more successful you will be. However, these tactical moves need to align with and be a planned part of an overall CE strategy, as we have discussed throughout this book. It is wasteful for individual business functions to approach customer experience in a siloed way; the positive impact on customer experience from one function can be offset by a negative experience from another touch point or function. Successful CE initiatives are synchronized, coordinated efforts that involve the entire organization.

The people in your organization will need to see and believe in the benefits of CE before they will be willing to change their thinking and behaviors in a big way. Working on these shorter-term initiatives and seeing the results is a good way to get them to do just that.

CHAPTER **11**

Measures
of Success

The top objective for nearly half of corporate social
strategists in 2011 is to create ROI measurements for
their social media strategies.
—ALTIMETER GROUP, 2010

MANAGEMENT GURU PETER DRUCKER had it right: if you can't measure something, you can't manage it. And with regard to the customer experience, he might have added, if you can't manage the effort, it's going to fail, sooner or later.

Of course, metrics is a topic that people seem to prefer reading about to implementing. And even when companies do use metrics, they often measure the wrong things. In most organizations, many employees are compensated based on metrics that actually work against improving the customer experience (average call-handling time, for example, rather than first-call resolution). Metrics are often shrouded in dysfunction.

It's understandable. Measuring is hard work, often subjective, and not as interesting as the mainline work of improving the customer experience. People are often tempted to skip measuring in favor of doing. Again, this may be human nature, but tracking your customers' experience and measuring your performance at improving that experience are at the very heart of obtaining the customer experience edge. Proceeding without confirmation that your customers appreciate what you're doing is part and parcel of the old way of doing business. You need to be absolutely certain, from your customers' point of view, that you are doing the right things.

The key is to select metrics that reflect your customers' state of mind and measure the activities that drive customer value. Think for a minute about the classic metrics upon which businesses have been run for decades. These include financial measures like revenue (per geography, per product line, per customer group, per unit of time); return on assets; return on investment; and earnings before interest, taxes, depreciation, and amortization. Of course, you have to pay attention to these things, but these classic financial metrics do not relate to the way your customers perceive you. They say nothing about whether your customers are about to buy more from you or jump to a competitor. Even a market leader's customers may be on the verge of defection—you can't tell by looking at market share alone. Traditional financial metrics also say nothing about whether your employees are empowered and given incentives to solve customer problems. That's why it is crucial that you start developing and using customer-centric metrics.

It is equally critical, however, not to track too many metrics. Measurement overload is akin to analysis paralysis—too many metrics take up too much time, confuse everyone, cloud insights, and stymie positive action. Metrics should be focused and well understood by the broader organization. Focus on a handful of metrics that matter—certainly, no more than 10.

Creating Metrics for CE: Guiding Principles

In a blog post, customer experience (CE) consultant Lynn Hunsaker advises companies to let the following four principles be their guide when creating customer experience metrics[1]:

1. **Connected.** Make sure you're measuring things that have a strong connection to overall business objectives (such as to increase profits or retain the highest-value customers). The goal is cascaded to each level of the program or organization, to identify successive contributions to the big-picture objective.

2. **Actionable.** Select strongly connected success measures that allow you to control outcomes. Metrics at an organization's lowest layer are the most actionable.

3. **Predictive.** Emphasize metrics that have a strong cause-and-effect relationship with objectives. Rather than focusing on customer satisfaction as measured by a survey after a transaction, for example, look at leading indicators of customer satisfaction, such as on-time delivery. This eliminates the pitfall of operating in reactive mode. "Most metrics look through the rearview mirror to say, what happened in the past? But you really need to look forward to where you're going to take your business," says Greg Langston, vice president of sales for the Harris Products Group, a subsidiary of Lincoln Electric Company that sells welding and brazing equipment.

4. **Sustained.** Set up the right environment for predictive measures to keep producing strong results. Your ability to sustain these results will depend in part on keeping the key metrics in front of everyone in the organization (via tools like dashboards and scorecards) so that they can see areas that need immediate attention, as well as how performance is trending.

Types of CE Metrics

Old-school metrics often track cost and other financial measures, reflecting a company-centric worldview. The best customer experience metrics relate to a customer goal, while also measuring how well your organization has furthered that goal.

First-contact resolution is a good illustration. The first and most important aspect of this metric is the number of times your customers' issues were resolved during their first call to the contact center or first visit to your website or store. This is directly tied to your customers' desire to minimize the amount of time spent getting their problem fixed. First-contact resolution stands in stark contrast to the old-school metric of average call-handling time, which can backfire because it gives customer service reps an incentive to wrap up calls quickly, even if the customer's problem has not been resolved. This metric speaks only to organizational imperatives such as cost efficiency.

But first-contact resolution doesn't stop at making customers happy. This metric also speaks to organizational efficiency. If the issue is taken care of on the first go, not only does the customer go away satisfied, but the company also saves money by avoiding subsequent calls. First-contact resolution is a prime example of a metric that aligns the customer's best interests with the company's.

Number of unsolicited leads is another such metric. Here, a customer seeks you out based on a recommendation. From your perspective, this person drops into your corporate lap as if heaven-sent—your organization did not have to spend any time or money chasing those who are not interested.

Not all your CE metrics will be so perfectly balanced, but a few should be. The key is to locate the areas where customer and corporate interests intersect and create metrics around those points. The principle that you can run your business better by serving your customers better should be the backbone of your customer experience metrics. A number of customer experience metrics are summarized in Table 11.1.

Net Promoter Score

Net promoter score (NPS) has become a very popular way of measuring the customer experience, based on its simplicity, and also on studies that have shown a correlation between a high NPS score and corporate success. NPS is obtained by asking customers a single

TABLE 11.1: **New Customer Experience Metrics**

Customer Experience Key Performance Indicator (KPI)	Primary Financial Metric Influenced	Secondary Financial Metric Influenced	Relative Impact
Net promoter score	Increased revenues	Pretax income	+++
Customer satisfaction survey scores	Increased revenues	Pretax income	+
Traffic on FAQ, knowledge base, and other online self-help resources	Reduced support costs	Selling, general, and administrative (SG&A) costs	++
Percent of orders considered perfect	Pretax income	Increased revenues	++
Increased sales to existing customers	Revenues	Pretax income	++
First-call resolution	Pretax income	Revenues	+
Number of help-desk calls per 1,000 users	Pretax income		+
Number of customers that had been detractors who are now promoters	Revenues	Pretax income	++
Abandoned shopping cart frequency	Revenues	Pretax income	++
Site abandonment	Revenues	Net income	+
Website usability	Revenues	Pretax income	++
Online conversion rate	Revenues	Pretax income	++

question on a 0 to 10 rating scale, where 10 is "extremely likely" and 0 is "not at all likely": "How likely is it that you would recommend our company to a friend or colleague?" Based on their responses, customers are categorized into three groups: promoters (9–10 rating), passives (7–8 rating), and detractors (0–6 rating). The percentage of detractors is then subtracted from the percentage of promoters to obtain the NPS. NPS is a key indicator, the theory goes, because a person's willingness to recommend your firm to a friend or family member is the definitive indicator of satisfaction.

Indeed, to loyalty guru and author Frederick F. Reichheld, "Would you recommend this company to a friend?" is *The Ultimate Question*, the name of his most recent book.[2] According to research that Reichheld conducted in conjunction with Bain & Co., a high NPS is correlated with higher profitability. The analysis shows that sustained value creators—companies that achieve long-term profitable growth—have an NPS two times higher than the average company. And in most industries, NPS leaders outgrow their competitors—by an average of 2.5 times.

To Reichheld, NPS is *the* metric around which every company should organize—it is more important by far than any financial measure or customer satisfaction score. The average company achieves an NPS of only +5 to +10, meaning that its promoters barely outpace its detractors. Many firms—and some entire industries—have negative NPSs, says Reichheld, which means that they are creating more detractors than promoters on a daily basis. Companies with bad NPSs cannot hope to achieve profitable, sustainable growth, no matter how aggressively they spend to acquire new business. Even companies that are at the top of the heap score NPS efficiency ratings of +50 to +80, leaving room for improvement. As with the rest of your CE journey, you should strive for continuous improvement in your NPS.

Although NPS is a great way to measure customer experience success, its detractors point out that it is limited. For instance, it is not actionable—there is no way to know from the score itself what a company is doing wrong. This is why many companies either add a section to their surveys asking for further comment or create a process to follow up with low-scoring respondents.

For Dell, even the mighty NPS is eclipsed by another metric: customers who were detractors who have turned around and are now promoters. This experience magnifies the positive effect, says Manish Mehta, vice president of social media and community for Dell. "You'll find someone who will say, 'I will never buy from Dell again.' If we can turn around that situation by solving their problem, that same person will say, 'I am now a Dell customer for life,'" says Mehta.

Organizational Metrics

Organizational metrics should be modified to better link employee compensation with the customer experience. At Synopsys, the leading supplier of software that helps semiconductor companies design new integrated circuits, for example, support engineers receive bonuses based on how many customers grade them as "exceeding expectations."

Even a company that tracks wrong-headed metrics like average call-handling time has the possibility of redemption if its employees are trained to see the bigger picture and have the tools necessary to take corrective action. Say, for example, a credit card customer calls, trying to get to the bottom of a problem with his account. He's told that he'll need to wait a few days while the fraud department investigates the issue. After numerous unsatisfactory attempts to straighten out the problem, the customer—dogged, if not optimistic—calls yet

TIP

Dell goes beyond the NPS metric by turning unhappy customers into promoters. It actively monitors social media sites and e-communities to discover influential individuals who are vocal about their negative experiences with Dell. Then, several times a year, the company invites 15 of its most unhappy customers to fly, all expenses paid, to corporate headquarters and participate in a Customer Advisory Panel. As it turns out, detractors are just as happy to vent in person as they are online, especially when they are surrounded by other like-minded individuals. But soon (usually by the second day) they begin to see that Dell is listening and working to resolve their issues, says Manish Mehta, vice president of social media and community at Dell. At this point, most are transformed from detractors to promoters. "After a while, when they see that we are listening, they start listening as well," he says. When negative experiences can be converted into positive ones, loyalty is even more guaranteed.

again. This instant is a moment of truth—the organization has the opportunity to turn things around.

This time, let's say the agent is able to see in the customer record that this person is a good customer and has called three times to resolve the same issue. If the agent is empowered to take ownership of the situation by saying, "I am going to stay on the phone with you until we sort this out," there is a good chance that the customer is going to feel taken care of by the end of the call. That kind of good feeling translates into true loyalty. As at Dell, a customer who started out unhappy but for whom the situation was turned around is probably going to be an advocate, someone who will tell people about the positive experience he had with your company.

Financial Metrics

As we've said, traditional measures of corporate performance are not the most accurate measures of the customer experience. However, you can spin these metrics so that they are aligned with your customer's point of view. Take the metric of customer profitability. Generally, you would interpret this from an enterprise perspective ("How much profit did we make from this customer?"), but you can and should view it from the customer's point of view, too. Customers who understand and buy into your value proposition tend to be of higher value from a profitability standpoint than those who don't.

Take someone who buys a luxury car for the first time. The customer has seen enough commercials to understand the car's value proposition ("This car is better than the rest, and I will look good driving it"), but in the end, it's not the right car for him. Let's say he failed to confer with his spouse prior to buying the car, they can't really afford it, and so on. Now, after the purchase, he has a major case of buyer's remorse that causes him to contact the call center to report on tiny flaws, in hopes of getting the deal reversed.

In this instance, there was never a true meeting of the minds. The customer thought he wanted the car, but he couldn't afford it. The dealership thought the sale was legitimate, but it turns out to be too much of a hassle to continue serving this customer. A dealership that is on the lookout for this scenario will rescind the sale. It simply costs too much to try to serve a customer who should never have bought the product in the first place. The relationship is not going to be profitable for either side, so the best thing is for both parties to walk away. Customer experience means delivering the right experience to the right customer, and metrics should measure how well you do that.

There is another important component: compensation for sales staff needs to be based at least in part on customer satisfaction or another customer-facing metric, not just sales numbers. Pay for salespeople will always be based on their numbers, of course, but it is imperative to add in some customer-centric measures as well. Otherwise, customers will view the relationship as adversarial rather than collaborative and mutually beneficial.

The salesperson and the customer service rep are prime examples of employees whose compensation needs to be aligned with the customer experience. But this is also true for employees in other roles. You need to break down what drives compensation for employees across the company and ask if each element contributes to or detracts from the customer experience. There should be some customer-centric metrics embedded in every employee's compensation model, such as customer satisfaction with the most recent transaction.

Social Media Metrics

Companies can use social media both to measure their customer experience and to improve their metrics. For instance, companies can leverage social media to learn about a prospect prior to making a visit or cold calling. You can unearth a lot of information about a person, such as her work experience and personal interests, just by examining her LinkedIn profile. Instead of making hundreds of calls per week (an old-school metric), your sales team might make 15 calls, but these calls are now much more relevant to the customer because of the background work. The new metric here would be something like, "How many calls result in a follow-up meeting or discussion?" When the customer or prospect opens the dialogue, you know you are onto something. You are not going to differentiate your business by getting your sales team to rack up the highest number of visits. When you can use social media to increase your relevance and convenience for customers, you are much better off from a customer experience standpoint.

Meanwhile, when it comes to measuring the success of your social media campaign itself, there are a number of metrics you could use. Cognizant suggests four KPIs that use social media traffic examples like sales leads (see Table 11.2).

TABLE 11.2: **CE Metrics for Social Media**

KPI	Key Elements
Channel effectiveness score	Number of interactions per channel
Opinion leader score	Number of posts by a user
Feedback sentiment	Number of positive and negative sentiments
Interest score	Number of sales leads generated

Source: Cognizant Technology Solutions.

Recent surveys show increased interest in creating ROI measurements for social media strategies. In a 2010 survey by Altimeter Group, 48.3 percent of 140 corporate social strategists named this as a top objective for 2011.[3] Evidence is beginning to accrue that a highly engaged social media strategy is related to higher revenue. According to a 2009 Altimeter Group study, companies that are heavily engaged in social media saw revenue growth of 18 percent that year, whereas the least engaged companies *on average* saw a decline of 6 percent in revenue during the same period.[4] The same holds true for two other financial metrics, gross margin and net profit.

The Altimeter blog post discussing this study was quick to point out that there may not be a causal relationship between revenue growth and the effective use of social media, but there is a clear correlation and connection. For example, a company with a mindset that allows broad engagement with customers probably performs better because the company is more focused on its customers than its competitors are.

While it isn't clear yet, the link between social media and sales is rapidly evolving into what some are calling social commerce. A social media dialogue between company bloggers and prospects, for instance, leads directly to incremental revenues. Dell's social media team is already talking about this as a phenomenon that it will be able to track in 2012.[5]

Predictive Metrics

Good customer experience metrics can produce actionable insights. Rather than saying what happened in the past ("Longtime Customer A has not ordered from us for 18 months"), these metrics can point the way to action before the damage grows too deep ("Longtime Customer A's order pattern has changed—it hasn't ordered from us in two months"). Marriott, for example, tracks two sets of measures, Ed French, senior vice president of Marriott Rewards, tells us. One set concerns satisfaction and the net promoter score, such as, "How satisfied were you with your recent stay?" and "Would you recommend Marriott to someone else?" And at the individual customer level, Marriott tracks financial metrics, including, "What type of revenue does this customer drive?" and "How much share of her wallet do we receive?"

"We can see when things drop off and act on that," says French. Most of the time, when an individual guest's revenue trends down sharply, it's because of a change in his personal situation, he adds, like a job change. "In a small number of cases, about 10 percent, we find an issue. What has been surprising is how effective simply reaching out to the guest can be." One part of the interaction is acknowledging that there might be an issue and asking if the guest would like to discuss it, to see if the hotel can do anything for her. "We might hear about the difficulty of reserving the type of room they want in the type of hotel they want. It doesn't take more than an e-mail to make it right for this guest," he says.

Avoid Measurement for Measurement's Sake

Lincoln Electric's Langston knows all too well the pitfalls of misaligned metrics. In late 2008, when he joined the company, his mission was to increase his wallet share with his customers. Lincoln Electric sells directly to distributors, which might stock brazing alloys from five different vendors. The only hope for increasing wallet (and therefore market) share, Langston says, was via a superior customer experience.

"Our products have a lot of commodity elements to them," he says. "Our value proposition is how close we are to our customers. We need to go beyond pricing to provide an experience customers like and want to replicate."

Langston's first step was to take a hard look at the metrics the sales organization had been using. Then he installed a structured sales process with metrics, followed by implementation of a SAP customer relationship management (CRM) system to give sales personnel visibility into customer accounts that they sorely lacked.

One problem was measurement for measurement's sake. "We had report after report that no one ever read. There was a level of granularity that would surprise the people that created the Sarbanes-Oxley Act," he says. Langston held an organizational review in which he spelled out metrics to be used moving forward. These were built on five key questions: What do we want to sell? To whom? What does a good order look like? Is there an incumbent vendor on this order? If so, why should a customer switch to us—what is our value proposition? "This helped create some clarity. Without that, people don't know if they are winning or losing," he says.

These metrics, especially the last one, helped keep the customer experience top of mind. And they were critical to turning the organization around, even in a negative economic climate, says Langston. "We saw double-digit sales growth in 2010 vs. 2009, and that is continuing in 2011."

Now, every Lincoln Electric salesperson tracks a Top 25 account list in the CRM system. These are the all-important customers that will generate the most business in the calendar year. Everyone pays much more attention to opportunity management, staging each prospect in the pipeline and tying his own sales calls to ripening prospect opportunities as well as visits to the most valuable customers.

Langston attributes much of the increased sales to the new "clarity and accountability," measuring and tracking the right things. "Specific behaviors drive profitability for the company," he says. "Now, that's what we measure."

CHAPTER 12

Emerging Economies: Exporting a Profitable Customer Experience

A large percentage of consumers in emerging markets report their customer service expectations are now higher than they were five years ago and even just one year ago.

— ACCENTURE, 2010

THE EYES OF THE BUSINESS WORLD are on emerging markets. Companies in mature markets are looking to emerging economies for growth opportunities, while those in emerging markets are seeking to attain the status of global players. In either case, the customer experience edge, driven by the smart use of technology, is a major factor in whether success is attainable.

For businesses in mature markets, the attraction of emerging economies is clear. After weathering the global recession better than most countries, Brazil, India, and China now account for an increasingly larger portion of the world economy.[1] According to the International Monetary Fund (IMF), each of these countries expects GDP growth of more than 6 percent in 2011, with China topping the sunny outlook with an expected growth rate of 9.6 percent. Other emerging markets (notably, parts of Africa, Russia, and some

Eastern European nations) are also growing quickly, but China, Brazil, and India are most significant because of their respective rankings within the top 15 world economies based on GDP, according to the IMF. As reported by Bloomberg,[2] the world's biggest private equity firms are looking to take advantage of regions with an expanding middle class, rising disposable income, and increased consumer sophistication.

Meanwhile, companies in emerging markets are looking to move beyond their traditional low-price competitive differentiation and sell premium products of higher value to consumers in mature markets. Examples range from introducing a new flavor to a mature market (such as the growing popularity of packaged tender coconut water from Brazil) to more sophisticated consulting services (such as Indian IT firms establishing a stronger onshore presence through foreign hiring practices). To succeed in this endeavor, they need to have a better understanding of their customers and surround their offerings with a more intimate experience.

Emerging-Market CE: No Shortcuts

For companies that are looking to expand in emerging markets, the customer experience (CE) edge is just as important as it is for differentiation in developed markets, and in some ways, it is even more difficult to achieve. Potential customers in emerging markets rely more on mobile devices and short message service (SMS) messaging than on e-mail and the Web. At the same time, in terms of personalized, meaningful experiences that fit their local needs and preferences, these customers are developing the same level of expectation as their counterparts in mature markets. So while all four customer experience essentials apply here (reliability, convenience, relevance, and responsiveness), relevance takes on renewed importance.

According to a 2010 Accenture report,[3] consumers in emerging markets are just as attuned to a strong customer experience as those in developed markets, if not more so. For instance, the report revealed that emerging-market customers are more inclined to switch providers as a result of poor service across all industries, but especially within the retail and banking industries. While the reasons for this were not specified, it may be that customers are less entrenched with their providers and thus are more open to experimentation and trying new things. A large percentage of consumers in emerging markets report that their customer service expectations are now higher than they were five years ago and even just one year ago. The consumer reigns, the world over.

TIP

No matter where you are in the world, a key technology for a profitable customer experience is short message service texting. Available on any mobile phone service, SMS has been used to its fullest potential in emerging markets and much less so in mature markets. To operate in emerging markets, companies will need to be much more sophisticated in their use of messaging or new variants of SMS, while emerging-market companies can adapt their advanced SMS expertise to their advantage in mature markets.

There is a widening gap, Accenture concludes, between what consumers expect and what they actually experience—a gap that threatens to hinder companies' growth in these parts of the world. Many people falsely assume that customers in emerging markets will welcome obsolete or simplified products—that they will be grateful for any technology, even if it isn't even close to state of the art. The Internet and social media have ended any opportunity for sellers to take advantage of customers' ignorance.

When selling into an emerging market, the most important thing a company can do is due diligence to ensure that the product and the experience are aligned with people's needs, lifestyles, and shopping behaviors. This means studying local trends and customs and what the people there value. In other words, will it play in

Peoria—or in Hyderabad, Shenzen, or São Paulo, for that matter? A real danger is allowing organizational hubris ("we know what's best, anywhere in the world") to lead to wasted investment and lost jobs. Gold-standard products and customer experience in your market may not even resemble the most popular products and best customer experience in another market.

If you don't already have employees in your target market, you will need advice and counsel from people on the ground who are intimately familiar with the local culture. Getting the nuances right requires insider knowledge and vetting every step of the way—we can call this LACE:

- Listen carefully.

- Analyze thoroughly.

- Co-create with your target customers.

- Engage locally in accordance with the customers' desires.

A car company selling into India, for instance, would have to design a more compact and fuel-efficient model than it would sell in North America. Most Indian consumers today need only basic transportation rather than larger, more luxurious automobile models.

Awareness building, which drives your offering's emotional value, also needs to emphasize the relevance of your product or service. Samsung has done a good job in this area, first by optimizing its products for its intended market and then by building up its brand image. For example, it built a small washing machine that can be used on a balcony in Africa, India, and other markets where most people do not have a separate laundry room, and then developed a marketing campaign for both online and traditional media, called "The Way You Live," that underlined that connection.[4]

A common mistake that large companies make is to think that the expensive ad campaigns that work in mature markets are transferable to emerging markets. An example is a company that used a soccer theme in its advertising; this played well in regions that love soccer, but it fell flat in India, which favors cricket. Pepsi's famous "Come Alive! You're the Pepsi Generation" campaign of the 1960s was an early example of something possibly having been missed in translation. While the error has now been elevated to the status of impossible-to-verify urban legend, this slogan may or may not have been interpreted by consumers in China (or Mexico, Thailand, or Germany) to mean that the soft drink would bring people back from the dead.[5]

Global trends don't necessarily apply in the particular market you are targeting. For example, traditional newspapers and other forms of print media have been losing their influence in most of the developed world for at least the past 7 to 10 years. However, in India, newspapers retain their supremacy, so no customer experience would be complete without newspaper advertising, as well as a celebrity spokesperson from the right sport. Similarly, don't assume that Facebook and Twitter have the same dominance as in established markets. Brazil and China, in particular, have their own established social networks. It would be folly not to include local sites in your emerging-market social media plans.

The bottom line is, go on a discovery mission to bring all of your assumptions about a market to the surface, and then question everything. Vet everything with local employees, experts, and consumers. No one is exempt from the risk of becoming yet another cautionary tale. For example, a large computer company that was planning a foray into India wanted to address the threat of counterfeit devices destroying its profit margins. To encourage consumers to make sure they were buying genuine products, company executives convened a meeting and devised the idea of offering one free support call to everyone running a validated system. There was just one problem: the free support call did not fit the way most Indian consumers buy computer systems. Most buy them from an individual or a small consulting company, which installs the computer and all the software at the buyer's house, then returns to help with any problems. In this environment, the offer of a free support call not only would be useless, but would also signal to consumers that the company did not understand common practices there.

Despite being one of the world's largest and most successful enterprises, this company went so far as to allocate the funds to build a major call center to provide the free support calls. Though it had sought advice from native consultants, these experts, out of respect, had only dropped subtle hints that the idea was faulty. The project was halted at the last minute when a manager finally got through to the executives that the effort was doomed. This goes to show that when it comes to delivering on the CE essentials in emerging markets, all four—reliability, convenience, relevance, and responsiveness—can have different meanings in different locales.

The experience of Best Buy in China and Turkey is another cautionary tale.[6] The world's largest electronics retailer in terms of sales closed all of its branded stores in China, highlighting a mismatch between its emphasis on service and the physical shopping experience and Chinese shoppers' price sensitivity. It was not convenient for Chinese consumers outside the major cities to get appliances repaired by the retailer, and it was impractical for a store repairperson to drive hundreds of miles to fix a refrigerator. Perhaps Best Buy could have saved its operations in this market by making an effort to better understand consumer behavior there—for instance, by seeking local partners to service its products.

Small product and service suppliers often play a major role in life in emerging markets. In India, for instance, cosmetics are sold at little shops on every street corner. So, while the cosmetics retail sensation Sephora has been looking into opening stores in India for the past few years, it has not yet done so. This caution may be wise, as the company is analyzing consumer life there and how its format might be adapted, rather than vice versa. You can't expect distribution channels in your target market to match those in your primary market. You may need to create alternative channels that are appropriate to the local market.

Mobile Phones and SMS: The Cornerstone of the Emerging-Market CE

The ubiquity of smartphones and other mobile phones in emerging markets makes it easier than ever to reach out to potential customers and expand the customer experience to these far-flung realms. With the penetration of these devices outstripping that of computers, laptops, or even TVs, it is safe to say that potential customers in emerging markets are more likely to have their customer experience shaped by smartphone or mobile phone interaction (and most likely through SMS messages) than by any other media. In a 2010 survey by Accenture, more than half (53 percent) of Chinese respondents currently own a smartphone, compared with one-third of U.S. respondents. Furthermore, smartphones are predicted to be the most purchased device in China in 2012, with 38 percent of those surveyed planning to buy one.[7]

Because of this ubiquity, any discussion of creating a strong customer experience in emerging markets would be incomplete without a mention of SMS—or, as it's known in the United States, text messaging. In most emerging markets, SMS is *the* way for companies to reach consumers, and its use is on the upswing. Consumers who are too poor to have a PC, an Internet connection, or even a bank account do have cell phones, virtually universally, and companies in those markets rely on SMS to reach them, whether for mobile couponing, status alerts regarding their current accounts or products owned, or alerts for special sales and discounts.

Globally, SMS traffic is expected to increase to 8.7 trillion messages in 2015 from 5 trillion messages in 2010, according to Informa Telecoms and Media,[8] with SMS revenues reaching $136.9 billion in 2015 compared with $105.5 billion in 2010. The organization says that SMS is increasingly being used by banks and financial institutions, brands, retailers, and transport providers to deliver alerts, information services, mobile marketing campaigns, appointment reminders, tickets, coupons, banking and payments, and loyalty programs.

Because messaging systems like SMS are relatively inexpensive, reliable, universal, and familiar to consumers in emerging markets, companies in mature markets can use them to target these customers. They would do well to watch and follow the lead of emerging-market companies, which are quite sophisticated in the way they use SMS compared with what their mature-market peers are doing. SMS in emerging markets already encompasses things like location-based coupons, surveys, quizzes, customer service, bill payments, and even rudimentary telemedicine applications. Approaching emerging-market consumers with an entry-level SMS strategy risks appearing naïve and out of touch.

In Africa, for example, counterfeit goods are rampant. Nearly 100 Nigerians were killed by a tainted batch of fake pharmaceuticals in 2010.[9] In response, a start-up called Sproxil created Mobile Product Authentication (MPA). Manufacturers put a unique code, hidden under a scratch-off panel, on their products. Potential buyers send the code to the authentication service via SMS, and the service sends an instant reply as to whether the product is authentic or counterfeit. Sproxil sells the scratch panels and SMS bundles to manufacturers.

Consumers pay nothing to use the service because the manufacturer covers the cost of both the query and response messages. Today, MPA is a business-to-consumer (B2C) offering, but Sproxil sees the market potentially expanding to business-to-business (B2B). For example, a manufacturer could use MPA throughout its supply chain, with scratch-off panels on cartons and pallets.

Necessity is the mother of invention, and with other communication channels being limited, emerging markets have learned to use SMS in increasingly inventive ways. Companies should study what is happening in their markets and include SMS and other messaging technologies as a primary component of their customer experience.

The Other Side of the Coin

Now let's look at the flip side: companies in emerging markets that want to use a differentiated customer experience as a way to sell into an established market. It used to be that emerging-market companies would sell their goods into mature markets at fire-sale prices, with no relationship with the end consumer. The only consideration was price. The typical scenario was selling products like cheap MP3 players, jeans, or toys. The customer experience was nil, but the price made the buyers happy. Low price used to be the primary mode of differentiation for emerging-market companies. This is no longer the primary case.

Thanks to the Internet and social media, emerging-market companies now have the ability to engage directly with global customers by creating a more sophisticated experience than they did in the past, when they largely didn't have a visible presence in mature markets. Emerging-market businesses can now put more of a face on their company and not just rely on low prices to attract customers. Like their competitors in mature markets, emerging-market companies have the ability (and therefore, an imperative) to establish the multi-channel presence and experience options that customers expect.

It is true that companies in countries like China, India, and Brazil still have low-cost production as one of their biggest advantages. However, price is no longer king. Customer requirements have become more sophisticated. According to the Accenture study, customers around the globe are unwilling to forgo product quality, product options, or customer service to get a low price, and they are more interested in personalized experiences and in products and services that have been customized to their needs. Companies in these countries have been reengineering their products and the attendant customer experience. For instance, product-assembly instructions written in subpar English have given way to slicker, more understandable documentation that is available online in a multitude of languages.

After-sale service is a clear area for improvement. There is an opportunity to provide value-added after-sale services or a different experience level according to customer type, something that has almost never been seen from emerging-market companies selling into the United States and other mature markets.

Whereas companies that are selling into emerging markets need to get up to speed with marketing via mobility and SMS, the converse may also hold true. Emerging-market companies selling into mature markets may be able to bring their unique SMS customer engagement practices to established markets. For example, while SMS use by companies is still in its infancy in the United States and other mature markets, emerging-market companies are more experienced and skilled at using SMS as a low-cost channel for customer engagement. These companies could very well drive the adoption of low-cost customer engagement using text messages.

Emerging-market companies that seek to move upmarket with their products and services must find a way into the buyer's value chain. Here, optimizing the channels of customer interaction is key. In addition to SMS, they need to elevate their status through sophisticated websites, smartphone applications, and social media presence.

Though hailing from Sweden rather than an emerging market, IKEA is an iconic example of a company that has succeeded in reproducing its distinctive customer experience in established markets. Its sleek furniture is undeniably cost-effective compared with other products on the market. But price is almost secondary to the experience of shopping in an IKEA store. The sheer size of the space is awesome, and Swedish touches like the yellow-and-blue flags, meatballs in the café, and native-language product names create a sense of cool *otherness*. With its emphasis on design, hipness, and creativity, IKEA foreshadowed the success of the Apple store. And it did this from across an ocean—a true achievement. While its retail stores are the cornerstone of its customer experience, IKEA also has an e-commerce website that succeeds in recreating the hip in-store vibe.

Whether you're starting from an emerging market or a mature economy, delivering relevant customer experience can open the doors of your next big market. Once again, the essentials can be summed up by the acronym LACE: listen, analyze, co-create, and engage.

CASE STUDY: **AKBANK**

The Customer Experience at Akbank
Is Surpassed Only by the Turkish Bank's Growth

Akbank T.A.S., one of the leading banks in Turkey, has seen dramatic growth, beginning in the late 1990s and continuing through 2011. Founded in 1948, the Istanbul-based bank employs 15,000 people, who serve customers through more than 900 branches, 20 regional offices, more than 3,000 ATMs, 260,000 point-of-sale terminals, a telephone banking center, and other technology channels.[10]

CE ESSENTIALS

- **Convenience.** Through Akbank's ATMs, customers can view banking offers, chat with service reps, purchase products, and receive an SMS confirmation. After leaving a branch, customers can use any contact channel to see the status of the issue.

- **Reliability.** Akbank offers consistent, efficient, and effective service across diverse channels, including telephone banking centers, branches, ATMs, mobile phones, and its website.

- **Responsiveness.** Akbank uses key performance indicators (KPIs) to ensure accuracy, courtesy, and compliance with service-level agreements. The reports are sent to managers in a scorecard format so that they can evaluate employees and assess whether they need further training. The bank has reduced average resolution time for issues from three days to two and increased first-contact resolution rates from 65 percent to 90 percent.

While Akbank's growth has been positive overall, a set of disparate service processes and ineffective customer communications were raising challenges. Akbank needed to find an efficient and effective way to handle the one million annual customer complaints, disputes, and suggestions that it receives each year from its disparate customer contact channels. A new customer relationship management (CRM) system, based on an integrated software platform with SAP CRM at its core, delivered an award-winning solution.

In 2010, Akbank was the first Turkish bank to receive the Oscar of CRM awards—the prestigious "CRM Excellence–Integrated Marketing Award" from research firm Gartner—for its customer relationship management system, dubbed ATOM.[11] ATOM helps provide a more efficient solution to Akbank's customers' needs and expectations, leading Akbank to attract a lot of attention in global banking circles for its operational excellence, including a 20 percent investment by global banking giant Citicorp in 2007.

A Need for Transparency

Akbank first started focusing on the customer experience in 2003 through data mining and campaign management. But as the products and services it offered increased, the bank needed to communicate better with its customers and to integrate contact data from the multiple channels through which it interacted with them, including its call center, the Internet, e-mails, faxes, and 877 bank branches.

Previously, the bank had been using multiple disparate platforms for its customer operations, which were costly and inefficient, said Yesukan Akinti, head of customer service operations at Akbank. Functionality was also lacking—customer service reps had limited capability to prioritize and classify customer contacts, no alerts, and no escalation process. Responses to customers and the original customer inquiries were stored in different places, he said. "We lacked sophisticated reporting, analysis, and monitoring tools," Akinti said.[12]

The bank chose to deploy a new technological infrastructure to optimize its planned customer experience improvements, according to Attila Bayrak, Akbank's CRM senior vice president.[13] Management charged the CRM business team with designing a multichannel, multifunctional, event-triggered sales force and marketing system. It also made sure to get buy-in on the new system from various departments.

End-user workshops were held with the departments that would use the system, including marketing, alternative delivery channels, the call center, and several operational departments. Senior leadership presented examples of the new CRM tool's capabilities and benefits at these meetings.

An organizational restructuring was also required to use the new system more efficiently. The reorganization included implementing segment-based portfolio management, then aligning the product management and marketing teams with the new segments. Previously, the CRM department, for example, had served only the retail and small/medium business segments, but now it works with all segments and product management teams.

Akbank also introduced more in-depth analytical approaches to support customer-centric marketing. The approaches include conducting value-based and behavioral clustering and predictive modeling to create cross-selling propensity models, build attrition models, decipher channel preferences and usage propensities, and develop customer lifetime value models. This more granular level of data enables Akbank to interact with customers in a more targeted way, so that the appropriate relationship manager can be aligned with the right customer segments.

Akbank is also using the CRM system to integrate all customer inquiries and route them to customer service agents who also take calls. The inquiries (or tickets) are opened by agents, who try to address the issues right away. If they cannot be resolved, the agents categorize and prioritize them and use the CRM system to transmit the information, including any attached documents, to more experienced or specialized customer service representatives. If the issue is complex, it is broken up into subtasks and escalated to the appropriate sources.

The software can also measure key performance indicators, such as average number of requests handled per day, accuracy, courtesy, and compliance with service-level agreements. The reports generated are sent to managers in a scorecard format so that they can evaluate employees and assess whether they need further training.

"We reduced the average resolution time for issues from three days to two days and increased first-contact resolution rates from 65 percent to 90 percent," said Akinti in a report. In addition, the bank increased its customer satisfaction index by 20 percentage points.

With the software in place, human capital has been freed up for more value-added work. Customer service representatives (CSRs) have less paperwork to handle and don't have to spend as much time on administrative tasks, enabling them to hone in on customer-related issues, Akinti said. Akbank's IT group also spends less time supporting multiple CRM platforms, meaning that it has more time to focus on solving business issues, he added.

Today, with ATOM, a customer can go to an ATM, view an offer from the bank, learn more about the offer by clicking on a chat button and talking to a CSR, purchase the product, and receive an SMS confirmation.

The customer experience efforts are paying off. Within the first six months of the implementation of the CRM system, Akbank sold more than 500,000 new products. In addition, it gained 200,000 new customers and reported a €2.2 million gain in gross profit and a savings of €3.5 million in service costs.

CE PILLARS

- **Operational excellence.** Through a corporate reorganization and system consolidation, Akbank's product management, marketing, and customer service organizations have been synchronized.

- **Interaction excellence.** Customers can contact Akbank through a wide variety of channels, including the Web and its call center, that provide a consistent experience.

- **Decision-making excellence.** The bank uses in-depth data analysis to make more customer-focused—and ultimately profitable—business decisions.

But most important, customers are clearly pleased with the bank's customer service, which has helped Akbank raise its stature and become the most profitable banking operation among privately owned banks in Turkey. "Strategically, our complaint management team has become an enabler for enhanced customer perception," said Akinti. "If a customer walks into one of the bank's branches to discuss a problem with a service specialist, the next day that customer can contact us through any of the integrated contact channels—like the call center or through the Internet—and easily determine the status of the issue."

Outlook

Akbank constructed a new banking center in Çayirova, with the goal of making it the highest-transaction-capacity operations center not only in Turkey, but also in the surrounding region. The center is equipped with state-of-the-art technology.

Akbank is also keeping a close eye on customers' changing needs to ensure that it delivers the best experience, said Bayrak. The bank is planning to use social media as a marketing channel and enhance its marketing solutions so that customers can receive more targeted offers from the various teams and broaden the overall CRM strategy.

CHAPTER 13

The Future of the Customer Experience

Within the next two years, you will design customer experience into every product or solution that you develop. That means when you are at the early stage of defining the product requirements, you will have the help of people who are very experienced in customer experience, as well as the customers themselves.
— PATRICIA SEYBOLD

WHEN IT COMES TO CUSTOMER EXPERIENCE (to borrow a sports and management analogy), it pays to skate to where the puck is going, not where it has been—or at least, to try to do so.[1] No one can predict the future, but keeping an eye on what lies ahead will inform you of how well your present-day plans will hold up to the needs of the future. Evolving the customer experience edge is guaranteed to be a continuous journey that (barring a major career change) will keep you busy for most of your professional life, whether that be five more years or five more decades. So, what sorts of changes can you expect to see in the coming months and years?

It is certain that people will look for companies that will help them make their lives easier—through the four customer experience (CE) essentials of reliability, convenience, relevance, and responsiveness—so that they can recoup some of their ever-shrinking amount of personal time. Customers of all types will also expect the companies and vendors that they patronize to understand them and cater to their individual needs. Everyone wants to feel understood, and in the future, this will no longer be a "nice to have," but will be one of the core components of the customer experience edge. And there will be ever more sophisticated ways to get inside customers' hearts and minds. Twitter, Google, and Facebook are just the beginning of customer interaction channels; as others emerge, they might be adopted at an even faster pace.

The advanced customer experiences of today point the way to those of tomorrow. Let's say, for example, that you're in the market for a new car. The traditional approach to car buying used to be to drive over to your local dealer, test-drive a few cars, listen to the salesperson's spiel, check with a few friends, and make a decision. It is amazing how this behavior, which went on for 80-plus years, has been transformed in just the last 10. Today, you are very likely to spend some time checking out Cars.com, ConsumerReports.org, or one of the many other online resources available. Even better, you could tap the ShopSavvy mobile app on your smartphone and get instant access to everything from dealer and model reviews to special offers, Blue Book information for your trade-in, comparative safety records, fan sites, and even directions to the nearest dealership. Via location-based services, the dealership can even push a special offer on the exact model you're interested in to your mobile app while you're standing in the car lot. This experience hints at what will be possible in the customer experience across many industries in the near future.

Rather than a car, for instance, let's assume that you want to explore the nagging feeling that $100 is too much to pay for that sea-algae-based face cream that the saleswoman at Sephora encouraged you to buy. Does someplace else sell it cheaper? Is it even worth spending the dough—has it been shown to work? Again, using a mobile social shopping application and technologies such as quick response (QR) codes—two-dimensional codes that transfer information to the mobile device when scanned—these answers are readily obtained.

Using your smartphone, all you have to do is scan the code on the back of the jar, and up will pop a plethora of information about this face cream—a veritable library of data. You can check everything from clinical study information to all the available online and offline outlets that sell the cream, sorted from low price to high. Even better, you can set up the system to receive an alert should the item go on sale.

All of this is possible today, and according to the ShopSavvy website, more than nine million consumers have downloaded this particular application. But let's take this one step further. Imagine that a company representative were able to interact with you via phone or videoconference and act as your personal sales consultant, sending you exactly the information you want to know, in your preferred format. It's not too much of a stretch to imagine future mobile shopping applications being linked with Facebook or a social shopping site, so that you can immediately see who among your friends bought your target item, where they bought it, and for how much. Younger generations are way ahead on this; they are already eschewing traditional shopping methods and relying instead on what their social network peers are buying for their own purchase decisions. Soon, shopping will be "social" for the population at large, as we all check out what our friends are buying, compare prices and reviews, and post photos and videos.

On the business-to-business (B2B) front, imagine a scenario where rather than having to fly out to the vendor's site to make a final quality inspection of a costly piece of capital equipment that you're purchasing, you can use voice- and data-annotated video to take a virtual tour and even make any final arrangements or conduct sensitive negotiations via PC or mobile-based videoconferencing. Another possibility: while you're visiting an existing supplier's website and checking on the availability of products that you've bought in the past, a window opens with a limited-time offer—10 percent off of a purchase made within the next 15 minutes. The vendor's integrated databases and analytics have determined that, as a prior good customer who hasn't bought in a while because of a slowdown in your industry, you will probably respond positively to a little price motivation.

It's hard to believe that not long ago, such capabilities were the stuff of science fiction. New technologies are appearing on the scene, being adopted en masse, and then morphing into unrecognizable forms—all in a few years or less. A mere decade ago, for example, there was no Facebook, no Skype, no Twitter, no iPhone, no iPad, no YouTube, no Groupon—these staples of everyday life had not even been invented yet. In fact, daily deal provider Groupon, which did not exist until late 2008, was valued at at least $15 billion as of mid-2011. Meanwhile, digital cameras, which were fairly new on the scene 10 years ago, have all but replaced film cameras, but now face obsolescence themselves, as people can use the cameras on their cell phones and smartphones rather than bothering with carrying a separate device. As much as we have been whipsawed by change in the last decade, the pace is likely to accelerate, making it difficult to anticipate not only what is coming next, but what form it will take.

Many different elements will combine to create the future of the customer experience, based on what we and others see.

1. The Future of Real-Time Computing

According to the market research firm International Data Corp., the amount of electronic data that exists in the world doubles every 72 hours, as of 2010. The world is already grappling with the massive proliferation of unstructured data—how to transport it, store it, manage it, secure it, and leverage it—which is partly attributable to user-generated content. The Internet must change to keep up. This expansion in network bandwidth is often called Web 3.0 (and there is no telling what future iterations will be called). According to a popular YouTube video posted by STI International and the Future Internet project, the next generation of the Internet will be mobile, ubiquitous, and pervasive.[2] Dr. Vinton Cerf, who is often called the "Father of the Internet" and is now chief Internet evangelist for Google, concurs, saying in a video that the Internet will be more mobile and higher speed than anyone can imagine today.[3]

As a consequence of these developments, the customer experience will become more and more real time. Today, most customer experiences have a great deal of built-in lag time. It might take you 30 seconds to sign up for a magazine subscription online, but it still takes several weeks, if not months, to see that first issue. The lag time that is built into traditional processes will disappear, as consumers who grew up downloading music, books, and video for immediate consumption will not tolerate delays that, from the outside, at least, are inexplicable. Print magazine publishing has indeed been struggling for the past several years as real-time forces are at work, along with the explosion in user-created content. No one wants to wait six weeks to read an issue that can be pulled up on an iPad in seconds.

Traditional business processes will also undergo a transformation. Today, for example, while you can apply for a mortgage online and obtain fast credit approval, the mortgage approval process is no faster than it ever was. In the future, bigger "pipes" will speed the flow of data, and an emerging technology called "in-memory" databases will allow much faster data analysis, enabling virtually instantaneous decision–making—think actual approval of a mortgage on a specific piece of property, including underwriting and property/market valuation (not just "preapproval" based on your creditworthiness), in 30 seconds. Taking this a step further, imagine that 10 banks (with your approval) can review your data in a split second and offer you competing approvals and mortgage terms on that piece of property. You will no longer have to shop around—the offers will come to you.

Or, imagine that your basement gets flooded, or your house burns down. If your insurance provider had instant access to a full listing—complete with photos and video—of every item in your home that was covered by insurance, the claims process would be speeded immeasurably.

The life cycle for all types of decisions will shrink, increasing the gratification of customers whose daily lives depend on those outcomes. Both companies and their customers will be able to take mountains of data and quickly turn them into insights and value. Data transparency and data sharing will become more pervasive throughout the customer value chain. Advanced database management techniques, including in-memory, will aggregate data at the point of decision, making analysis much more fluid. So, for example, the time it takes to process a customer invoice will decrease from a few seconds (a veritable lifetime in the future of the customer experience) to close to zero.

2. The Future of Social Media Use

Although this is already happening, we predict that social media will merge even further with mobility. Both consumers and business users will look to their smartphones and other mobile devices to see what their friends and colleagues are buying or selling. Not surprisingly, Apple is ahead of this curve: it recently published a patent describing a shopping-oriented social network that would allow users to solicit feedback from friends while they were in a store. As envisioned, the system involves image sharing, enabling iPhone and iPad users to send photos of a potential purchase to a friend, colleague, or group and receive comments, votes up or down, or other types of feedback.[4] One can expect B2B uses of social shopping to involve their peers in recommendations and pricing reality checks. E-commerce giants such as Amazon are already working on allowing shopping within Facebook (with other social media sites being presumed to follow). There is every reason to believe that social media and mobility will merge so as to become virtually indistinguishable.

Though social media to date are used largely in consumer applications, the borders are beginning to disappear. Business users' experience is already informed by the consumer experience, and this distinction will completely fade over time. In the meantime, though, B2B marketers must become much more savvy in their use of social media.

According to a survey of 2,100 companies in July 2010 by Harvard Business Review Analytic Services, 69 percent of businesses will increase their use of social media significantly over the next five years. That's no surprise, considering that two-thirds of respondents currently have no formalized social media strategy in place. Once they understand how social media can support their business objectives, their use will skyrocket. And before long, there will be no way to provide a customer experience of any kind without the use of mobile social media. Looking to the future, 41 percent of survey respondents said that a primary goal will be to integrate social media monitoring solutions with other marketing solutions, so that they can understand not just what is being said, but who is saying it and its impact (see Figure 13.1).

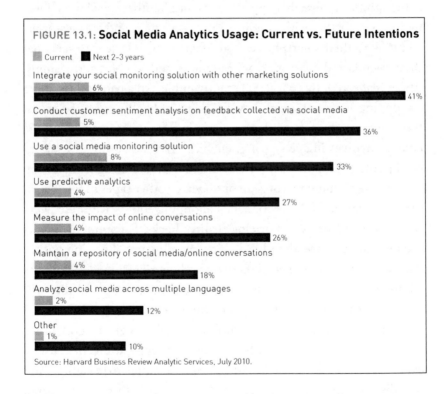

FIGURE 13.1: **Social Media Analytics Usage: Current vs. Future Intentions**

Current   Next 2–3 years

Integrate your social monitoring solution with other marketing solutions
6%
41%

Conduct customer sentiment analysis on feedback collected via social media
5%
36%

Use a social media monitoring solution
8%
33%

Use predictive analytics
4%
27%

Measure the impact of online conversations
4%
26%

Maintain a repository of social media/online conversations
4%
18%

Analyze social media across multiple languages
2%
12%

Other
1%
10%

Source: Harvard Business Review Analytic Services, July 2010.

3. The Future of the Mobility/Online Customer Experience

Anyone who has given any thought to the future of the customer experience agrees that mobility will be its key characteristic going forward. As discussed in Chapter 12, short message service (SMS) is already the central tool for delivering the customer experience in emerging markets, and this technology—along with other messaging technologies—is expected to be increasingly adopted in mature markets as the more sophisticated SMS techniques developed in emerging markets cross into established markets. Banks and financial institutions, retailers, and transportation providers will look to SMS and other messaging technologies to deliver alerts, information services, mobile marketing campaigns, appointment reminders, tickets, coupons, payments, and loyalty programs. Mobile payment—from consumers to businesses, consumers to consumers, and even businesses to businesses—are poised for takeoff. According to In-Stat, there will be as many as 375 million mobile payment users worldwide by 2015. Examples of mobile payments range from an individual paying bills on his smartphone, to an employee in a retail store helping customers check out via an iPhone, to a retailer zapping coupons to customers while they are in the store. Contactless payment is an especially fast-growing area in emerging markets.

According to a blog post by Forrester vice president and research director Moira Dorsey, Web-based applications and experience are evolving away from their initial format, the Web "page," which was an attempt to mimic familiar paper in the earliest days of the Web.[5] Additionally, today's default Web platform (a browser running on a PC) is rapidly giving way to diverse online environments, she writes. The types of devices used to connect to the Web today range from PCs to laptops to netbooks to now-exotic form factors like Internet radio and even Wi-Fi appliances. There is no telling how these devices will evolve. Portable devices are rapidly getting more powerful; as a result, the trade-off between mobility and capability is shrinking, according to Dorsey. And as the hardware evolves, the interfaces on the devices we use to connect to the Web are becoming more and more customizable.

According to Dorsey's blog post, the future of the online/mobile customer experience can be handily summed up by the acronym CARS:

- **Customized by the end user.** Not only will consumers control what they get online, but they'll control the form that they get it in to a much greater degree than they do today.

- **Aggregated at the point of use.** Content, function, and data will be pulled from different sources and combined at a common destination to create a unique experience.

- **Relevant to the moment.** This customized, aggregated content will appear on the device that's best suited to the customer's context at a given point in time.

- **Social as a rule, not an exception.** Social content will be integrated into most online experiences, not segregated into today's blogs, microblogs, and wikis.

According to Jonathan Zittrain,[6] author of *The Future of the Internet—And How to Stop It*, people will begin moving away from PCs as their platform of choice in favor of what he calls "contingently tethered" devices like the iPhone because of the specter of increasing security vulnerability. Because smartphones and tablets are relatively closed platforms, unlike the PC, they cannot be compromised as readily, he says. "Generative" technologies, like the Internet combined with a traditional PC, unleash an enormous amount of creative force as people use them as a means of expressing their own individuality and ingenuity. This compares sharply with what Zittrain calls "sterile networks," which means that they work the same way on their last day of usage as on their first day (the earliest computers, for example). Zittrain predicts that the use of semiclosed devices like the iPhone and iPad will increase exponentially as data security and privacy threats burgeon. This message is in line with other predictions that mobile devices will become the preeminent delivery mechanism for the customer experience, both for consumers and for business customers.

Some futurists, such as Dr. Michio Kaku, a theoretical physicist and author of *Physics of the Impossible*, see mobile computing expanding to even more unexpected delivery mechanisms, such as your eyeglasses, an eyepiece, or even a retinal implant. Kaku foresees the day when we'll be able to download information and images and view them on a tiny LCD display right on the eye's surface. The final image would appear to float in front of your nose.[7] Imagine that extended to an array of products that you are interested in, along with their price and availability.

Others see the friendly, intuitive interfaces made ubiquitous by smartphones and tablets beginning to appear in entirely new places. Volkswagen's Bulli concept van features an iPad mounted on the dashboard, allowing the user to control everything from the interior lights, to the heating and cooling systems, to the entertainment system—even receiving alerts when maintenance is needed.[8] There is every reason to believe that tablets or their next iterations will come to control everything from your refrigerator to your alarm system. Tabletlike interfaces will also figure for B2B in industries like oil and gas and manufacturing, which rely on controls of various sorts.

4. The Future of Customer Service

From the earliest days of Twitter, companies have been using the microblogging site as a means of delivering better customer service. The specter of harm was clear enough: if someone with lots of followers complained about your product, the damage could be incalculable. Companies, especially those serving consumers, got a crash course in how to use social media to discover consumer problems and help fix them. Now, companies of all types and sizes have been learning how to do customer service on social media. That's good, as these platforms will become a premier forum for customer service in a few years.

For some companies, that future is already here. Gatorade, for example, has the edge with its Gatorade Mission Control Center.[9] As part of its mission to interact with "millions" of athletes and influencers, the company built an Internet command center in which a room full of people track brand mentions and online consumer sentiment in real time, monitoring the pulse of the Gatorade brand, according to a YouTube video. Their task:

- Monitor online discussions.

- Monitor sporting events.

- Track media performance.

- Be proactive in social media outreach.

- Track campaign analytics.

- Track website analytics.

- Track social media analytics.

The information gathered at Mission Control influences not only Gatorade's communications, but its product as well. Observers like Altimeter Group analyst Jeremiah Owyang insist that the traditional call center will give way to a social media command center like Gatorade's.[10] The next generation of customer service will proactively go out and help customers in their native environments, rather than expecting customers to call in to a call center, says Owyang. But social media are not just another channel for interacting with customers, he cautions. Characteristics of customer service in the future will be that it is outbound rather than inbound, real-time rather than post-issue, based on lifestyle content rather than incident-resolution scripts, long-term rather than one-off, and social-media-oriented rather than support-oriented. Measurements will be equally as critical to the customer service organization of the future as they are today, focusing on customer satisfaction and issue resolution rate, Owyang adds.

A few other organizations have geared up to monitor what customers are saying about their products more closely. Dell's Social Media Listening Command Center, established at its Texas headquarters in 2010, is listening to its computer users around the world. "A team of Dell employees monitors the thousands of conversations about Dell that occur on all social media platforms around the clock, delivering the company's systemic early warning system, ensuring listening consistency across Dell's business, and coordinating best practices across the company," according to Adam Brown, Dell's executive director of social media, at an electronics industry conference sponsored by Microsoft in February 2011.[11]

5. The Future of Product Development

Leading-edge companies already develop their next product and service offerings in tandem with their customers. The customer experience piece will no longer be tacked on at the end, as with classic R&D processes, Patricia Seybold tells us. "Within the next two years, you will design customer experience into every product or solution that you develop. That means when you are at the early stage of defining the product requirements, you will have the help of people who are very experienced in customer experience, as well as the customers themselves." Customers know what they need. They know what they want. Customers will lead product design and development from the inception of an offering to its release. "The whole development cycle will be done intertwined with customers," says Seybold. "They will be co-designing the products and co-designing the entire experience around the new product or service."

A by-product of these close working relationships between the customer and the company will be greater trust. As customers feel more open to telling companies what they need in order to get to the next step of their own evolution and experiences, companies will better be able to fill those needs. There is the potential for a productive symbiosis between the two in which customers and companies coexist and have a mutual dependency. There will be organizational and other types of ramifications to this development. For example, there may no longer be a need for a traditional marketing function. Demand-led companies will not have to do much marketing, as they will provide only what customers have already requested. An organization's central focus will become creating the product and supplying it to customers that need it. Demand generation will happen in e-communities and on social media.

Ideally, customers will become evangelists, significantly changing the role of both sales and marketing. When your best customers bring their needs directly to you and evangelize your company to others, traditional marketing campaigns will become all but obsolete. Marketers will no longer push information to prospects and customers—their role will be to understand customers' perspectives, sense what is being said, and then influence, enable, engage, and nurture evangelists. The new marketer will be an orchestrator, listener, and analyzer. The days of disseminating an annual or quarterly marketing campaign and then sitting back to make your own projections will end, and the communication and interaction with customers will resemble a natural conversation rather than a broadcast in its fluidity and immediacy.

For years, across industries, the sales function has been evolving into an exercise of building trust as opposed to getting a deal. We see sales shifting to a largely consultative role, in which the company representative helps customers figure out the solution or service that will best help them meet their own objectives. Building and retaining trust will be crucial to survival. Salespeople and the companies they work for will align with the customer's needs and those of the larger supply chain. In many industries, competition will rise to the level of Supply Chain A vs. Supply Chain B as opposed to Company A vs. Company B. The new salesperson will be given incentives for listening, gathering insights, and creating personal connections with customers.

6. The Future of Business Models

A few innovative start-ups are already using an entirely consumer-driven business model in which everything from new product recommendations, to pricing, to customer support is determined and handled by consumers. For example, the U.K.-based virtual mobile network operator giffgaff.com provides free texting and mobile Internet service while selling SIM cards. Customers participate in various aspects of giffgaff's operation, including sales, customer support, and marketing. The community is officially (rather than informally, as in other organizations) the first line of customer support. This is a new type of corporate business model, one in which the voice of the customer governs all.

As we said at the very beginning of this book, the customer experience will become an increasingly critical differentiator for all companies. Truly, there is no future for companies that fail to find their customer experience edge by providing customers with an experience that is difficult to replicate in a profitable way.

CHAPTER 14

Action Items for Achieving the Customer Experience Edge

Businesses that cannot adapt to the new business realities that demand customer centricity will be faced at best with second-class status, and at worst with defeat.

CAN YOUR CUSTOMERS LIVE without you? This question (asked in Gallup customer engagement polls)[1] is at the heart of the customer experience edge that we've discussed throughout this book. But while many companies are working to strengthen their customer experience, few are achieving the customer experience edge.

To recap, today's business world is characterized by rampant commoditization, sluggish growth in mature markets, increasingly digital channels of interaction, democratization of information, and changing customer behavior. In this environment, business executives are coming to realize that a new approach to doing business is required. Their only hope for growth and survival is to differentiate themselves based not on traditional competitive factors like product features or pricing but by offering customers an experience that they value so much that they are eager to engage with the company and have no reason to turn to the competition.

This cannot be achieved simply through a new marketing initiative or an optimized call center. An improved customer experience requires a holistic strategy encompassing the entire enterprise, its ecosystem, and its customers. It requires a new approach to doing business that centers not on products, cost cutting, and efficiencies but on understanding, anticipating, and fulfilling customer needs. Research from Bloomberg Businessweek Research Services (BBRS) reveals that the four elements of the customer experience (CE) that customers value most highly are reliability, convenience, relevance, and responsiveness—what we call the four customer experience essentials. If you shape your customer experience around one or all of these essentials, you will establish a trusted relationship with your customers, building a bond that cannot be replicated by anyone else. Through this bond, you can begin to engage with customers in a whole different way, such as co-innovation, word-of-mouth evangelizing, and customer advocacy.

But to create a differentiating experience in a sustainable, scalable, and profitable way (the customer experience edge), companies need to rely on technology: a well-conceived foundation of integrated applications that can execute complete processes plus disruptive technologies that advance the game. Such a framework alone will help to ensure that processes operate reliably, customer needs are identified in real time, business decisions are based on accurate customer insights, the right insight is available to anyone who needs it, and customers receive a personalized, relevant experience that is consistent across all channels of interaction.

Just as there is no universal customer, there is no universal customer experience strategy. But a close look at the leading companies highlighted in this book reveals some common approaches that any reader of this book can apply to his own situation. We've summarized these into a list of action items that we hope will prove inspirational and perhaps even profitable for you.

Action Item 1: Define a Vision for a Customer Experience That Differentiates Your Company from the Competition

Companies can no longer compete on price and product alone; they need to develop services and experiences that truly matter to customers *and* that are difficult for their competitors to replicate. This is true even for companies that are performing well. Colmobil, Coop, CEMEX, Synopsys, Akbank, The LEGO Group, Cardinal Health, and many others discussed in these pages were leaders in their industries when they decided to aim for a customer experience edge.

In the words of Ven Bontha, customer experience management director for CEMEX USA, "Anyone can make cement or concrete. We wondered, How can we de-commoditize this? How can we make it easier for our customers to do business with us?"

Action Item 2: Earn Customer Trust with the Four Customer Experience Essentials

Trust is the glue that bonds any relationship, personal or business. Only when you have established customer trust can you begin to form the emotional bond—the "stickiness"—that cannot be replicated by anyone else. We have identified the building blocks of trust (which we've deemed the four CE essentials): reliability, convenience, responsiveness, and relevance. The companies highlighted throughout this book exemplify these four essentials, earning their customers' trust.

Reliability ("Live Up to the Promise")

Once CEMEX determined that on-time delivery was its customers' top priority after quality, it set out to ensure that it could meet that expectation. This involved increasing the visibility of its delivery operations and streamlining its bill of lading process. Accomplishing this involved implementing an enterprise resource planning (ERP) and customer relationship management (CRM) system that reveals key pieces of data about process flows, installing cameras on its truck loading docks, and setting system alerts when delays are likely. Not only has this increased on-time delivery, but CEMEX also notifies customers proactively of delays and how it intends to resolve them.

Convenience ("Offer Choice, Consistency, and Timeliness")

In Switzerland, stores close early in the evenings and are closed all day on Sundays. So, Swiss grocer Coop developed an iPhone-based shopping application that enabled customers to shop while commuting to or from work and allowed them to specify the delivery time within a 60-minute time window while they shopped. The iPhone was a good choice, as 13 percent of the country's citizens owned one, and adoption is increasing rapidly.

Responsiveness ("Listen and Respond Quickly")

When customers contact a call center, they want a quick resolution. At Cardinal Health, any agent is able to help any customer who calls, thanks to a CRM system that centralizes all pertinent customer information, no matter how it comes in, in a single interaction record. If the inquiry is related to a shipment, it is automatically sent to the right distribution center, enabling faster response times.

Relevance ("Ensure that Offerings and Interactions Are Personalized and Meaningful")

Purchasing an automobile or dropping off your car for servicing is an inconvenience, and Colmobil took that into account when it transformed its organizational structure and processes to center around the customer. Many auto dealers simply add extra parking spaces, free coffee, or valet service. Colmobil looked more deeply into customer needs, enabling sales agents to offer special discounts to repeat customers, for instance, because the system gives them a full history of the customer's previous interactions and lets them know whether the person is a high-value customer. Other elements of a personalized experience include simply welcoming customers back, knowing their names, and apologizing for any past issues. Colmobil also fitted new cars with radio frequency ID (RFID) tags and placed tag scanners at its entrance gates. When a customer arrives, reception agents can offer a personal greeting rather than a request for identification. When the customer leaves, the exit gate opens automatically, without further inquiry.

Action Item 3: Get Your Technology House in Order before Trying to Optimize the Customer Experience

You can have the most customer-centric culture and the highest levels of passion for customers, but if your technology is working against you—if it's too complicated, too costly, or simply broken—you won't be able to gain a sustainable and profitable customer experience edge.

Before you make a purchase decision on a new piece of technology, pause and think what implications it may have for your existing infrastructure. Is it going to easily coexist with and support your existing systems, or will it add another animal to the zoo? Across the board, the companies profiled in this book moved from a patchwork of disconnected business applications (with customer information spread across multiple systems) to one or a handful of connected systems that share customer and business information. These integrated systems provide a full view of the customer, visibility into front- and back-office operations, consistent information across channels, and the flexibility to respond to unexpected customer actions or needs. When a customer interaction triggers a process, such as placing an order, there's a centralized way to orchestrate the many pieces of that process (including product selection, purchasing, fulfillment, logistics, distribution, billing, payment, product return, and after-sale support). In fact, the global BBRS survey conducted in December 2010 showed that respondents with a foundation of tightly connected systems and applications ranked their customer experience 20 percent higher than other respondents.

Profiled companies also made smart use of more "disruptive" technologies, including the mobile Web, social media monitoring and engagement, mobile applications, rich Internet applications, just-in-time information, voice analytics, and unified communications, to name a few. The choice of which technologies to implement was guided by the four customer experience essentials and the three pillars of customer experience: operational, interaction, and decision-making excellence. In other words, how does this technology turn insights into action and better decisions? How does it make every interaction count? Does it make my operations run more smoothly?

Action Item 4: Empower Employees with Flexible Processes, Accurate and Timely Information, and Easy-to-Use Tools

The customer experience edge requires a new focus on employee empowerment. In most cases, employees are motivated to satisfy customers' needs and desires, but they often do not have the technology tools, data access, or organizational standing to do so. Businesses need to provide their employees with information, such as customer order status, customer financial history, and product inventory levels, and with the tools required to respond to customer requests. Answering customer questions and providing speedy access to relevant information is a clear customer experience priority.

Furthermore, companies need to introduce process flexibility so that employees can handle exceptions and make decisions in real time. Tools must be easy to use and must be the right match for employees' jobs and roles.

At Synopsys, sales reps can alert customers to issues before those issues are even apparent to the customer. They can do this because the Synopsys field consultants set up notifications and subscriptions in the CRM system, so that the rep who is in charge of the account will know if an issue comes in via a different channel. For example, if three individuals from one customer have open issues, the sales rep might call the field application consultant to obtain relevant information about the account. As a result, Synopsys customers sometimes discover things they did not know about what their own colleagues on the other side of the world are doing.

Action Item 5: Adopt New Hiring and Training Practices for Support Personnel

An empowered workforce might require a different kind of employee, especially for customer-facing positions. Nearly any employee today can be an "agent of experience," meaning that she fulfills customer expectations and can even be a prime source of insight that can be fed back into product development, marketing, and customer service.

At Zappos, new customer service employees take an intensive four-week training course that immerses them in the company's culture and processes. At the end of their training, they are offered a $3,000 bonus to quit that day, with the idea being that only those who are truly passionate about the company's approach will stay. Synopsys staffs its customer call centers with electronics engineers, most of them with master's degrees, who have done chip design work at other companies, rather than with traditional service representatives. "We look for designers who like the people side of the business and recruit them," says Vito Mazzarino, vice president of field support operations. "It takes a special kind of person." CEMEX also works hard to hire the right people. Recently, the customer care team interviewed

200 candidates before hiring two new people. "We're looking for that service attitude," says Bontha.

Action Item 6: Segment Your Customers and Deliver Differentiated Experiences

Many of the companies profiled also segmented their customers, categorizing them based on their particular relationship with the company or on other measures, including lifetime value. The idea is to focus resources on the customers in the top tiers while providing relevant experiences to each tier. You can also work to get closer to the highest-value customers by learning about and even anticipating their needs. These customers are your most valuable, not only because they buy from you, but also because they value what you offer and think highly of your company. When you build trust with these customers over time, they become more likely to engage with you, tell you their needs, and even co-create innovative new products and services.

The LEGO Group has a fine-tuned customer segmentation strategy, and it engages with its "lead users" to incorporate the experiences and product features that these enthusiasts want to see into its new offerings. A select group of LEGO Ambassadors arranges events all over the world, attended by 2.5 million customers a year. In this way, the company's "lead users" demonstrate the brand's potential even more strongly than the company itself can.

Action Item 7: Ensure Multichannel Consistency

A dramatic shift for all companies has been the need to keep up with not just existing touch points, but also the new ones that are continually being created in digital channels. The customer experience edge requires an experience that is uniform across all channels—physical stores, the call center, the website, e-mail, chat, social media, social communities, and the like. These channels need to be synchronized with one another to ensure consistent data, such as pricing, product availability, and customer status information.

At Akbank, for instance, customers can visit an ATM, view an offer from the bank, learn more about the offer by clicking on a chat button, purchase the product, and receive a short message service (SMS) confirmation. In addition, if a customer walks into one of the bank's branches to discuss a problem with a service specialist, that person can later determine the status of the issue through any of the integrated contact channels. Similarly, CEMEX customers who prefer self-service via the Web can see exactly the same information that customer care agents see, including order status, invoice status, tickets issued, last 15 interactions, and pending support issues.

Action Item 8: Develop and Use New, Outside-In Metrics

Measuring how well your customer experience efforts are paying off is at the very heart of being a customer-focused organization. Many of the old metrics used to measure company performance don't tell you how you're doing from the customer's point of view. The key is to measure activities that drive customer value. The companies that we profiled are working to incorporate new metrics such as first-call resolution, number of unsolicited leads, and net promoter score.

At Cardinal Health, for instance, the CRM system itself measures key performance indicators such as "on-time delivery" and "ease of doing business with Cardinal," so the company can track trends and make needed modifications quickly. Additionally, Zappos has developed an employee dashboard to show people how they're doing from a cultural perspective and in terms of living up to the company's 10 core values, such as an "obsession" with customer service and bringing passion, fun, and a sense of adventure to the job. The customer experience edge requires that employees be compensated for driving outcomes, not just fulfilling a set of prescribed tasks.

Action Item 9: Move beyond B2B and B2C to P2P, or Peer-to-Peer

Many people equate the customer experience with business-to-consumer (B2C) companies, such as Netflix, Best Buy, and Apple. However, we've profiled several business-to-business (B2B) companies (Synopsys, CEMEX, and Cardinal Health, for example) that have honed their customer experience edge. B2B companies, like their B2C brethren, can no longer compete on new product offerings and lower prices alone, and they are just as susceptible to commoditization. It's just as important for these companies to become indispensable to their customer base; in fact, the impact of an inconsistent customer experience is potentially more damaging to them in terms of downstream implications. Consider the detrimental effects of mistimed deliveries, shipment delays, and incorrect quantities. Any time a supplier is unable to honor its contract commitments, this can lead to thousands of dollars in budget overruns because of labor costs, waste, or other avoidable costs.

Nearly everyone who uses a B2B product or service is also connected to the digital world. The ease of 24/7 information access has changed the dynamics between B2B companies and their customers. So, when it comes to the customer experience, there is less and less distinction between B2C and B2B. In fact, we should simply think in terms of P2P—people-to-people—or, as R. "Ray" Wang of Constellation Research calls it, peer-to-peer.

Action Item 10: Gather Customer Intelligence from Numerous Sources and Incorporate These Data into Your Processes and Your Product or Service Offerings

There are many ways to obtain customer insights by capturing solicited and unsolicited feedback, including social media monitoring; analysis of your own internal data; transactional surveys; and analyzing customer e-mails, chat sessions, blog commentaries, and calls into the call center. Companies need to take a three-pronged approach: create the mechanisms to listen to actual customers, analyze this feedback, and act on it.

Continually refreshing your insights into your customers enables you to align your efforts with their needs and desires. The key is to discover everything possible about your customers—psychographics as well as demographics.

At Dell, two Social Media Listening Command Centers—one at headquarters and one in China—coordinate and manage the company's response to 22,000 online customer conversations per day, in nine languages. Critical conversations are routed to one of the 7,000 social media–trained Dell employees, who have the technical expertise and language skills to respond. For example, an engineer who is designing laptop hinges can see conversations about hinge-related issues, while a shop floor manager might monitor conversations about the build quality of the products produced in his shop.

Action Item 11: Identify Your Customers' Moments of Truth and Excel at Them

Part of being customer-centric is seeing your company the way your customers do.

What does a customer go through in buying from you, from researching what he needs, deciding to purchase it from you, placing an order, receiving it, paying for it, and obtaining post-sale service? There are hundreds of these touch points that make up a customer journey. At each of these points, the customer can have either a negative or a positive impression of your company.

Companies that have honed the customer experience edge work to identify the most important touch points, sometimes called "moments of truth" or "trigger points." They then need to assess how well they perform during those key interactions and lay out a plan to fill the gaps and strengthen weak links. Classic examples are flight attendants handing out pizza during a delay on JetBlue Airways, which passengers continue to recount as a "moment of truth" that makes them think positively of the airline.

Once companies can consistently deliver a highly valuable, relevant, and cost-efficient experience at their high-impact touch points, they are on their way to establishing the customer experience edge. The rule of thumb is that for every two profoundly bad moments of truth, you need to outweigh them with three profoundly good ones.

Action Item 12: Design Processes from the Customer's Perspective, Not for Internal Efficiencies

Companies with the customer experience edge have analyzed their processes from the customer's perspective and redefined them with the customer in mind. They also realize that they can't always predetermine customers' behavior or train customers to take certain actions. For instance, even though they've developed a self-service component on their website, they still invest in their phone-based customer support, and vice versa.

Furthermore, they design their processes to accommodate things that go wrong. CEMEX, for instance, has a system that tracks abandoned calls and automatically generates a report that is routed to supervisors, who then call the person who hung up to see if they can help. Meanwhile, at Marriott, if a decline in a top-value customer's total revenue or number of reservations is detected, an agent calls or e-mails that customer to see if there are issues that need to be resolved.

These companies realize that recognizing and fixing a problem can actually lead to a higher degree of loyalty than if the problem had never happened.

Action Item 13: Have Clearly Stated Financial Goals as a Prominent Part of the Customer Experience Strategy

Improving the customer experience involves creating wins for your customers, but behind those customer-focused wins need to be financial goals for your company. Financial drivers can range from reducing customer churn, to acquiring new customers, to reducing the cost of sales, to decreasing the sales cycle. "It has to be something you can point to and say, 'We have moved the needle on either revenues or expenses," says Lior Arussy, president of Strativity Group, a customer experience research, strategy design, and implementation firm.

For all the talk among CE advocates of passion, obsession, and devotion to customers, embarking on a CE program cannot be backed by the idea that "if you build it, they will come." You need to have a clear sense of what your return is going to be.

Comcast, for instance, reduced its service calls by four million in the first four months of 2010 compared to 2009 as a result of its social media monitoring and follow-up response, which has translated into reduced operating expenses, according to the company. At Marriott, its repeat customers (Rewards members) account for half of the company's revenue, and an even smaller subsegment of its top-value customers, called Platinum members, provide a significant revenue base, according to Marriott.

Meanwhile, Synopsys attributes many cost efficiencies to its customer experience edge, such as a reduction in the amount of time that application consultants spend on reactive support from 33 percent to 20 percent. This enables the company to shift support to more accessible channels and leverage a broader global talent pool. And at Akbank, within six months of launching a centralized CRM system to support its customer experience strategy, the company sold 500,000 new products and had an increase of 200,000 new customers, a €2.2 million gain in gross profits, and a savings of €3.5 million in service costs.

Action Item 14: Think "Personalization"

In the future, the customer experience will involve providing customers with personalized treatment, personalized service, and even customized products. In financial services, customers are designing their own products and services, such as designing the layout of their mobile banking graphical user interface. In insurance, Progressive Insurance offers customers the option to pick their own monthly premium cost and coverage. In hospitality, Marriott call center agents have at their fingertips enough information about top customers' preferences that they can deliver a personalized experience. In the B2B world, CEMEX USA agents can identify incoming customer calls by their cell phone, home phone, and work phone. Customers are often routed automatically to the same agent that they spoke with in their last call, and Spanish speakers are routed to Spanish-speaking agents. "We want them to feel, 'CEMEX is doing this for *me*,'" says Bontha.

Action Item 15: Select New Technologies to Raise the Customer Experience Bar

The companies profiled continue to sharpen their customer experience edge through the use of new and emerging technologies, particularly as customers in both the B2B and B2C worlds are increasingly expecting to use social networking and mobile devices to make buying decisions, initiate and complete transactions, obtain information, and interact with companies. In customer experience surveys, business executives increasingly agree that technology now underpins and shapes the entire customer experience.

Best Buy, for example, announced new initiatives in 2010 to expand its mobile strategy, including increasing its SMS initiative and making more product information, customer reviews, and ratings available via mobile, such as through quick response (QR) codes.

It also launched a new mechanism for obtaining real-time customer feedback through store associates.

Similarly, The LEGO Group continues to fine-tune its customer experiences through technology. In addition to its in-depth and extensive customer interaction, The LEGO Group is also working to strengthen its online community, and future plans include making further use of sentiment analysis tools, as well as launching a Facebook page.

Surviving and growing in today's business environment is not for the meek, and there is simply no room in the global economy for any business that is unwilling to take bold steps to outsmart the competition. With newly empowered consumers, the battle is no longer about price and product offerings; there is a new battlefield, and it's all about the customer experience.

At the same time, there is little forgiveness for costly innovation that does not hold the promise of a measurable and profitable outcome. That is where smart technology choices come in. When you lay the right groundwork, you are freed from constantly having to ensure that the basics are operating correctly, so you can successfully make use of game-changing technologies to create a profitable, sustainable, flexible, and differentiating customer experience. That is the customer experience edge.

Businesses that cannot adapt to the new business realities that demand customer centricity will be faced at best with second-class status, and at worst with defeat. So, be bold—establish a strong vision, prepare your organization for constant change, execute iteratively, experiment as much as possible, and don't be afraid of small failures. Every journey starts with one step, and any step toward the customer experience edge is a step toward your future business success.

To continue reading about customer experience and to join in the discussion, please visit us at http://www.thecustomerexperienceedge .com.

The Customer Experience Edge and SAP

WHEN REZA, VINAY, AND VOLKER talked to us about their ideas for *The Customer Experience Edge*, we were more than just curious about the topic, and that is because we ourselves have been on a journey to consistently deliver a superior experience to the multitude of our own customers around the globe.

Indeed, several of the ideas in this book about providing a reliable, positive, and appropriate experience for customers are being used by SAP today. We have learned over time that we have to build and maintain our brand every day by exceeding our customers' expectations, since in today's world of aggressive global competitors, just meeting their expectations is not good enough. We have embarked on a journey to transform everything we do to deliver a unique customer experience—the SAP experience. We are aligning our organizations, job descriptions, individual objectives, communication strategy, sales engagement, and other activities to become truly customer focused.

It is easy to deliver a great customer experience to a select few—for example, to your top 100 customers. However, that is not the SAP promise to our customers. Our promise is to make every business, no matter what size it is or where in the world it is situated, a better-run business. So, we have the challenge of delivering a superior customer experience to every one of our valued customers every day. The only way we have been able to scale up and deliver this promise is by leveraging technology. Strategic use of technology is the secret sauce that is enabling us to deliver on our brand promise to our more than 100,000 customers and millions of users worldwide so that they can operate profitably, adapt continuously, and grow sustainably.

We embrace and support our customers through traditional channels and online and physical communities, listen to our customers and prospects, and co-innovate with our customers to build the next generation of SAP solutions. Our online SAP Community Network has grown to more than two million regular participants. We have also transformed our annual customer conference, SAPPHIRE NOW, so that it is highly interactive and relevant to the more than 60,000 participants who are either on site or participating remotely. We engage actively through social media channels like Twitter and Facebook. We continually strive to deliver a unique experience—the SAP experience.

SAP today does more than deliver software solutions for our customers. Our solution experts, customer communities, employees, and partners have become a trusted advisory network to solve complex business problems. This broader role is widely acknowledged, as evidenced by the doubling of our brand value in the past 10 years and our becoming the third most recognized German brand in the world. In the process, we're also helping the world run better.

It all begins by focusing on providing the best customer experience consistently to everyone, every time. This is why the customer experience edge is so important. We hope that you have found some valuable nuggets of information from the various discussions and case studies in this book that you can apply to your particular situation. While you may find that there are several things you could do at the same time, it is often best to start by focusing on a few key issues, addressing them successfully, then taking on the next few things, and so on. Taking a bite-sized approach gives you more flexibility and more control over the outcomes. Achieving the customer experience edge is a continuous journey, not a one-time project.

—Jonathan Becher, chief marketing officer, SAP

—Anthony Leaper, senior vice president and general manager for sales, marketing and service solutions, SAP

Bloomberg Businessweek Research Services North American Survey on Customer Service Experience: Survey Questionnaire and Methodology

Background Information on the Customer Experience Surveys (North American)

Bloomberg Businessweek Research Services (BBRS) launched a survey and research program in late 2010 to discover and analyze the views of C-level and line-of-business executives in North America on customer experience. The research sought to determine these executives' perceptions of the importance of creating competitive differentiation by providing powerful customer experience, thus growing the business.

The research also sought to identify the importance of technology as a tool to maintain or even improve customer experience.

The specific goals of this program included:

- Determining the level of recognition of the importance of a positive customer experience.

- Defining the elements of a positive customer experience that contributes to the financial well-being of the company offering that experience.

- Identifying the challenges of developing and maintaining a positive customer experience for the long term while increasing profits.

- Understanding the technological foundation for a positive and profitable customer experience.

- Determining the impact of new technologies on the customer experience, such as data analytics, social media and mobile computing.

This research program included both quantitative and qualitative components:

- A survey of director-level or above executives at large and midsize B2B and B2C companies in North America who are members of the Bloomberg Businessweek Market Advisory Board, an online panel of 25,000 business executives. A total of 307 director-, vice president-, and C-level executives responded to the December 2010 survey. The demographics of the respondents are as follows:

By title:

- 24 percent were C-level executives, such as chief executive officer, chief financial officer, chief information officer, chief operating officer, president, board member, or board chair.

- 39 percent were either a vice president or director.

- 37 percent were an executive vice president, senior vice president, or general manager.

By company size:

- 40 percent were from companies with at least $5 billion in annual revenues.

- 20 percent were from companies with at least $1 billion but less than $5 billion in revenues.

- 17 percent had revenues of at least $200 million but less than $500 million.

- 14 percent had revenues of at least $500 million but less than $1 billion.

By industry:

- 28 percent from manufacturers.

- 18 percent from financial services.

- 11 percent from business services.

- 8 percent from healthcare, including pharmaceutical makers.

- 5 percent were retailers or wholesalers.

- 30 percent were from other industries, including utilities, transportation, government, and education.

- A poll of 1,004 senior managers and directors from companies with at least $500 million in annual revenues. Two-thirds of those responding to the poll were at the vice president and executive levels. Approximately 30 percent of the respondents were from the United States, 30 percent from Europe, 30 percent from Asia, and 10 percent from the rest of the world. The industry sector representation was similar to the survey of North American executives noted above.

- In-depth telephone interviews with C-level and other senior executives at large and midsize companies. The companies involved include:

    - Arizona Cardinals Football Club

    - Cardinal Health

    - CEMEX

    - Citi

    - Coop

    - Colmobil Corp.

    - Comcast

    - Disney Institute

    - The LEGO Group

    - Marriott International Inc.

    - Reliant Energy

    - Synopsys

    - Verizon Wireless

- Interviews with leading independent consultants, industry analysts, and academics, in addition to survey data from research firms, to provide context and additional insights. The experts include individuals from the following firms:

    - Beagle Research Inc.

    - Constellation Research, Inc.

    - Convergys

    - Deloitte Consulting

    - Diamond Advisory Services at PricewaterhouseCoopers

- Forrester Research Inc.

- David Gardner, Mass-customization-expert

- Great Brook Consulting

- Live Path

- Patricia Seybold Group

- Peppers & Rogers Group

- Smith+co

- Strativity Group

- TARP Worldwide

- Temkin Group

- Charles Patti, University of Denver

Triangle Publishing Services Co. Inc. supported BBRS in the development of the survey questionnaires, in addition to providing the in-depth telephone interviews and the writing, editing, and production of five reports. BBRS and the authors of these reports, Lauren Gibbons Paul, Mary Brandel, and Bill Roberts, are grateful to all of the executives who provided their time and insight for this project.

This research project was funded by a grant from SAP but was written independently of this sponsor. The editorial department of Bloomberg Businessweek magazine was not involved in this project.

Five research reports and four case studies were developed based on the surveys and in-depth interviews. They will be available on the website for *The Customer Experience Edge*. To review the reports, please visit this website:

www.thecustomerexperienceedge.com

Bloomberg Businessweek Research Services Report on the Value of Global Integration: The Right Foundation for Growing Global

LANDMARK RESEARCH REVEALS new insights into the real business value of integrated business applications, including cost reductions, data visibility, and net income increases.

Excerpts from an exclusive survey and research report from Bloomberg Businessweek Research Services.

Executive Summary

Not too long ago, the idea of "globalizing" was the exclusive concern of large companies with widespread operations. In today's new world economy, everyone is looking to get into the global game, with countries like China, India, and Brazil growing at two and three times the rate of established economies.

Based on the remarkable findings of a worldwide survey of more than 1,000 executives, one of the key strategies for becoming a truly global player is suddenly clear: creating a global operating model supported by a foundation of integrated financial, customer relationship management, human capital management (HCM), and other business applications. A decided majority of respondents—a whopping 89 percent—intends to increase application integration in 2011. And no wonder: In the survey, a clear link was established between integrated applications and cost savings, in addition to a positive impact on net income benefit.

As large and midsize companies alike work toward global growth, they are realizing they need to adopt a global operating model, in addition to unified, standardized and integrated applications to support that model. Of course, there are barriers to overcome with global application integration, and a substantial number of survey respondents noted this challenge. But the future is clear: Integrated applications have become a prerequisite for success, whether your company operates in three countries or 30. The way to grow globally is to build a global operating model and an integrated platform to support it.

This research report provides new insights, examples and research on how integrated financial customer relationship management and HCM applications are crucial if large and midsize companies are to emerge as truly global players. Key findings include:

- More than half of respondents with tightly integrated applications (51 percent) report a substantial positive impact on net income.

- Cost savings are a top benefit of an integrated platform. A majority of respondents (58 percent) reduced operational costs, while nearly half of those with tightly integrated applications (49 percent) lowered IT costs.

- Most organizations claim moderate levels of integration (3.4 on a scale of 1 to 5), and only a small subset (11 percent) report having tightly integrated applications.

- Few respondents (18 percent) have achieved integrated end-to-end processes, and less than half (45 percent) have an enterprisewide view of data. Those with tight integration say it is easy to obtain a consolidated view of enterprise data.

- Most respondents (74 percent) have at least half their enterprise applications from a single vendor, while one-third (37 percent) claim they will replace best-of-breed applications with an integrated suite.

Methodology

Bloomberg Businessweek Research Services (BBRS) launched a survey and research program in mid-2010 to discover and analyze the views of C-level and line-of-business executives around the world on enterprise application integration.

The goals of this program included:

- Determining the current state of application integration.

- Identifying which business applications are the most important for integration.

- Discovering respondents' plans to achieve tighter integration.

- Defining the business value expected and realized from application integration.

Methodology

This research program included both quantitative and qualitative components:

- A global survey of director-level or above executives at large and midsize companies who are members of the Bloomberg Businessweek Market Advisory Board, an online panel of 25,000 business executives. A total of 1,004 director-, vice president-, and C-level executives responded to the November 2010 survey.

Here is more information about the demographics of the survey:

Titles:

- 42% of the respondents were executive or senior vice presidents or general managers

- 34% of the respondents were C-level executives (CEO, CFO, CIO, CMO, COO, etc.)

- 24% were directors or vice presidents

Company size:

- 59% were from companies with at least $1 billion in annual revenue

- 41% were from companies with $500–$999.9 million in annual revenue

Region:

- 30% from the U.S.

- 30% from Europe

- 30% from Asia

- 10% from the rest of the world

Industry:

- 21% from financial services

- 16% from manufacturing

- 12% from business services

- 10% from computer/internet/software development

- 6% from nonprofits

- 6% from healthcare/pharmaceuticals

- 5% from telecom

- 5% from advertising/pr media

- 5% from construction/engineering/architecture

- 14% other

- In-depth telephone interviews with C-level and other senior executives at the following large and midsize companies:

  - Arcelor Mittal Temirtau

  - Bodal Chemicals

  - Charles and Maness Investments

  - International American Group (IAG)

  - Lorbec Metals

  - Merck Sharp & Dohme, a subsidiary of Merck & Co.

  - Nelsen China

  - Platinum Holdings Co.

  - A diversified, worldwide manufacturing and technology company

  - An IT services group

  - The retail arm of a diversified corporation

- Interviews with leading independent consultants, industry analysts, and academics, in addition to survey data from research firms, to provide context and additional insights. The experts include individuals from the following firms:

  - The Hackett Group (thehackettgroup.com), a global consulting firm and leader in providing data and advice on business best practices and benchmarking

- Human Capital Collaborative (HC3)

Triangle Publishing Services Co. Inc. supported BBRS in the development of the survey questionnaire, in addition to providing the in-depth telephone interviews and the writing, editing, and production of the following research report. BBRS and the author of this report, Bill Roberts, are grateful to all of the executives who provided their time and insights for this project.

This research project was funded by a grant from SAP but was written independently of this sponsor. The editorial department of *Bloomberg Businessweek* magazine was not involved in this project.

The report will also be available on the website for *The Customer Experience Edge*. To review it, please visit this website: www .thecustomerexperienceedge.com.

Introduction

A German machine-tool manufacturer builds a factory in China to achieve low-cost production for its major markets in Europe and Japan. A U.S. computer company launches a call center in India to provide cost-effective support to American customers. A UK consumer goods producer opens a sales office in Brazil, knowing there is not much of a market—yet.

Do these strategies sound familiar? They are examples of what executives used to mean when they uttered the words, "going global." Onsite managers who have profit-and-loss responsibility and a lot of autonomy run the plant, the call center, and the sales office. Corporate executives need basic financial data—a spreadsheet sent by e-mail suffices—but otherwise, "just send the money."

Today, going global means something entirely different. The factory has grown into a worldwide strategic network of plants, with a supply chain crisscrossing continents. The computer company is opening R&D centers in Eastern Europe and China to tap new pools of talent and harness round-the-clock product development. Brazil has exploded into a huge market for the consumer goods producer, as have several other growth economies.

Managing in this truly global environment requires much more than the e-mail and spreadsheets that so many companies still rely upon. It demands a global operating model, with integrated enterprise applications to support it. Over the next few years, companies will transition from merely "going global" to "growing the global operating model." In other words, they will standardize on a worldwide basis and integrate the policies, standards, processes, definitions, and information technology (IT) to support access to the data and analytics that allow agile decision-making anywhere, anytime.

Some among the new breed of global companies already have made progress toward integrating their applications—from financials to supply chain management to CRM to human capital management (HCM). And those that have achieved tight integration report surprisingly robust benefits, including a substantial impact on net income, according to groundbreaking findings from a worldwide survey by Bloomberg Businessweek Research Services (BBRS). Most respondents say there is a clear link between improved net income and the timely and accurate data insights gleaned from tightly integrated applications (see Figure B.1, "Timely and Accurate Data Drives Net Income").

Another resounding win of an integrated platform is reduced costs. More than half of all respondents (58 percent) reduced operational costs by integrating applications, while nearly half of those with tightly integrated applications (49 percent) lowered IT costs.

The survey, based on responses from 1,004 executives worldwide, reveals many other new insights into how enterprise application integration is a key success factor for companies moving to a global operating model.

Application integration reduces costs and provides more transparency, better decision-making, and more timely and accurate insights, all of which contribute to positive income statement bene-

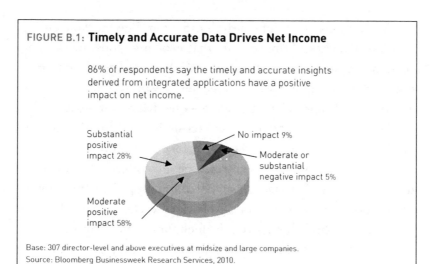

FIGURE B.1: **Timely and Accurate Data Drives Net Income**

86% of respondents say the timely and accurate insights derived from integrated applications have a positive impact on net income.

Substantial positive impact 28%

No impact 9%

Moderate or substantial negative impact 5%

Moderate positive impact 58%

Base: 307 director-level and above executives at midsize and large companies.
Source: Bloomberg Businessweek Research Services, 2010.

fits. In fact, application integration is at the top of most respondents' priority lists, with 89 percent planning to improve integration in 2011 (see Figure B.2, "Much Integration in Coming Year").

FIGURE B.2: **Much Integration in Coming Year**

When asked about integration plans, only 11% of respondents plan to do nothing, with the remaining 89% naming a variety of activities.*

Question: How do you plan to improve integration in the next 12 months?

For new applications, continuing the standardization process of our solutions portfolio by reducing the number of application vendors	39%
For existing applications, considering replacing existing disparate solutions with an integrated suite from one vendor	37%
For existing applications, adding funding to develop additional integration points	30%
Investing in new IT architectures such as service-oriented architecture	28%
Moving existing or new applications to SaaS or cloud computing	21%
No additional actions planned	11%

*Respondents could select two responses, so totals do not add up to 100%.
Base: 1,004 director-level or above executives at large and midsize companies worldwide.
Source: Bloomberg Businessweek Research Services, 2010.

Michel Janssen, chief research officer at The Hackett Group, a business advisory firm, concurs that evolving global markets are "causing companies to rethink the way they operate, moving from operating on the international basis they've worked under forever to a more global approach to managing—one that requires data visibility they've not had in the past." As a result, he says, "policy and standards are being revamped and tech platforms transformed."

The Hackett Group's own research also offers substantial evidence of this trend. A Hackett survey of top executives at 175 multi-billion-dollar global companies—provided exclusively to BBRS for this analysis—finds similar trends, including plans to move rapidly toward the global operating model in the next two years by applying the global approach to everything from policy and strategy standards to customer service to HCM processes to software platforms.

Barriers to Integration

- Although enterprise application integration is the technological key to the global operating model, the BBRS survey finds that only a small subset of respondents (11 percent) consider their applications and data to be tightly integrated. This group of 110 respondents will be referred to throughout this research report as the "tight integration group" (see Figure B.3).

For overall respondents, the resulting weaknesses are apparent. Consider the following:

- Only the tight integration group reports data flows and processes that operate flawlessly.

- About 1 in 10 respondents say enterprise data is all online and either easy to find or automatically delivered.

- Less than half of the executives report having an enterprise wide view and the ability to analyze data.

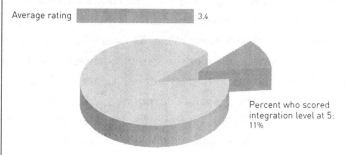

FIGURE B.3: **Tight Integration Group**

When asked to describe the current level of integration from their organization's various operating and line departments, most respondents give a mediocre rating. However, 11% give the highest score available.

Scale of 1 to 5, with 1 being "our systems barely communicate with each other, and data routinely has to be reentered numerous times" and 5 being "tightly integrated—our data flows and processes operate flawlessly."

Average rating   3.4

Percent who scored integration level at 5: 11%

Base: 1,004 director-level or above executives at large and midsize companies worldwide.
Source: Bloomberg Businessweek Research Services, 2010

- By far, the tightest application integration is found in finance, with fewer respondents reporting integrated supplier relationship management, customer relationship management (CRM), and talent management applications. This is slated to change in the next two years.

Some companies and entire industries are closer than others to achieving a global operating model. One industry example is electronics manufacturing services. Companies like Sanmina-SCI and Jabil Circuits, which have factories, suppliers, design centers and OEM customers around the world, were forced earlier than most to achieve greater visibility through tighter application and data integration by using standard processes and platforms.

"What is changing is the need to manage beyond the local geography," The Hackett Group's Janssen says. "The trick is not to go too far. You have to manage globally, but you have to do some things locally—pay, holidays, etc. The difference might be subtle, but it goes to where spend decisions get made and for what purpose."

Consider the flow of information. Companies that are 'internationally managed' may not have fully integrated platforms for the consolidation of worldwide financials or other operating information—revenue, expenses, inventory, staffing, etc. Their information flows happen in a fragmented way, with no way to easily consolidate data or drill down seamlessly on all of the required information for truly informed decision-making. There may be additional local P&L views based on product and/or business unit, but they are not the primary mechanism for decision-making, Janssen says. "In the 'internationally managed' company, most of the spend is managed locally or regionally, with separate marketing strategies, separate sales staffs, separate customer service and separate corporate support functions."

The global operating model, on the other hand, emphasizes the product or service from a more holistic global information and delivery model perspective. If a company is building a technology widget destined to be a global product, it needs "to be managed based on the global revenues and expenses for that product," Janssen says. "There is a global roll-out timeline, a global marketing budget (with a component for local spend), a global product support staff, global customer service (with local language support) and a global view of the success or failure." That is the view many companies simply do not have today (see Figure B.4, "Few Have Enterprise View").

"To accomplish that, companies must be able to break down the business by region, division, country, sub-country business unit, channel, product, or customer segment," says Martin Kuhn, the Australia-based executive director for strategic marketing operations and commercial support for the Asia-Pacific region of Merck Sharp & Dohme (MSD). MSD is a subsidiary of Merck & Co., a $27.4 billion pharmaceutical company.

Regionally and globally, Merck has traveled far along the path to application integration and, as such, is well aware of both the promises and difficulties of this endeavor—particularly for a large company that has grown through acquisitions. It is in the midst of rolling out standard back-office financials and currently has a global inte-

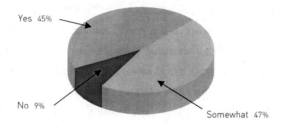

FIGURE B.4: **Few Have Enterprise View**

Less than half of respondents say that executives and managers have an enterprisewide view of data.

Question: Do executives or managers have an enterprisewide view and ability to analyze operating and historical data?

Yes 45%

No 9%

Somewhat 47%

* Total exceeds 100% due to rounding.

Base: 1,004 director-level or above executives at large and midsize companies worldwide.
Source: Bloomberg Businessweek Research Services, 2010.

grated digital assets system, a global HCM platform, and a regional data warehouse to overcome some of the integration issues. "Usually you can get a vertical slice of the business or a horizontal slice by type of spend," Kuhn says. "The weakness with this type of breakdown is that you cannot cost projects or activities well." Most commercial ERP systems have sub-code features that allow companies to set up product or project codes so spend can be viewed that way, he notes.

Kuhn says his region has P&L by business units that roll up to the country and then to the region. His group also is working on developing an accurate P&L by product within a country or regional roll-up. The additional capabilities will improve pricing and resource allocation decisions, Kuhn notes.

A Need for Visibility

One classic example of the data visibility problem is the executive who cannot get an accurate headcount or cash flow figure because the company has different systems in each region. "In our research, we asked about cash forecasting, and the spreadsheet is still the number-one tool," The Hackett Group's Janssen says, despite the fact that most accounting software can automate cash forecasting, he adds.

With more than 10 systems in his Asia-Pacific region, visibility is an issue MSD's Kuhn contends with. "If I wanted to know key customers—the key accounts—across a brand in the region, I can't do that straight out of the system."

"I can't even extract good sales data in terms of number of units, what price you sold for, and connect that to the customer," he says. Some of the systems are from the same vendor, but they are operating as separate instances, Kuhn says. Merck's Asia-Pacific region has embarked on a large data warehouse project to resolve the issue.

Lack of visibility impacts line managers, too. Miguel Ramirez is the MIS manager for a plant in Guadalajara, Mexico, one of more than 200 factories owned by a diversified worldwide manufacturing and technology company. The firm was trying to integrate with a single ERP vendor globally. But "with the economic situation last year," Ramirez says, "the project was postponed and does not appear to be resuming in 2011." With better integration, he adds, "we would save money on IT maintenance and administration. We would probably have more expertise in IT as a company and get better and faster at solving problems."

The financials are integrated globally and some sales information is visible across the company, but "we don't share parts or inventory information with other plants," Ramirez says. "We have an interface with suppliers but not among ourselves. Too often, we try to solve our problems with spreadsheets."

Kuhn and Ramirez are not alone. In the BBRS survey, 56 percent of respondents agree that while data about raw transactions flows through their companies' financials, sales, operational, or HR systems, they do not function as a group of integrated end-to-end processes. Respondents from large companies are more likely to use a combination of automation and manual data crunching, while mid-size companies are more likely to have an enterprisewide view with automated processes. However, even many midsize companies are not where they want to be.

Intent to Integrate

Testimonials like those corroborate another BBRS survey finding. When respondents were asked how concerned they are about the level of integration of enterprise applications and data at their organizations, the average response is 3.64 on a scale of 1 to 5. The mode (the most common response) is also telling: 6 out of 10 respondents rate their concern as a 5.

The vast majority (89 percent) says they plan some integration activity in the next 12 months. One in five will look to integration solutions from cloud computing and software as a service (SaaS). More than one in three is considering replacing disparate systems with an integrated suite from one vendor. (More than two-thirds already have at least half of their enterprise apps from a single vendor.)

Lorbec Metals is consolidating from three ERP systems to one at its six sites, says Jay Goldstein, president of the privately held scrap-metal recycling business, with operations in North America and sales of reprocessed metals worldwide. "We will be able to see what is going on in each location, what is in inventory, make joint decisions on sales and purchase jointly what we need for our order book."

Integration challenges are ever present at privately held International American Group (IAG), says CEO Chris Bylander. IAG owns various worldwide companies in computer manufacturing, telecommunications, and consumer goods, with operations in 90 countries and more than $1 billion in revenues. "In a perfect world, we would want our enterprise applications to be uniform across all holdings. However, it is easier said than done," he says.

For example, when IAG bought several rival companies in similar markets, management's impulse was to integrate the old and new tools at the acquired companies. However, "those operating under the old had no depreciations left, which hurt cash flow," Bylander says. "Those operating under the new had them but were undercapitalized. In both cases, we would have to infuse capital."

The solution: "We started from a clean slate. It became a single new project, which spoke to our desire to engage with just one systems vendor," he says.

The $450 million retail arm of a diversified corporation in India took the opposite approach but achieved tight integration, according to Arun Gupta, group chief technology officer. Gupta relies on a few vendors for most of his applications, with a small and select group of best-of-breed tools layered on top. One of these tools is a B2B Web portal now used by 99 percent of the company's 2,300 suppliers. His staff builds the integration points and, a few years ago, installed a data warehouse for the enterprisewide view of data that management needs from and among its 100 locations across India. "We are very tightly integrated," Gupta says.

"We deal with five or six technology partners," he says. "When we consider new technology, after functionality and price, the next thing we look at is integration. We need to be able to resolve it internally or by working with the vendor."

Merck's data warehouse project is its solution to integrating the various systems through the Asia-Pacific region. The original idea was to tackle this integration globally. "When we looked at 90 countries, and the connectivity and complexity in each region, it just couldn't be done," Kuhn says. "That didn't stop people from trying. But after a few false starts, we had to agree it was best to work within certain geographies."

In other cases, Merck has achieved global integrated systems. "We manage digital assets in one system globally," he says. "About 50 or 60 percent of material—promotional, brand image, clinical information—is generated globally and then adapted and modified, or what we call 'derivative,' locally." Merck is rolling out standard back-office financials. "The data model in each instance will be similar or exact," Kuhn says.

Top Benefits: Cost Savings, Net Income Boost

World economic developments are driving the need for the global operating model. After weathering the recession better than most, China, Brazil and India account for an increasingly larger portion of the world economy. According to the International Monetary Fund, each expects gross domestic product (GDP) growth of more than 6 percent in 2011—9.6 percent for China. Other emerging markets also are growing quickly, but China, Brazil, and India are the most significant due to their respective rankings as the No. 2, No. 8, and No. 11 economies, based on GDP. When these economies mattered less, most companies did not pursue a global operating model because "they didn't have the need," The Hackett Group's Janssen says. "Once China, Brazil and others became a bigger part of the whole, they became important in this regard. We reached the tipping point where they matter."

Consider how Merck's geographical sales are changing. In 2007, 39 percent were outside the U.S.; in 2008, it was 44 percent; and in 2009, sales outside of the U.S. were 49 percent of the total, according to Merck's 10-K for the fiscal year ended Dec. 31, 2009. "As a result of the [Schering-Plough] merger, Merck has expanded its operations in countries located in Latin America, the Middle East, Africa, Eastern Europe and the Asia-Pacific region. Business in these developing areas, while sometimes less stable, offers important opportunities for growth over time," the 10-K says.

The changing priorities require the characteristics of a global operating model, and this is implicit in BBRS survey respondents' answers about the factors that drive integration investments. Asked for reasons they undertake integration efforts, "agility and faster response times," "operational process improvement" and "free up knowledge workers" are top responses. The tight integration group differs a bit from the whole. "IT cost savings" is more important for this group than it is for the total sample, whereas "free up knowledge workers" is less so.

As for the actual benefits of integration, the tight integration group has a different view of the benefits achieved vs. those who merely aspire to that state. While just over a third of the entire sample anticipates reduced IT costs, for instance, nearly half of the tight integration group (49 percent) says they have achieved that goal and name it as the most important benefit. IT cost savings appear to be fully realized only after achieving tight integration. Overall, however, a big win of an integrated platform is reduced costs, with more than half of all respondents reducing operational costs by integrating applications (58 percent) (see Figure B.5, "Top Realized Benefits from Application Integration").

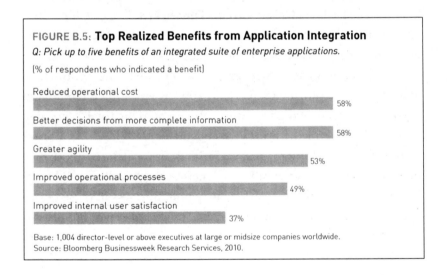

FIGURE B.5: **Top Realized Benefits from Application Integration**
Q: Pick up to five benefits of an integrated suite of enterprise applications.
(% of respondents who indicated a benefit)

Reduced operational cost — 58%

Better decisions from more complete information — 58%

Greater agility — 53%

Improved operational processes — 49%

Improved internal user satisfaction — 37%

Base: 1,004 director-level or above executives at large or midsize companies worldwide.
Source: Bloomberg Businessweek Research Services, 2010.

In addition, more of the overall group of respondents (58 percent) thinks they achieve better decision-making capabilities from more complete information vs. the tight integration group (39 percent). Perhaps the difficulty of measuring "better decisions" becomes evident only after tight integration has been achieved. Other acknowledged benefits are similar between the two groups.

Remarkably, 86 percent of respondents report a positive impact on net income from the ability to obtain timely and accurate insights about operational or historical business process data. Among the tight integration group, the response is even more resounding—with more than half realizing a substantial positive impact on net income.

The tight integration group notes a number of other net income driving benefits. For instance, they derive greater benefit to net income from tightly integrated SRM, CRM, and PLM processes.

Research by The Hackett Group's Janssen suggests that general and administrative (G&A) cost savings are possible from the finance, HR, IT, and procurement departments when an organization adopts a global operating model. He finds that a typical Global 1000 company—$26.6 billion in revenue and 67,000 employees—can save between 25 percent and 42 percent of G&A.

Comments from the survey respondents indicate both tangible and intangible benefits:

- At the Indian retailer, overall IT visibility has helped the company work with partners to improve gross margins by 1 percentage point and reduce selling, general, and administrative (SG&A) costs by 3 percentage points in the last three years, Gupta says. "In the last four years, we doubled our size, while manpower in the back office increased only 20 percent," he says. "And, the CEO can look at each store by product category."

- At IAG, clear net income benefits have been primarily realized when a new project has been initiated, Bylander says. It is not so much a function of accrual of benefits as it is of starting from a clean slate. "Virgin projects create fewer problems, saving man-hours initially and additional integration costs going forward," he says. "At each new, or higher, level of system integration we have won a bottom-line victory. It has not always come from lower operating costs or a smaller maintenance burden. We were surprised to find that our employee confidence grew and gave them pride, much as they might when trading in an old Ford for a new Cadillac."

Conclusion and Recommendations

A global operating model, based on an integrated application foundation, is a prerequisite for success and for thriving in today's new world economy. Clearly, the only way to grow in this environment is to have not just a global focus but also an integrated foundation of policies, processes and applications to support it.

According to new data, an integrated foundation also results in the following benefits:

- **Net income boost.** Over half of respondents with tightly integrated applications report a positive impact on net income. A majority (86 percent) says the timely and accurate insights achieved through integration improve net income.

- **Reduced costs.** More than half of all respondents reduced operational costs with integrated applications, while nearly half of those with tightly integrated applications (49 percent) lowered IT costs.

With a global operating model, Hackett Group's Janssen argues, decisions must be made quickly when it comes to redeploying resources, and this requires visibility into knowing where those resources are, how many you have, and what they are capable of doing. "Truly global means to have a set of enterprise strategies that allow you to make decisions in all parts of the organization, wherever they are," Janssen says. "You can have an enterprise strategy, but without integrated applications, you can't make the most effective decisions."

Notes

Quoted material that is not referenced is from personal interviews.

Introduction

1. Jon Stokes, "Lawsuit: Dell Knowingly Shipped 12 Million Faulty Computers," *ARS Technica*, 2010, http://arstechnica.com/business/news/2010/06/suit-alleges-that-dell-shipped-12-million-faulty-computers.ars; Michael Krigsman, "Dell Lawsuit: Pattern of Deceit," *ZDNet*, June 30, 2010, http://www.zdnet.com/blog/projectfailures/dell-lawsuit-pattern-of-deceit/10165; Ashlee Vance, "Suit over Faulty Computers Highlights Dell's Decline," *New York Times*, June 28, 2010, http://www.nytimes.com/2010/06/29/technology/29dell.html?pagewanted=2&_r=1.
2. Dan Ackerman, "Costco Kills Return Anytime Policy," *CNET*, February 27, 2007, http://news.cnet.com/8301-17938_105-9691796-1.html.

Chapter 1

1. Bloomberg Businessweek Research Services conducted two surveys in late 2010 to determine the views of C-level and line-of-business executives on the customer experience. In one survey of 307 U.S. respondents, nearly half (48 percent) said that improving customer experience was one of their company's three highest priorities for 2011. An additional third (33 percent) ranked it among the top five. In a second survey of 1,004 global respondents, 80 percent said that getting closer to customers and providing them with a differentiated experience was a top strategic objective.
2. Timothy H. Hannan, "Consumer Switching Costs and Firm Pricing: Evidence from Bank Pricing of Deposit Accounts," Federal Reserve Board, May 12, 2008, http://www.federalreserve.gov/pubs/feds/2008/200832/200832pap.pdf.
3. Lisa DiCarlo, "Dell Satisfaction Rating Takes a Deep Dive," *Forbes.com*, August 16, 2005, http://www.forbes.com/2005/08/16/dell-customersatisfaction-falls-cx_ld_0816dell.html.
4. Jeff Jarvis, "Dell Learns to Listen," *Bloomberg Businessweek*, October 17, 2007, http://www.businessweek.com/bwdaily/dnflash/content/oct2007/db20071017_277576.htm.

Chapter 3

1. Ashwin Nayan Rai, "From Brick to Click: E-Commerce Trends in Industrial Manufacturing," Cognizant Technology Solutions, 2010, http://www.cognizant.com/InsightsWhitepapers/From-Brick-to-Click.pdf.
2. "SAP Helps Companies of All Sizes Become Customer-Centric Businesses," SAP press release, August 3, 2010, http://www.sap.com/solutions/business-suite/crm/newsevents/press.epx?pressid=13707.
3. Lior Arussy, "Creating Customer Experience in B2B Relationships," Global Customer Experience Management Organization, http://www.g-cem.org/eng/content_details.jsp?contentid=2203&subjectid=107.
4. Richard Tait, "What's Different About the B2B Customer Experience," blog post, August 16, 2010, http://winningcustomerexperiences.wordpress.com/2010/08/16/whats-different-about-the-b2b-customer-experience/.

Chapter 4

1. "Three Secrets of Success for Customer Experience Organizations," Forrester Research, Inc., April 29, 2010, www.forrester.com/rb/Research/three_secrets_of_success_for_customer_experience/q/id/55871/t/2.
2. Tony Hsieh, "Your Culture is Your Brand," *Huffington Post*, November 17, 2010, http://www.huffingtonpost.com/tony-hsieh/zappos-founder-tony-hsieh_1_b_783333.html.
3. Keith McFarland, "Why Zappos Offers New Hires $2,000 to Quit," *Bloomberg Businessweek*, September 16, 2008, http://www.businessweek.com/smallbiz/content/sep2008/sb20080916_288698.htm.
4. "Big Think Interview with Tony Hsieh," BigThink.com, October 11, 2010, http://bigthink.com/ideas/24388.
5. "Customers Trust Real Friends and Virtual Strangers the Most," Nielsen Global Online Consumer Survey, NielsenWire, July 7, 2009, http://blog.nielsen.com/nielsenwire/consumer/global-advertising-consumers-trust-real-friends-and-virtual-strangers-the-most/. The study surveyed more than 25,000 Internet consumers in 50 countries.
6. Rebecca Reisner, "Comcast's Twitter Man," *Bloomberg Businessweek*, January 13, 2009, http://www.businessweek.com/managing/content/jan2009/ca20090113_373506.htm.
7. Rick Germano, "Your Call Is Important to Us," *Comcast Voices* blog, November 5, 2010, http://blog.comcast.com/2010/11/your-call-is-important-to-us.html#more.
8. Barney Beal, "NPS, Follow-Up Helps SONY Canada Improve Customer Experience," *SearchCRM.com*, May 20, 2010, http://searchcrm.techtarget.com/news/2240018770/NPS-follow-up-helps-Sony-Canada-improve-customer-experience.
9. Derek Kreindler, "Saab to Let Customers Watch Their Cars Get Built via Webcam," *AutoGuide.com*, October 18, 2010, http://www.autoguide.com/auto-news/2010/10/saab-to-let-customers-watch-their-cars-get-built-via-webcam.html.
10. "Introducing Boutiques: A New Way to Shop for Fashion Online," Google blog, November 17, 2010, http://googleblog.blogspot.com/2010/11/introducing-boutiques-new-way-to-shop.html.
11. http://www.reebok.com/US/custom-shoes/mens/listing?f.ProductId=50.
12. *Cognizanti Journal*, vol. 4, no. 1, March 2011, http://itunes.apple.com/us/book/cognizanti-journal-volume/id426466251?mt=11.
13. Lauren Gibbons Paul, "Made to Order," *Managing Automation*, November 3, 2006, http://www.managingautomation.com/maonline/magazine/read/view/Made_to_Order_917515.

Chapter 5

1. Paul Hagen, "The Right Customer Experience Strategy," http://blogs.forrester.com/paul_hagen/10-10-05-the_right_customer_experience_strategy.
2. "What Is the Right Customer Experience Strategy?" Forrester Research, Inc., September 28, 2010, www.forrester.com/rb/Research/what_is_right_customer_experience_strategy/q/id/57673/t/2.
3. Norm Brodsky, "Learning from JetBlue," *Inc. Magazine*, March 2, 2004. http://www.inc.com/magazine/20040301/nbrodsky.html.
4. http://www.pkwy.k12.mo.us/homepage/theller/File/Best_Buy.pptx.
5. Andrew McInnes, "Customers' Problems Are Companies' Loyalty-Building Opportunities," Forrester Research, Inc., blog, December 6, 2010, http://tinyurl.com/3bq8gxa.

Chapter 6

1. Bloomberg Businessweek Research Services survey, 2010.

2. Shaun Smith, "The Eight Brand Traits Separating the Best from the Rest," *mycustomer* *.com*, March 7, 2011, http://www.mycustomer.com/topic/customer-intelligence/shaun-smith-eight-brand-traits-separating-best-rest/121029.

3. "Why Is 37Signals So Arrogant," blog post, Don Norman's jnd.org, http://jnd.org/dn.mss/why_is_37signals_so_arrogant.html.

4. "Tesco: A Case Study in Supermarket Excellence," Coriolis Research, July 2004, http://www.coriolisresearch.com/pdfs/coriolis_tesco_study_in_excellence.pdf.

5. Bruno Aziza, "Learn How a Major Retailer Boosts Customer Satisfaction," MSDN blogs, February 11, 2011, http://blogs.msdn.com/b/bi/archive/2011/02/07/learn-how-a-major-retailer-boosts-customer-satisfaction.aspx.

6. "Tesco Shines at Loyalty: An Interview with Clive Humby," *CustomerThink*, January 28, 2004, http://www.customerthink.com/interview/clive_humby_tesco_shines_at_loyalty.

7. Bruno Aziza, op. cit.

8. Sarah Shannon and Clementine Fletcher, "UK Market is 'Challenging' This Year, Retail Chiefs Say," *Bloomberg Businessweek*, March 25, 2011, http://www.businessweek.com/news/2011-03-16/u-k-market-is-challenging-this-year-retail-chiefs-say.html.

9. "Progressive Reaches Concierge Levels of Claims Service Milestone with Opening of 50th Service Center," Progressive press release, November 15, 2006, http://www.progressive.com/newsroom/2006/november/akron-service-center.aspx.

10. Michael De Kare-Silver, "Does Investment in Digital Pay Back?" conference speech, http://dekaresilver.com/downloads/speeches/digital_investment.pdf.

11. "Progressive's Name Your Price Tool Aims for Cost Transparency," *Hartford Business* *.com*, June 29, 2009, http://www.hartfordbusiness.com/news9372.html.

12. E. J. Schultz, "Progressive's Flo Thumbs a Ride with Drivers," Advertising Age, March 14, 2011, http://adage.com/article/news/progressive-s-flo-thumbs-ride-snapshot-device/149367/.

13. "Progressive Says February Income Rose 16 Percent," CNBC, March 16, 2011, http://www.cnbc.com/id/42119304.

14. Megan Burns, "The Business Impact of Customer Experience, 2011" July 7, 2011.

15. Bill Doyle, "Customer Advocacy 2011: How Customers Rate U.S. Banks, Investment Firms, And Insurers," Forrester Research Inc., March 8, 2011.

16. "Cultivating Super Loyalty," Convergys survey, 2010, http://www.convergys.com/insights/research/downloads.php.

17. Lance Whitney, "Major Outage Hits Comcast Customers," CNet, November 29, 2010, http://news.cnet.com/8301-1023_3-20023949-93.html.

18. Elizabeth Glagowski, "CEMEX USA Constructs a Concrete Competitive Advantage," 2011 Gartner & 1to1 Media CRM Excellence Awards, http://www.1to1media.com/downloads/2011_Gartner&1to1Awards.pdf.

Chapter 7

1. "The CMO-CIO Alignment Imperative: Driving Revenue through Customer Relevance," Accenture and the CMO Council, October 2010, https://microsite.accenture.com/AccentureInteractive_CMOCouncil/Pages/default.aspx.

2. In a recent global survey of 1,004 respondents by Bloomberg Businessweek Research Services, only 11 percent of respondents said that they had achieved "tight integration" among applications, including financial, human resources, talent management, customer relationship management, supply chain management, supplier relationship management, and product life-cycle management. The survey was designed to discover and analyze the views of C-level and line-of-business executives on enterprise application integration. See Appendix B for an extract from this survey.

3. Kate Leggett, "Nine Ways to Enhance the Customer Experience," *Baseline Magazine*, January 28, 2011, http://www.baselinemag.com/c/a/CRM/Nine-Ways-to-Enhance -the-Customer-Experience-687244/.

4. *Cognizanti Journal*, 2011.

Chapter 8

1. "More than Half of U.S. Handset Shipments Will Be Smartphones by 2012, Worldwide Smartphone Shipments Move toward One Billion by 2015," In-Stat, June 24, 2011, http://www.instat.com/newmk.asp?ID=3012&SourceID=00000501 000000000000.

2. "Best Buy Launches Multi-Channel Network," *Twin Cities Magazine* blog, January 6, 2011, http://tcbmag.blogs.com/daily_developments/2011/01/best-buy-launches -multi-channel-network.html.

3. Bill Briggs, "Best Buy Plans to Double Its E-Commerce Business," *Internet Retailer*, April 14, 2011, http://www.internetretailer.com/2011/04/14/best-buy-plans-double -its-e-commerce-business.

4. Kate Leggett, "Nine Ways to Enhance the Customer Experience," *Baseline Magazine*, January 28, 2011, http://www.baselinemag.com/c/a/CRM/Nine-Ways-to-Enhance -the-Customer-Experience-687244/.

5. Volker Hildebrand and Vinay Iyer, "Why a Traditional Siloed CRM Approach Is Doomed," *SAPInsider*, Wellesley Information Services, January–March 2010 issue.

6. "Industry Market Barometer," ThomasNet, September 2010. ThomasNet's "Industry Market Barometer" (IMB) is a semiannual survey of buyers (engineers and purchasing agents) and sellers (owners, managers, and sales and marketing executives) at the manufacturers, distributors, and service companies that make up the industrial sector. The majority of respondents are from small and midsized companies, mirroring the makeup of the industrial/manufacturing segment. The IMB serves to measure companies' performance, uncover the strategies they are employing to grow their businesses, and present an overall segment outlook. This is the third consecutive IMB. There were a total of 3,243 survey respondents, of which 95 percent were located in the United States. The majority were from the Midwest (20 percent) and Mid-Atlantic (19 percent), followed by the Pacific Northwest (15 percent) and Pacific (12 percent), http://www.thomasnet.com/pressroom/Industry_Market_Barometer.html.

7. Ashwin Nayan Rai, "From Brick to Click: E-Commerce Trends in Industrial Manufacturing," Cognizant Technology Solutions, 2010, http://www.cognizant.com/ InsightsWhitepapers/From-Brick-to-Click.pdf.

8. "Apple Sells One Millionth iPhone," press release, Apple Computer, Inc., September 10, 2007, http://www.apple.com/pr/library/2007/09/10iphone.html.

9. "Apple Sells Three Million iPads in 80 Days," press release, Apple Computer, Inc., June 22, 2010, http://www.apple.com/pr/library/2010/06/22ipad.html.

10. "More than Half of U.S. Handset Shipments Will be Smartphones by 2012."

11. "Anywhere Enterprise: 2010 U.S. CIO Priorities FastView Survey Snapshot," Yankee Group, December 2010.

12. Rimma Kats, "Mobile Coupon Redemption Rates to Rise This Year," *Mobile Commerce Daily*, April 21, 2010, http://www.mobilecommercedaily.com/2010/04/21/mobile -coupon-redemption-rates-to-rise-this-year.

13. "U.S. Consumers Significantly More Likely to Respond to Location-Based Mobile Ads than Other Mobile Ad Types," Mobile Marketing Association, April 21, 2010, http://mmaglobal.com/news/us-consumers-significantly-more-likely-respond -location-based-mobile-ads-other-mobile-ad-types.

14. "CMO Council State of Marketing," CMO Council and Deloitte, 2010, http://www
    .deloitte.com/assets/Dcom-UnitedStates/Local%20Assets/Documents/us_
    consulting_CMOCouncil_050510.pdf.
15. "Five Rules of Real-Time Marketing," *Retail Customer Experience.com*, February 28,
    2011, http://www.retailcustomerexperience.com/article/179628/Five-rules-of-real
    -time-marketing.
16. John Goodman, *Strategic Customer Service: Managing the Customer Experience to Increase
    Positive Word of Mouth, Build Loyalty and Maximize Profits* (New York: AMACOM,
    2009).
17. Gary Curtis, "Give Your Workplace a Millennial Makeover," *CIO Magazine*,
    September 3, 2010, http://www.cio.co.uk/article/3238071/give-your-workplace-a
    -millennial-makeover.
18. Analytics is "the extensive use of data, statistical and quantitative analysis, explanatory
    and predictive models to drive decisions and actions," Thomas Davenport and Jeanne
    Harris, *Competing on Analytics* (Boston: Harvard Business School Press, 2007).
19. Andrew McInnes, "Customers' Problems Are Companies' Loyalty-Building
    Opportunities," December 6, 2010, http://tinyurl.com/3bq8gxa. The survey base was
    North American consumers who had a problem while doing business with a company
    in the past three months and had it fully resolved.

Chapter 9

1. Ray Wang, "The Four Personas of the Next-Generation CIO," *The Conversation* blog,
   Harvard Business Review, March 3, 2011, http://blogs.hbr.org/cs/2011/03/the_four_
   personas_of_the_next-.html.
2. "2010 CIO FastView Survey: CIOs Make Business the Priority," Yankee Group, March
   2010, http://web.yankeegroup.com/rs/yankeegroup/images/2011CIOPriorities_
   Fastview_Snapshot.pdf.
3. "Accenture Survey Finds that High-Performing IT Organizations Hit the Ground
   Running Following the Economic Downturn," Accenture, November 2010, http://
   newsroom.accenture.com/article_display.cfm?article_id=5102.
4. "The Future of Work Has Arrived: Time to Re-Focus IT," Cognizant Business
   Consulting, February 2011, http://www.cognizant.com/RecentHighlights/CBC_
   FoW_Refocus_on_IT.pdf.
5. "What Makes a Centralized Customer Experience Team Successful?" *Megan Burns'
   Blog for Customer Experience Professionals*, Forrester Research, Inc., May 14, 2010, http://
   blogs.forrester.com/megan_burns/10-05-14-what_makes_centralized_customer
   _experience_team_successful.

Chapter 10

1. http://www.sethgodin.com/sg/books.asp.
2. Shaun Smith, "The Eight Brand Traits Separating the Best from the Rest,"
   MyCustomer.com, http://www.mycustomer.com/topic/customer-intelligence/shaun
   -smith-eight-brand-traits-separating-best-rest/121029.
3. Linda Rutherford, "My Conversation with Kevin Smith," *Nuts About Southwest* blog,
   http://www.blogsouthwest.com/blog/my-conversation-with-kevin-smith-0.
4. Forrester Research, Inc., "Three Secrets of Success for Customer Experience
   Organizations," April 29, 2010, http://www.forrester.com/rb/Research/three_secrets_
   of_success_for_customer_experience/q/id/55871/t/2.
5. Douglas MacMillan, "Best Buy, Other Retailers Tap Tech to Boost Sales," *Bloomberg
   Businessweek*, February 8, 2009, http://www.businessweek.com/bwdaily/dnflash/
   content/feb2009/db2009028_712098.htm.

Chapter 11

1. Lynn Hunsaker, "Driving Sustained Customer Experience Improvement: Four Metrics Tips," *CustomerThink*, March 6, 2009, http://www.customerthink.com/article/four_metrics_tips_drive_sustained_customer_experience_improvements.
2. Frederick Reichheld, *The Ultimate Question* (Boston: Harvard Business School Press, 2006), http://www.theultimatequestion.com/theultimatequestion/home.asp.
3. Amy Porterfield, "Study Reveals Top 6 Social Media Goals for 2011," *Social Media Examiner*, February 11, 2011, http://www.socialmediaexaminer.com/study-reveals-top-6-social-media-goals-for-2011/.
4. "New Study: Deep Brand Engagement Correlates with Financial Performance," Altimeter Group, July 20, 2009, http://www.altimetergroup.com/2009/07/engagementdb.html.
5. Fred Sandsmark, "From Social Media to Social Commerce," Microsoft Global High Tech Summit II, Spring 2011, http://tinyurl.com/3r48aty.

Chapter 12

1. For a full treatment of the subject of globalizing business, please see Appendix B, "The Right Foundation for Growing Global," Bloomberg Businessweek Research Services, February 2011.
2. Jason Kelly, "Private Equity Managers Aim for Emerging Market Economies as Deals Shrink," *bloomberg.com*, May 3, 2011, http://www.bloomberg.com/news/2011-05-03/private-equity-managers-aim-for-emerging-market-economies-as-deals-shrink.html.
3. "Global Consumer Research Executive Summary 2010," Accenture, 2010, http://www.accenture.com/SiteCollectionDocuments/PDF/Accenture_2010_Global_Consumer_Survey_Executive_Summary_v4.pdf. The survey includes online responses from more than 5,800 people in 17 countries. Respondents were asked to assess their experiences with up to four service providers in 10 industries: retail, wireless service providers, Internet service providers, banks, airlines, hotels, home telephone service providers, utility companies, cable/satellite television service providers, and life insurance providers.
4. http://www.samsung.com/africa_en/consumer/home-appliances/washing-machine/index.idx?pagetype=type_p2&.
5. http://www.snopes.com/business/misxlate/ancestor.asp.
6. Patti Waldmeir, "Best Buy Brand Closes Shop in China and Turkey," *Financial Times*, February 22, 2011, http://www.ft.com/intl/cms/s/0/62fda500-3eb1-11e0-834e-00144feabdc0.html#axzz1O2flM8dc.
7. "Consumers' Purchases of Computers, Mobile Phones to Dip, Newer Gadgets to Soar," *DailyFT*, Feb. 15, 2011, http://www.ft.lk/2011/02/15/consumers%E2%80%99-purchases-of-computers-mobile-phones-to-dip-newer-gadgets-to-soar/. The Accenture survey, conducted in October and November of 2010, sought to cover a demographically representative sample across all geographies. Accenture conducted a quantitative online consumer study of 8,002 consumers in eight countries: Brazil, China, France, Germany, India, Japan, Russia, and the United States. Survey respondents in emerging countries represent key urban markets rather than the population as a whole. Survey respondents were asked about the following 19 technologies: computers, mobile phones, digital photo cameras, DVD players, regular TV, high-definition TV, portable music players, game consoles, VCRs, smartphones, GPS, digital video cameras, portable gaming devices, digital video recorders, netbooks, BluRay players, tablet computers, e-book readers, and 3D TVs.
8. "Global SMS Traffic to Reach 8.7 Trillion in 2015: Study," Inquirer.net, January 29, 2011, http://newsinfo.inquirer.net/breakingnews/infotech/view/20110129-317304/Global-SMS-traffic-to-reach-87-Tr-in-2015study.

9. "Emerging Markets Make the Most of SMS," Pyramid Research, February 3, 2010, http://www.pyr.com/points/item/100204.htm.
10. Akbank 2010 Annual Report, page 6. http://www.akbanknv.com/docs/2010_Annual_Report.pdf.
11. "Akbank's Customer-Centric Imperative," 2011 Gartner & 1to1 Media CRM Excellence Awards, http://www.1to1media.com/downloads/2011_Gartner&1to1 Awards.pdf"
12. "Turkish Bank Uses SAP CRM to Manage Multichannel Customer Queries," SAP, 2009.
13. "Akbank's Customer-Centric Imperative," op. cit.

Chapter 13
1. "I skate to where the puck is going to be, not where it has been," Wayne Gretzky, NHL hockey player.
2. "The Future Internet: Service Web 3.0," YouTube, October 15, 2009, http://www.youtube.com/watch?v=off08As3siM.
3. "Vint Cerf's Top YouTube Videos," YouTube, May 9, 2010, http://www.youtube.com/watch?v=zulDYxyv4KQ.
4. "Apple Planning Mobile Shopping Social Network for iPhones?" *PocketNow.com*, December 30, 2010, http://pocketnow.com/iphone/apple-planning-mobile-shopping-social-network-for-iphones.
5. "Forrester's Moira Dorsey: The Future of Online Customer Experience," 1to1 Media, February 3, 2010, http://blogs.forrester.com/moira_dorsey/10-01-29-future_online_customer_experience.
6. "Jonathan Zittrain, The Future of the Internet," YouTube, April 15, 2008, http://www.youtube.com/watch?v=o7UlYTFKFqY.
7. Michio Kaku, "This Is Your Future," *Newsweek*, March 13, 2011, http://www.newsweek.com/2011/03/13/this-is-your-future.html.
8. Robert Anthony, "No Bull: Volkswagen Bulli Concept Electric Van Powered by iPad," *PC World*, April 21, 2011, www.pcworld.com/article/225894/no_bull_volkswagen_bulli_concept_electric_van_powered_by_ipad.html.
9. "Gatorade Mission Control," YouTube, June 15, 2010, http://www.youtube.com/watch?v=InrOvEE2v38.
10. Jeremiah Owyang, "Social Media Mission Control, The Contact Center Must Evolve," *Web Strategy*, October 14, 2010, http://www.web-strategist.com/blog/2010/10/14/social-media-mission-control-the-contact-center-must-evolve-social support/.
11. "From Social Media to Social Commerce," *Journal of the Microsoft Global High Tech Summit*, Spring 2011, http://download.microsoft.com/download/9/4/A/94A04B64-7EB4-4754-BD82-A148D341549D/MSGHT%20Summit%2011-From%20Social%20Media%20to%20Social%20Commerce.pdf.

Chapter 14
1. http://gmj.gallup.com/content/745/constant-customer.aspx.

Bibliography

1. Lior Arussy, *Customer Experience Strategy: The Complete Guide from Innovation to Execution* (Strativity Group, Inc., 2010).

    Arussy provides a practical soup-to-nuts blueprint for understanding what the customer experience is, determining how to measure current experiences, and coming up with an action plan for developing greater customer experiences.

2. Shaun Smith and Joe Wheeler, *Managing the Customer Experience: Turning Customers into Advocates* (London: FT Press, 2002).

    The authors offer practical advice on how companies can build the power of the brand, not through advertising, but by the experience and value that they offer their customers. The book provides analysis and concrete methods for increasing loyalty and advocacy in customer experience in a targeted way.

3. Shaun Smith and Andy Milligan, *Bold: How to Be Brave in Business and Win* (Philadelphia: Kogan Page, 2011).

    This book highlights 14 businesses that illustrate what the authors say is necessary to stand out in business today: putting purpose before profit, going beyond what customers expect, and relentlessly differentiating.

4. John A. Goodman, *Strategic Customer Service: Managing the Customer Experience to Increase Positive Word of Mouth, Build Loyalty and Maximize Profits* (New York: AMACOM, 2009).

    This book focuses on the strategic alignment of customer service with overall corporate strategy. It draws on research from the author's work with the likes of Chik-Fil-A, USAA, Coca-Cola, FedEx, GE, Cisco, Nieman Marcus, Toyota, and Cisco Systems. It includes both case studies and formal research. Many aspects of conventional wisdom are challenged with hard data that show how any company can increase loyalty, win customers, and improve the bottom line.

5. Patricia Seybold, *Outside Innovation: How Your Customers Will Co-Design Your Company's Future* (New York: HarperCollins, 2006).

    Seybold explores how businesses can unleash innovation by inviting customers to co-design what they do and make.

6. Denis Pombriant, *Hello Ladies: Dispatches from the Social CRM Frontier* (lulu.com, 2010).

7. Paul Greenberg, *CRM at the Speed of Light*, 4th ed. (New York: McGraw-Hill, 2009).

    Greenberg reveals best practices for a successful social CRM implementation and provides examples of the new strategies for customer engagement and collaboration being used by cutting-edge companies, along with expert guidance on how your organization can and should adopt these innovations.

8. Seth Godin, *Purple Cow: Transform Your Business by Being Remarkable* (New York: Portfolio, 2009).

    Run-of-the-mill TV commercials and newspaper ads are no longer effective for reaching consumers because consumers are tuning them out. So you have to toss everything and do something remarkable, the way a purple cow in a field of Guernseys would be remarkable, according to Godin. He uses examples of companies including HBO, Starbucks, and JetBlue to illustrate new ways of doing standard business with measurable results.

9. Frederick Reichheld, *The Ultimate Question: Driving Good Profits and True Growth* (Boston: Harvard Business School Press, 2006).

Reichheld argues that customer satisfaction is more important than any other business criterion except profits and that the best measurement of customer satisfaction is whether you would recommend a business to a friend—the foundation of the widely used net promoter score.

10. Tony Hsieh, *Delivering Happiness: A Path to Profits, Passion, and Purpose* (New York: Business Plus, 2010).

The CEO of online shoe giant Zappos, Hsieh details his rise from Harvard student entrepreneur to the creator of a hugely successful brand. Customer service became the focus of the start-up retailer, even when funding dried up. The book recounts how Zappos survived, eventually being acquired by Amazon for more than $1.2 billion in 2009.

11. Jim Joseph, *The Experience Effect* (New York: AMACOM, 2010).

Joseph focuses on how to create "the experience effect," which is a combination of marketing message, advertising, sales approach, website, interaction with company personnel, and more.

12. Brian Solis, *Engage! The Complete Guide for Brands and Businesses to Build, Cultivate, and Measure Success in the New Web*, rev. & updated (Hoboken, N.J.: Wiley, 2011).

Solis's updated primer focuses on how to use social media to succeed in business. Learn about the psychology, behavior, and influence of the new social consumer, and define and measure the success of your social media campaigns. It features a foreword by actor Ashton Kutcher, who has more than five million followers on Twitter.

13. Bernd H. Schmitt, *Customer Experience Management: A Revolutionary Approach to Connecting with Your Customers*, (New York: Wiley, 2003).

Schmitt examines how customer experience management increases growth and revenues and remakes companies' image and brands. The book offers a five-step approach to customer experience to connect with customers at every touch point, and offers case studies in various B2B and consumer industries.

14. Gerald Zaltman, *How Customers Think: Essential Insights into the Mind of the Market* (Boston: Harvard Business School Press, 2003).

Zaltman, a Harvard Business School professor, says that about 80 percent of all new products either fail within six months or fall short of their profit forecast. The reason? A disconnect between the customer experience and the way marketers collect information about how customers view their world. Analysis, success stories, and advice on rethinking marketing approaches are included.

15. Joseph Pine and James Gilmore, *The Experience Economy: Work Is Theater and Every Business a Stage* (Boston: Harvard Business School Press, 1999).

The authors make a case for focusing on the service economy and learning "to stage a rich, compelling experience" by adding service to differentiate products.

16. Chip Bell and John R. Patterson, *Take Their Breath Away: How Imaginative Service Creates Devoted Customers* (Hoboken, N.J.: Wiley, 2009).

A comprehensive look at what it takes to keep customers in today's market as well as gain new customers. The book provides real-world examples of how 12 brands create customer practices leading to "irrational loyalty," and explains how these techniques work and how to implement them.

17. John R. DiJulius, *What's the Secret? To Providing a World-Class Customer Experience* (Hoboken, N.J.: Wiley, 2008).

An inside look at world-class customer service strategies at top companies, such as Disney, Nordstrom, and Ritz-Carlton. The book provides steps, best practices, and service standards needed to build a customer service machine that consistently delivers.

18. Jeanne Bliss, *Chief Customer Officer: Getting Past Lip Service to Passionate Action* (San Francisco: Jossey-Bass, 2006).

The author offers advice to companies that think they've committed to customer experience but haven't.

Resources

1. Ashwin Nayan Rai, "From Brick to Click: E-Commerce Trends in Industrial Manufacturing." Cognizant Technology Solutions, 2010, http://www.cognizant.com/ Insights Whitepapers/From-Brick-to-Click.pdf.
2. "Customer Experience Boosts Revenue," Forrester Research, Inc., June 22, 2009.
3. "The State of Customer Experience, 2010," Forrester Research, Inc., February 19, 2010.
4. "Three Secrets of Success for Customer Experience Organizations," Forrester Research, Inc., April 29, 2010.
5. "What Is the Right Customer Experience Strategy?" Forrester Research, Inc., September 28, 2010.
6. "The Six Laws of Customer Experience: The Fundamental Truths That Define How Organizations Treat Customers," Temkin Group, July 2010.
7. "Profiling Customer Experience Leaders," Temkin Group, September 2010.
8. "The Evolution of Voice of the Customer Programs," Temkin Group, September 2010.
9. "2010 Consumer Experience Study," Strativity Group, September 2010.
10. "2010 Customer Scorecard Series," Convergys, 2010.
11. "Q1 2010 Customer Experience Tracker," Beyond Philosophy, 2010.
12. "Social CRM: The New Rules of Relationship Management," Altimeter Group, March 5, 2010.
13. "Empathica Consumer Insights Panel: 2010 Year in Review," Empathica, 2010.
14. "2010 State of Marketing," CMO Council and Deloitte, 2010.
15. "Global Consumer Research Executive Summary 2010," Accenture, 2010.
16. "Worldwide CRM Applications 2010–2014 Forecast: First Look at a Market in Recovery," International Data Corp., May 2010.

Index

About the Authors

Reza Soudagar has more than two decades of experience in business consulting, IT strategy, and the development of customer relationship management (CRM) solutions. He held senior leadership positions at Accenture and Oracle, serving clients in high-tech and communications industries, and was responsible for a number of products in Oracle's CRM suite. Currently, Reza is an executive in SAP's global marketing unit and focuses on customer experience. Reza has a bachelor's and master's degree in Electrical Engineering from the École Polytechnique Fédérale de Lausanne and completed an executive education program at Harvard Business School.

Vinay Iyer brings more than 20 years of experience as an engineer, product manager, sales and business development manager, and marketer to this book. He currently is the Vice President of Global Marketing at SAP.

Prior to joining SAP, Vinay held roles in product marketing and product management for over five years at Siebel Systems in the United States and in Europe. He is a frequent speaker at customer engagement conferences and is now championing SAP's rapid growth in the market in the overall customer experience management space. Vinay has a master's degree in Electrical Engineering and an MBA from the Wharton Business School.

Dr. Volker G. Hildebrand has two decades of experience as an expert on CRM as a researcher, author, professor, and software industry professional. With a doctorate in business economics, an MBA from the University of Mannheim, and a degree in business and technology from the University of Stuttgart, Volker has been an instructor and pioneering researcher on how to optimize the relationship between a customer and its suppliers. In addition, he has been a CRM consultant for large international companies and held various leadership positions at SAP in sales, marketing, and product management for CRM and e-commerce applications. Volker is currently Vice President for CRM Solutions at SAP.

Volker is the author of several books and more than 100 articles on CRM. *Database Marketing & Computer Aided Selling* was published in 1993, and his articles have appeared in many journals: the German edition of the *Harvard Business Review, absatzwirtschaft* (Germany's leading sales and marketing journal), and the *CRM Project, HMD, Marketing ZFP,* and *SAP Insider* journals.

Lightning Source UK Ltd.
Milton Keynes UK
UKOW04n1848110914

238415UK00001B/1/P